C000017603

UNFIT TO FLY?

A civil pilot's lucky career.

Written by Hugh Thompson
2010.

Hugh Thompson. June 2014.

**Every Noble Life Leaves the
Fibre of it Interwoven
For ever in
The Work of the World.**

(John Ruskin 1819-1900)

Copyright: Hugh Thompson 2010

First published September 2010 by Hugh Thompson
Additional Orders and comments please to e mail:
thompsonmilson@talk21.com

Text and illustrations are copyright and remain the property of the author. All rights reserved. No part of this book may be reproduced, stored in a retrieval system, or transmitted in any form or by any means (electronic, mechanical or otherwise) without prior permission in writing of the copyright holder.

A Catalogue record of this book is available from the British Library.

ISBN 978-0-9566749-0-6

Set in 10pt Arial and printed in England by Orphans Press Ltd., Arrow Close, Leominster Enterpise Park, Leominster, Herefordshire HR6 0LD.

Forward.

It is a great pleasure for me to write this forward to Hugh Thompson's very well written book "Unfit to Fly?"

Hugh came into my life when he started his regular Sunday afternoon walks from Lucton School to Shobdon Airfield in 1967; although I held an Assistant Flying Instructor's rating for a number of years, Hugh had finished his Private Pilot's Licence training before I qualified as an AFI, but I do see his name in my logbooks for a number of type checks at later dates.

When Hugh moved on from his regular instructing and parachute pilot duties at Shobdon in 1974, I lost touch with his career, even though he used to come back to visit us from time to time.

Each time that I have read through the various drafts of this book, I have become more fascinated by the great variety of flying, both paid and unpaid, that Hugh has undertaken in his 43 year flying career; and each time I have found more intriguing snippets that I had missed on previous readings.

This book is different from most aviation stories; not only is it well researched and well written but it gives readers an excellent example of what determination, good flying and good instructional discipline, can achieve - and Hugh does not hide his occasional mistakes, nor spare us from his occasional red-faced moments.

There are several well know sayings in aviation, one of which is "I learned about flying from that..." In my case I learned about flying my self-built Shaw Europa from Hugh - for his instruction I am eternally grateful, after almost 10 years of incident free flying in my magical aeroplane.

Thank you, Hugh, for writing and publishing this excellent story about your flying career - and for all you have done for General Aviation over the years. You have shown enormous initiative and courage in pursuing your career against all the medical odds - and we must be very grateful to you for sharing your experience and your adventures with your readers. I wish you every success with this book.

David Corbett.

Shobdon. August 2010.

This book is dedicated to my parents Guy and Edna, whose generosity provided the funding for this publication;

and

All the users, past, present, and future, of my "Legacy to Aviation", Milson Airstrip.

List of some of the abbreviations used in the book.

AAIB	Air Accident Investigation Branch
ABZ	Aberdeen
Agl	Above Ground Level
AFI	Assistant Flying Instructor
Amsl	Above Mean Sea Level
AOC	Air Operators Certificate
ATC	Air Traffic Control
ATIS	Automatic Terminal Information Service
ATPL	Airline Transport Pilots Licence
BBC	British Broadcasting Corporation
BEB	Benbecula
CAA	Civil Aviation Authority
CFI	Chief Flying Instructor
CPL	Commercial Pilots Licence
CVT	Coventry
DHFS	Defence Helicopter Flying School (Shawbury)
DME	Distance Measuring Equipment
EMA	East Midlands
FAA	Federal Aviation Administration
GMT/UTC	Greenwich Mean Time/Universal Time Co-Ordinated
GPS	Global Positioning System
IFR	Instrument Flight Rules
ILS	Instrument landing System
INV	Inverness
I/R	Instrument Rating
LBG	Paris, Le Bourget
MATZ	Military Aerodrome Traffic Zone
METAR	Meteorological Aerodrome Report
Notam	Notices to Airman
NDB	Non Directional Beacon
PPL	Private Pilots Licence
QFE	Altimeter setting to give Height above airfield
QNH	Altimeter setting giving Altitude above sea level
RAD	Radar
RAF	Royal Air Force
ROC	Royal Observer Corps
RVR	Runway Visual Range
TAWS	Terrain Awareness Warning System
TCAS	Terminal Collision Avoidance System
VOR	Very High Frequency Omni Direction Range

UNFIT TO FLY?

Index of Chapters.

Prologue.	Friday 13th!
Chapter One.	Early Years, Farm Life, and Schooling.
Chapter Two.	The Early Shobdon Years.
Chapter Three.	Early Years as an Instructor at Shobdon.
Chapter Four.	The Cardiff Years; Twice!
Chapter Five.	My Army Experiences in Cyprus and West Germany.
Chapter Six.	American Adventures.
Chapter Seven.	Commercial At last.
Chapter Eight.	The Flight One, Twin Pioneer Years.
Chapter Nine.	The Twin Otter Years.
Chapter Ten.	My Legacy; Milson Airstrip.
Chapter Eleven.	Other Matters.
Chapter Twelve.	The Shorts SD-360 Years.
Chapter Thirteen.	Captain at last; and Scottish Memories.
Chapter Fourteen.	Other Flying.
Chapter Fifteen.	A Non-Flying Future?
Statistics.	Aircraft Types Flown, Log Book Hours, And Companies Worked for.
Postscript.	Last Minute Additions
Quote Source	Ruskin Quote explained

UNFIT TO FLY?

Index of Appendices.

Appendix One.	**Shropshire Star Engine Failure Report.**
Appendix Two.	**NFU Farm Report; November 1954.**
Appendix Three	**Shobdon Navigational Competition Results.**
Appendix Four.	**CAA Medical Consultation Letters.**
Appendix Five.	**VFR Trip around Europe.**
Appendix Six.	**Linkman Hugh Keeps Things Going!**
Appendix Seven.	**Where Sheep may safely graze…….**
Appendix Eight.	**Personal Reflections on Flying the Shaw (Monowheel) Europa.**
Appendix Nine.	**Instrument Flying Summary.**
Appendix Ten.	**British Aerospace Work Reports; in Three Parts.**
Appendix Eleven.	**Milson Airstrip; a Planning History Summary.**

Author's Introduction.

I have been thinking about writing this book about a civilian pilot's flying career for some time and have finally decided to put the computer to a good use. In my time, I have read a lot of very interesting pilot autobiographies but apart from a few, most have been written by ex-military trained aircrew who were lucky enough to have their early career paid for by the taxpayer. I have long felt that another book about the career of a purely civilian pilot's flying experiences, one paid for largely out of their own private funds, would be a worthy effort; giving inspiration and hope to anyone thinking of following a similar path.

The demise of a small regional airline in Scotland called Highland Airways in early 2010 convinced me that it was unlikely that I would find another commercial flying job quickly. Having been made redundant for the sixth time in June of 2009, and approaching 58 years of age, the uncertain economic times in aviation has finally persuaded me to record, on paper, my varied flying career. I write it now, in the hope that my parents, who are still living, will be able to read it before it is too late. The unusual title will become self explanatory as you read the book. I had considered a title, **"Never Assume, Always Check"** as that was my motto when working as a flying instructor, but when having a meal with a close friend on a night off flying in Scotland in 2006, he suggested the title; and I agreed it would be an appropriate and eye catching heading for the flying story which follows!

It is my intention, in writing this book, to give encouragement to anyone who might wish to pursue a career in aviation, especially any person who has had a poor education; or who has some kind of medical handicap; it does not automatically prevent you from achieving success. By showing sheer determination and working hard, you should be able to achieve your aims; more so when you enjoy what you are doing and want to succeed. I also wish to write about flight safety matters; based on the experiences of myself and other pilots. There is a saying: **"There are Old Pilots and Bold Pilots, but No Old Bold Pilots"**. I have had a number of lucky escapes during my flying career and have always been prepared to tell others of my misfortunes; to prevent it happening to them. I hope that the reader will enjoy this autobiography. I have used my 23 small private pilot type log books as my lifetime diaries which, together with the recollections of friends and family, have helped me to compile the following account of my life. The idea of having 23 log books, so far, was a safeguard in case one was lost at any time.

I hope the reader will find the content interesting, that the flight safety tips and hints will be useful to you, and that some young men and women will take up a civil career in aviation as a result of reading my story. The significance of some of my comments on my medical condition will become apparent during the course of the book.

The content of the book may appear a little technical at times but for any reader wanting to become a pilot themselves, it should give them encouragement to enquire further and to read other literature about flying matters. In the chapter about my legacy, Milson airstrip, I am perhaps a little harsh in my comments about a certain persistent objector and did consider revising or removing it altogether, but I have decided that it is a fundamental part of the story as the outcome might well have been very different had he not come to live close to the farm and airstrip. I have therefore left those comments as they were originally written.

Whilst the majority of the photographs are from my own sources, a number have been downloaded from the internet, especially the CAA G-INFO website. If any copyright has been infringed then I would like to apologise to the holder but beg forgiveness as this is a genuine book on someone's flying history where the writer has had a direct connection with the aircraft concerned. I also apologise if there are any factual errors as most of the detail is based on memories and recollections.

I would like to thank my partner Wendy for tolerating me while I wrote the book, the local college where I did an Information Technology (IT) course on computing and wrote the text at the same time; and most importantly of all, my father Guy for agreeing to give me an expensive birthday present, paying for its printing and publication costs!

Happy reading and safe flying for any reader thinking of learning to fly; or for those who can already fly, you should find my story interesting? Janette Schönburg, who flew a Cessna 150 from London to Australia in 1980, calls me "A total aviation person". I hope you will agree with her as you read my book. Finally, the "Pegasus" symbol of a flying horse was chosen as it reflects my two main interests, flying and horses!

Hugh Thompson. August 2010.

Prologue. Friday 13th!

Unlucky Friday 13th June 2003 started bright and sunny for me. The forecast for the forthcoming weekend was very good with a large "High" centred over the United Kingdom. I had planned to fly up to a small private airstrip in Lancashire to complete an aircraft type rating conversion training for an elderly gentleman who had recently purchased a small Kitfox aircraft; something I had been waiting for weeks to complete due to weather delays, etc. On the previous evening I had been up to my home airstrip, Milson, where I had kicked the tyres, checked the oil, topped up the fuel, and carried out a short ten minute test flight in preparation for the following day. My own Kitfox, G-BTNR, was then left outside and tied down, ready for an early morning departure. Little did I realise what was to occur the following day; an eventful one to say the least!

As the battery on my aircraft was a little weak, I had the habit of always starting the Rotax 582 engine using an external battery for the initial start when cold. Once warmed up, and for the rest of the day, starting was normally fine. After, using the internet to check the weather and local "Notam" information relevant to my route, I set off towards the private airstrip; at about 09.00 Hours local time. Note that today there are numerous internet websites available when planning a flight, including the Met Office itself; but three sites which I use regularly are avbrief.com, xcweather.co.uk (which is particularly good for the winds), and ippc.no/ippc/aerodromes, which gives both the local weather and airfield Notams together.

After settling down on course, I checked a few weather reports using both the radio Volmet and local ATIS reports for the latest weather and to obtain an accurate altimeter setting. I have always preferred to use actual QNH values rather than the regional one which will always be the lowest forecast value and hence not entirely correct. As RAF Shawbury was on my route, I called them for a MATZ (Military Air Traffic Zone) penetration, and was given a clearance to pass through their airspace at 2000 feet on their QFE setting; which gives you your height relative to the airfield elevation. As my own altimeter had an indication error, I had always reduced the given setting by 4 millibars (about 120 feet).

I was asked to make a call when entering the MATZ area but made an additional call out of courtesy when overhead the local town of Hodnet in order to give an accurate position fix prior to passing through the Ternhill airfield aerodrome traffic zone (ATZ). My aircraft did not carry a secondary surveillance radar transponder so I could only be monitored using primary or basic radar. Up to now, all had gone according to plan and I had passed by both Sherlowe and Tilstock airstrips; places I could have landed at. All the time, I had been making small adjustments to the throttle to keep the engine rpm at about 5000; something I found I needed to do regularly. Suddenly, there was a distinct sound change and reduction in rpm (revolutions per minute) which caught my eye. "Oh dear I thought, this engine is giving notice of a seizure". In recent months, I had become suspicious of the engine as the maximum rpm on take off had fallen from 6200 to about 6000. Based on the experience of another Rotax engined Kitfox owner whose engine had failed only a few weeks before, I had asked my engineer to check the engine over. All had appeared to be fine with the measured crankshaft tolerances being acceptable, and a change of spark plugs had made a slight improvement in the max power rpm. However, seconds later, there was:-

A sudden surge in rpm, then the engine stopped dead. "S**** (an expletive) I thought, Engine Failure". I collected my thoughts, trimmed the aircraft for the glide at about 60 mph, tightened up my full harness, and turned slightly right to see Ternhill airfield behind me. I considered flying towards it but decided against it as it was into wind and crossed over a built up industrial area. Do not stretch the glide came to mind. It was too far away to be a safe option. I then made a quick call to the Shawbury MATZ controller stating that I had suffered an engine failure, was just north of Market Drayton, and was turning east to look for a field to land in. His immediate response was to ask me to call again when on the ground if able to do so, and instructed other air traffic to cease making any calls. I did not use the internationally recognized "Mayday" call for an emergency as I was already in contact with the controller. I learnt later on that the Shawbury controller did consider directing me towards Ternhill airfield but concluded that I would already be aware of it having passed over it just a minute or so earlier. I then either turned off the radio completely, or reduced the volume, in order to concentrate on the flying, and the forthcoming forced landing.

I continued to turn on to an easterly heading as what little wind there was, was from the west. I have always believed that unless you have an obvious field choice immediately, turning downwind in the event of an engine failure, gives you a better chance of finding a suitable landing area as you cover more ground while looking. I did not notice a perfectly good private airstrip directly below me and continued heading east until I chose an area of relatively small fields. At this time of year (June) I consider the type of surface to be important; I did not want to end up in a cornfield with a soft surface or in a crop of hay. Thinking of the 5 "S", **s**ize, **s**hape, **s**urface, **s**urroundings and **s**lope, I chose what turned out to be a small but recently cut, grassland and predominantly level field.

I concentrated on flying the aircraft, planning my descent profile which seemed to take an awfully long time, and did not make any further use of the radio. I did turn off the magneto switches but failed to turn off the main fuel selector as it would have meant having to loosen or undoing my shoulder harness. I probably closed the throttle but do not recall doing so. I was conscious of being high on the approach profile but this did not bother me too much as the Kitfox sideslips very well and you can loose height very rapidly if required. I aimed the aircraft about 30 metres into the field and varied the sideslip angle to achieve this. On rounding out with an indicated speed of about 60 mph, I found I floated on for a while despite having a dead prop. I was reluctant to force it down in case of a bounce.

As I landed, about half way down the field length, I noticed to my horror for the first time, that electricity wires crossed the field at the far end. I found myself heading directly for an electricity pole but stopped about 20 metres short of it. I could have applied the brakes to avoid it but did not do so and came to a gentle stop. Relieved at having made a perfect forced landing with no further damage, injury, or fire, I congratulated myself. I then made an immediate call to the Shawbury ATC controller on the radio, and with good two way contact, said all was well! I then noticed that the altimeter read exactly zero; which rounded things off very nicely.

Shaking a little, I then got out and thinking that the engine had suffered a piston seizure, checked the oil tank level and saw it had fallen by about an inch after roughly 40 minutes of flying. I could still turn the propeller with difficulty but there were some hasty noises coming from the engine. Before doing anything else, I then made a number of mobile telephone calls to my home airfield and intended destination where they had originally expected me to come by car, but I quickly found that my battery had run down. The RAF in the meantime, had diverted a DHFS/CFS Squirrel helicopter to the scene. After landing alongside, one crew member got out, and kindly offered assistance in case I had been injured in any way. That gesture was much appreciated and sincere thanks were later sent by letter to the crew involved. I subsequently met one of them at RAF

Shawbury a few years later when I took part in a visit to the Defence Helicopter Flying School. I just knew the face but could not place it initially, until we talked about the incident. After seeing that I was safe, and obviously elated at having pulled off a perfect forced landing, they flew away and confirmed that all was well to air traffic control.

The aircraft secured by a hedge with no apparent damage!

As there was no livestock in the field I moved the aircraft and parked it under a tree close to the roadside access gate on to a public road. After tying the aircraft down, removing the GPS and radio for safe keeping, securing the flying controls, and locking it, I then proceeded to find the landowner and farmer. The lady farmer kindly allowed me to use her own telephone to clarify events and after exchanging telephone numbers, names, etc, I then walked down the country lane to the main road where I successfully got a lucky lift in the right direction; all the way from Market Drayton to Wigan, which was very near to where I had to go. After two more lucky lifts, I arrived at my intended destination at about 14.30 some four hours later than intended, and was able to complete the other Kitfox conversion later the same day.

Good training, 5000 hours on light aircraft and a little luck played an important part in this successful landing. I kept a cool head, flew the aircraft well and did not, as many attempt to do, pick the largest field around. If you fly a good approach at the correct airspeed, you can land most light aircraft in a very small area; especially if it is into a good headwind. Being a little high and rolling into the far end hedge after landing at say 20 mph is better than stretching the glide, and possibly stalling at about 30 feet as you try to reach the one and only field you have chosen! In some RAF notes relating to the Harvard, a wartime training aircraft, which I managed to fly a few times during my flying club days at Cardiff, there was the following note relating to glide approaches. It said, **"Remember:**

To make you're landing the end of a journey, not the end of everything!"

Friday the 13th June 2003, was a lucky day for me, even if the date is normally associated with superstition and concern.

Newspaper Report:-

The event found itself on the front page of a widely read local newspaper, the "Shropshire Star" later that same day. Just 30 minutes after I had rung my partner at home to tell her the news, our immediate neighbour came round with a copy of the paper asking "Is this your Hugh"? I did not ring immediately after the landing as I did not want to worry her at work. How lucky I was to have telephoned the news in time. The actual Shropshire Star report is **Appendix One** at the end of this book.

Engineering Report:-

After recovery home by trailer, an advantage for a Kitfox as the wings can be folded easily; the engine was removed and stripped down. There were no obvious signs of damage externally, apart from a crack in the crankcase. Fully expecting to find a big end failure or a hot piston seizure, we actually found the engine to be in a very good overall condition.

However, a complete failure of the magneto end of the outer web of the crankshaft had occurred, and it was obvious that the failure had been a progressive one over many hours. It was due to a torsional vibration caused by having a propeller reduction gearbox at one end, and a starter motor at the other. The problem was a known fault and a non mandatory modification had been recommended by

Rotax recommending that a rubber based "Hydro Damper" should be fitted to overcome the vibration effect. Unfortunately, I had never been made aware of the fault, either by the engineering inspector appointed by the Light Aircraft Association (LAA) who had twice checked the aircraft during my ownership, or by the previous owner. When asked about it later, he admitted knowing that a "Hydro Damper" had not been fitted but did not think it necessary as he had not done very much flying on the aircraft! I was angry with him that he had not told me this when I had decided to buy the aircraft. Inadvertently, I had in fact been flying a ticking time bomb waiting to go off at any moment.

I made enquiries with both the Civil Aviation Authority (CAA) and the LAA about the legal implications had I been seriously injured or killed, and learned that as the owner of the aircraft, it was my responsibility to ensure that all necessary maintenance and modifications were carried out. I replied by asking, "How long was a piece of string"? If you do not know about a potential problem, how can you possibly do anything about it! Let my experience be a lesson to any reader wishing to own his or her own aircraft. Be sure you check the current modification state of your engine and airframe, together with all the documentation, before taking delivery!

Recorded engine Log book hours for my Rotax engine was just 242 Hours 20 Minutes, of which I had flown about 40 hours during my ownership. Needless to say, I sold the airframe engineless and lost about £2000. I calculated that after paying hangarage, insurance, "Permit to Fly" renewal fees, inspection costs, fuel and other things, it had cost me about £125 an hour to fly. Be sure you really want to own your own aircraft; it might be better to just hire a flying club aircraft, or become a part owner in a flying group.

Finally, I would like to include a note about my one and only total engine failure. When I informed the United Kingdom Air Accident Investigation Branch (AAIB) of the failure, they did not want to know about it as it was not an accident. As no additional damage had been done, it was classed as an engineering fault, and no report was ever issued about the failure. A similar torsional vibration failure had occurred to another Kitfox for the same reason (no Hydro damper fitted) a year or so earlier where the aircraft had been seriously damaged during the landing. As that was an accident, a report was issued by the AAIB, but I had never seen it for myself. Had I done so, I might have been more cautious about the engineering status and records of my own aircraft.

Chapter One.
Early Years, Farm Life, and Schooling.

As a result of my mother being a hard working farmer's wife, I was born about six weeks premature on the 18th July 1952 and christened Hugh, weighing in at just 4 Pounds. Shortly after birth, I was found to be suffering from acute Yellow Jaundice and required an almost immediate blood transfusion. According to what the local doctor said at the time, I should have been "knocked on the head" at birth. However, my parents, Guy and Edna Thompson had more faith in me than that as I had a good set of lungs and cried loudly; and luckily I survived. A sister, Janet, followed on the 22nd May 1954 but she arrived on time with none of the medical problems that I had encountered.

Guy Maxwell Hartill Thompson, had first met my mother at the local cattle market at Tenbury Wells, where she had walked a few Heifers the four miles to market from her farming home at Hillwood, near Eastham, in the Teme Valley. Unfortunately, one of the cattle, with a good set of horns, had caught my mother's nose causing a nasty cut and Guy came to her aid. This first meeting was recalled recently in a local newspaper article written on their 50 wedding anniversary.

My father had been born at Eyton Mill near Leominster and to start with, lived at a number of public houses around Herefordshire and Worcestershire where his own father had been a butcher, milkman and lastly a publican. One home was at the "Boat Inn" at Whitney on Wye which still remains a popular place on the banks of the River Wye. He developed a lifelong interest in fishing and countryside matters while living there, deciding eventually to become a lifetime farmer.

One of his most cherished memories of those early days is recorded with a drawing saying "They'll Never Believe Me" when he is reputed to have caught his first Salmon with a stick and piece of string? His main schooling was at a boarding school named Lucton, which he still visits regularly some 70 years later as one of the oldest surviving Old Luctonians. This school had no heating whatever in the dormitories, something I myself had to put up with when I attended the same school 23 years later, it being my third boarding school. However, more will be said about those days later.

During the war years he was exempt from military service as he had trained to become a cowman but had to be a member of the local Home Guard. He also worked nights in an armaments factory in nearby Worcester where, on one occasion, a German aircraft dropped a bomb from a very low altitude. Luckily for him and me, it did not explode, but simply bounced back out through the roof. As a member of the Home Guard, while on lookout duty one day at the top of Abberley Clock Tower, a prominent local landmark in the Teme valley, he was one of four soldiers on duty to report seeing parachutists falling from the sky. This caused a full scale alert which became known locally as the **"Battle of Bewdley"**; and which was the subject of a separate local book written some years later.

When the war started in 1939, he started working for a farmer at Orleton Court, near Stanford Bridge on the banks of the river Teme, and was told to go and find the thrashing machine which at harvest time travelled around all the local farms to extract the corn. He found himself travelling up the long drive to Hillwood Farm, Eastham, on a motor bike where on arrival he was invited in to the kitchen for a bite of lunch. Low and behold, my Mother was there, so they had met again. From then on, a courtship began in earnest; leading to what has turned out to be a long, happy, and hard working marriage. They became engaged, and were both married at Eastham Church in September of 1947.

The picture above which was taken in 1947 at Hillwood Farm, Eastham on the front lawn, shows my Mother at the bottom left with my father standing in the middle of the back row. Her elder and younger sister's, Mary and Betty are also shown as well as her parents standing with my father in the centre.

My Mother was born at Hillwood, the second of five children, one of whom died tragically during childhood when he was electrocuted trying to save a bird caught in some wires. She was educated locally and travelled daily by bicycle and train to Ludlow School, then becoming one of the famous "Land Girls" during the war years carrying out all manner of jobs. While at Hillwood she witnessed a terrible air crash when a cousin of hers, Tony Brettall, flew round the farm in a Mitchell Bomber, carried out some unauthorised low passes, and clipped the chimney of the farmhouse with the propeller tip. This caused the one engine to become detached and led to a fatal crash in the cherry orchard in the valley below. This event was to become a major concern of hers when I first learnt to fly myself. She feared I might do something similar and show off over our own farm at Milson, but I was a good lad and never flew low when flying over the area some 30 years later.

Before they were married, Guy had a nasty accident on horseback when the rider wanted to go one way at a pathway junction in the woods, and the horse the other! He ended up in the local cottage hospital at Tenbury where he had to lie almost perfectly still for about six weeks while the thigh bone he had broken healed naturally. Edna visited him regularly where they discussed their future together. It was decided that they would begin farming 103 acres of pasture and rough ground at Milson, a small village on the southern slopes of the Clee Hills in South Shropshire, which Edna's father had acquired some years earlier. It had been purchased by a family friend Mr Brinton, whose son, after wartime service as a pilot in RAF coastal command, married her older sister Mary. They took on the farming there, and over a number of years paid for the land by instalments whilst developing a reasonable dairy herd of Shorthorn cows.

The farm itself had a small stream running through it which provided valuable drinking water for the stock. There was also a marshy area in the centre which in earlier years had been used to soak wood for making paper. This area was later developed into two fish pools where eventually a holiday chalet was built. When my parents sold the farm in 1992, they retained the pools and chalet area, and virtually retired there for about 15 years until their health declined and the remainder of the land was transferred to the new owner. They had planned to be there for at least 15 years, and that was reflected in the agreement they made when selling the rest of the farm, but declining health caused them to leave in late1996, two years earlier than hoped.

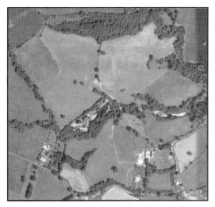

The two aerial photos above show the farm area with the fish pools and chalet area taken in 2007 after my parents had sold the farm, and the print to the right which was taken from the Twin Pioneer in 1981 when I was doing Ordnance Survey work flying out of Cardiff on this particular flight. A close study of the two pictures will show numerous changes have been made including a new farmhouse and buildings as well as the complete removal of the old orchards. Some of the field shapes have changed as well.

The various fields on the farm were given names to reflect their nature and use. Spring Bank, Patisley, Dark Orchard, the Doctors Field, Middle Laze, and the Stony Field are some which come to mind and, I wonder if any of those names remain today. Obviously as time has gone on, some hedges have been removed and fields combined due to more modern farming methods.

There was also one small strip of land which protruded into the stream which was used as a camp site on at least two occasions when my sister and I were about 11 and 13 respectively. For a week in the summer, we camped out, taking the horse, cats, and dogs with us; cooking all our own food, and generally enjoying ourselves: until that is, we had a torrential thunder storm which washed the whole lot away as the stream flooded the site. A diagram of the site layout is shown on the next page, which considering I drew it when I was about 11 years old is quite remarkable and detailed. I remember that we used to invite Mum and Dad, together with our Grandparents, down to the camp site for a camp fire cooked meal. If I remember correctly, we managed two summer camps before a flood ruined the third attempt.

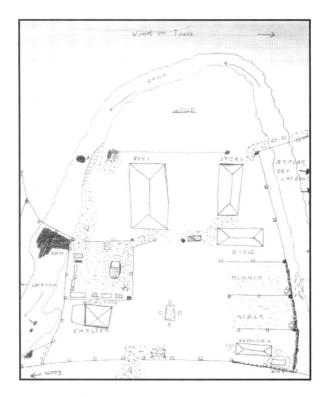

To begin with, they lived at a nearby cottage called "The Butts" where there was no running water, an outside loo at the bottom of the garden, virtually no furniture or heating, and life was hard by today's standards. They started farming with 10 cows and suckled calves were brought in from Scotland and delivered by train to the nearby Neen Sollars railway station. These animals were sent in bags with their heads showing. As new and keen young farmers, they were one of the first modern farming families in the area to have a tractor, tipping trailer and muck fork. This modern equipment, which was in high demand by all the neighbours, kept Dad busy and helped provide them with additional income.

When holidaying in Cornwall one summer, then saw what turned out to be one of the very new mobile "Simplex" milking parlours. This gave them the idea of starting a milking herd, and in due course, a new milking parlour which remained in use until 1985, was delivered to the local railway station in 1949. It was then towed on some metal wheels about two miles to the farm where it was then put to good use.

During this time, a completely new house was built using special grants of materials provided by the government during the harsh and difficult years after the war, when bricks and timber were severely rationed. A self starting, diesel electric mains generator was installed which provided electrical power to the house and farm buildings. I can remember, as a child, the lights slowly starting to brighten as the generator started itself up when a light switch was put on.

Shown above is the "New House" just after construction in 1947 with the view I had from my bedroom window for the first 20 years of my life looking towards the Clee Hill and the Little Down Farm where the airstrip was to be developed some 30-40 years later.

This new house was a perfectly good farmhouse which was later extended as my sister and I grew up. Sadly, it was later demolished after the farm was sold in 1992 and replaced by a monstrous mansion house which the new owners ironically called "The Old Hall". To quote a friend, this was a gross misuse of industrial money and not what the planning authority had authorised; "Extensive alterations to the existing dwelling" was stated but no evidence remains of what was a perfectly good farmhouse. It upset my parents to see the old house completely disappear as it held so many happy memories.

During the summer months (in those days the summers were summers) the milking parlour was taken out to the middle of the farm and established close to the small stream which passed through the area. Here, all the milking was done and the milk churns were then put into prepared trenches within the stream for cooling. I can remember that being done, and used to try and help. See the photograph shown on the next page. An article was written about their farming methods and ideas and published in an agricultural journal which is shown as **Appendix Two**. Even I got a mention.

I can just be seen in the back of the Land Rover.

Unfortunately for me, I was always present during milking time, either in the farm buildings during winter or near by the parlour during the summer and spent many hours in a pram or pushchair close by the small petrol engine and the "Thump, Thump" of the compressor unit. This together with my premature birth might have had, or probably did have; a bearing on my subsequent poor hearing but that was not to be known about at that time.

As my sister and I grew older, we were left in the house during milking time and sometimes had an Auntie, Alice Butcher, who lived at the nearby cottage, "The Butts", to look after us but to make sure we were safe, Philip Bozon who worked for my Father on the farm designed an amplifier so they could listen for sounds of movement in the house. A microphone was positioned at the top of the stairs next to our bedrooms with a large loud speaker placed by the milking parlour. Later on an old but very good radio was used for many years to provide music while you work; and milked the cows!

Another of my earliest memories which I can remember was travelling to Aberyswyth in winter time when both my sister and I had heavy colds. The doctor had advised a complete change of air to help both of us get well again. My mother and her younger sister

Betty, who was a nurse, took us there in the Land Rover in the most appalling conditions. On the return I remember following a car which just disappeared as we drove through a snow drift. We all thought it must have gone over the edge of the winding mountain road as we never saw it again.

Janet and I spent some very happy and interesting early years, living in an open countryside setting, doing all kinds of activities you would expect on a typical farm. A summer camp (already mentioned) was held at least twice. All the animals were pets to us, so the pig, for example, had to go to market when we were away for the day; or at school! We became friendly with another local family's children and had a good general upbringing. On one occasion when we went to visit our local vet, he gave us about 10 Bantam Chickens which we hid in the back of the Land Rover. My Mother could not understand why, for once, we volunteered to sit in the back but all was revealed just as we arrived home and they started chuckling.

As I grew up, the mains electricity from the National Grid was eventually installed in the area. I distinctly remember having the crazy idea of wiring all the farm buildings myself. This meant that over time, yards of electric fencing wire was strung from pillar to post all over the place. I suppose it was lucky that I did not try and interfere with the real wires! Also, I took to digging up the road, even the public one; putting "Road Works Ahead" signs up and then charging the postman or anyone else, to pass by. What a cheek! Another habit was enjoying taking things to pieces. An old Fordson tractor, for example, was parked by the house after ploughing one season and never moved again, except to the scrap man. I took it all to pieces which was a shame as it would have been worth a small fortune today.

As young children, we also took up horse riding for a while and our first horse was an old white Arab named "Tommy". Later on, my father acquired a Welsh Cob named "Minnie" off the nearby Clee Hills. We both had lessons with the local Pony Club but our interest declined while we were away at boarding school but I took to it again in the late 1970's and 80's when I had plenty of time on my hands while working for Flight One Ltd, but more about those days later in the book. My father had a strong interest in horses and when he could afford it, and had more time available, took to breeding his own. He became a regular fox hunter for many years. The true cost of having a large number of horses for some years was hidden by the fact that you had your own ground, stable block accommodation, and made your own Hay for winter feed.

I distinctly remember being sent away to my first day school in the autumn of 1957, because I cried as I put on to the bus. As I appeared to be backward at school and did not socialize well, I did not do at all well at the local day school in Cleobury Mortimer. After one term, it was decided to send me to a small private boarding school called "High Tree", which was about 20 miles away at Lentwardine on the Welsh border. I remember those days well. It was run by a Headmaster who had been a teacher at Lucton during the pre war years and had taught my Father there. One important memory of my time at this school was when, having been excused a class to visit the toilet, I was frightened to knock on the door to re-enter the class room as I found it difficult to hear the teacher say "Come In". As I got more scared, I eventually went and hid behind the nearby cloak room door where I must have remained for several hours until someone wanted their coat and found me. I remember the local police being called as they all thought I had run away. That event was another indication that I had a hearing loss, yet nobody had noticed or realized that the problem existed.

While at Hightree School, I formed a friendship with one boy, Charles Chatfield which was to last for many years until his family emigrated to South Africa. He went to all the three boarding schools I attended but I must admit that our likeness for each other did diminish over time. Also, at the school we were encouraged to get out and about in the countryside and we both found a cave in Mocktree Hays, a wooded area in the hills. I managed to crawl through the one entrance and come out at another, but almost got wedged in. When I found it again years later, it had been sealed up with concrete blocks so others must have had the same idea of exploring it as I did?

One possible reason for missing the fact that I had difficulty hearing was that I had serious eyesight trouble as well. In my early years I had spent a lot of time in and out of hospital trying to have a serious squint corrected, where my right eye was off set to the right and I had no monocular vision. I remember one occasion when, on visiting Kidderminster Hospital for a check up, something was found to be seriously wrong and I had to have immediate surgery. I was found to be allergic to ether which was poured on to a cotton gauze placed over my mouth and nose to put me to sleep. I hated it and still think of it today. Although this problem was largely corrected, I still do not have any perception of distance even today in the normal sense. I manage to judge distance based on experience and the everyday things around me. Surprising perhaps, when, as you will see, I have had a lifetime's career as a fixed wing aircraft pilot. Modern thinking with children having a similar problem is to leave any major surgery until that person has stopped growing.

During the first part of my life, up to about 14 years of age, we all had an annual holiday at Borth, a small seaside resort just north of Aberyswyth, where we always stayed in the same place "Tyroll House" for about a week. Some very happy times were enjoyed there. One regular feature was that we always took an inner tube of a large tractor tyre with us, and had it blown up and made into a boat by tying a large rope around the middle. However, as we grew up it was decided to spend holidays elsewhere, so in later years we had visits to Amroth in South Wales where we stayed in a Caravan, Newquay in Cornwall, and the Isle of White to name just a few locations. As I became more interested in all kinds of aircraft, I was often dropped off outside the perimeter of an airfield for the day to watch aircraft arrivals and departures.

On one occasion while on the Isle of White holiday in about 1968, I decided to make my way to the Army Air Day at Middle Wallop in Hampshire and was duly put on a Hovercraft to Portsmouth. I then made my way to Portsmouth airport and asked if anyone was flying to the show, only to learn that a pilot was planning to fly just a few miles to the Lee on Solent Naval Air Day just a short distance away. I therefore went with him across the bay on a five minute flight and enjoyed a good but different air show elsewhere for free.

After High Tree, which was considered a success, I was then sent, in 1961, to a very nice but unusual school called Aymestrey, near Worcester. A good colour painting of this school is shown in the pictures section. It was a very nice country house converted into a school and set in wonderful gardens and woodland. It was run by a very strict headmaster named Dan Asterley who was a very keen Boy Scout's leader. He gave us very little in the way of comfort.

As there was no running water in the dormitories, we had to fetch water for washing in a jug from a stand pipe tap; and also had to strip our beds every morning, making them again in the evening. Half term was just one day away and quarter term was allowing parents to visit the school for an hour within the school grounds. We all ran around outside with no shoes on to harden our feet during the summer months, and all our reading material had to be passed by Dan before we could read it. Just one comic of the day was allowed, the "Eagle", which had Dan Dare the spacemen in it. Once I, and my friend Charles, returned to school a day early which was funny to us but an annoyance to our respective parents. I remember the delight of having to go home again for 24 hours, during which I went to pay a surprise visit on my Aunty Alice who then lived at the "Butts" where Mum and Dad had first lived when they first came to Milson. On one half term visit, my parents turned up very unexpectedly, driving a Rolls Royce, which was a surprise to me. The Headmaster did allow me to go for a short drive in it on that occasion.

There were some good ideas as well. For discipline, you were awarded a nuisance mark if you did something wrong like dropping litter, but for more serious misdemeanours like swearing you got a minor mark; and four nuisance marks became a general minor mark. These results were all given to the school assembly once a week so it soon became known who the trouble makers were. Your parents were given the results as well! You could also be given a punishment by having to stand in a corner of the main school hall for all to see; for up to an hour or more. One such corner was facing the Grand Father Clock which I remember well. For school work, Dan wasn't bothered if you could not get on well with a particular subject, but gave you Alfa marks if he and the other teachers thought you had tried your best, and awarded you with Gamma marks if you did not bother to even try or make an effort. Aymestrey was a happy school which sadly had to close eventually as changing school regulations prevented the school keeping its strict environment of cold dormitories etc. However, the school did me some good and I was grateful for having spent time there, after I had left.

At about the time I went to Aymestrey School, I was taken to see a film at the local cinema during the Christmas Holidays. The main film was a Dorothy Lamour/Bob Hope classic where he found himself flying to the Moon in a spaceship originally intended for an Ape. I distinctly remembered Bob Hope being fed a constant stream of Bananas and squirts of water which made us all laugh, but it was the first film that was to have such a profound influence on my life. A drama documentary film on the X-15 Rocket Plane was shown which captivated me; and from that moment on, I wanted to fly.

My father says that, in actual fact, my first interest started when I was given a Flight International magazine to read, by a fruit merchant named Harold Drew who regularly came to the farm to collect the Damsons and Plums at harvest time. He and his brother, who continued to fly a full career as an airline pilot, had both been in the RAF during the war. However, I cannot recall that event but can certainly remember the X-15 film shots which are, to this day, vivid in my memory.

As I became interested in aircraft and flying from about 1961 onwards, I started to take an interest in the aerial activity which took place over and around the farm. Up until the time I went to see the X-15 film, I do not recall having any particular interest in aviation at all and just did what all children do on a farm at a young age. Father tried to get me interested in fishing but I found the pace too slow and not to my liking; I just was not patience enough and got bored easily.

In the late 50's and during the next twenty years when the "Cold War" was at its peak, the Royal Air Force was much larger than it is today and as a consequence, there was much more flying going on. RAE Pershore and RAF Gaydon near Warwick were both still open for many years after my close association with Gaydon had ended. Also, the United States Air Force had more military bases in the UK including the one at RAF Upper Heyford, north of Oxford.

The departure and arrival routing for aircraft from these two airfields in particular were to the North West passing over South Shropshire and the farm. We were regularly entertained by Vickers Varsity aircraft from Gaydon and McDonnell Douglas R-101 Voodoo's from Upper Heyford but these were later replaced by the General Dynamics F-111 swing wing bomber. These aircraft used to fly over at a very low height heading for the Clee Hills and used to pull up over the high ground ahead. In fact, on the day when the planning committee visited the farm to consider the planning application for my airstrip in the late 1980's, two F-111 aircraft happened to pass directly over the strip at low level impressing the visiting councillors and helping me to convince them that the noise and disturbance from light aircraft using the airstrip was minimal compared to the military who might pass over. Some thought I had arranged it!

There appeared to be a low level route running from north to south which happened to pass over the farm and, so I thought at the time, Aymestrey School; but I learnt later that the area was used widely by all kinds of aircraft. One day while having a Sunday lunch at home with my Grandparents present during the school holidays, I heard an unusual sound, and rushed outside to see the Battle of Britain Memorial Flight Lancaster pass overhead with a Hurricane and Spitfire on each wingtip. By the time the others came outside they were gone but it left me with a lasting memory of the occasion. During fruit picking time, I used to spend a lot of time at the top of the ladder looking for aircraft and later on had an air band radio in my bedroom with a tall aerial on the roof with which I used to listen to two way conversations between air traffic control and various aircraft at Pershore, Gaydon, Birmingham, Shobdon, Halfpenny Green, and as the Clee Hill radar site was developed, other places as well.

Another event of importance which developed my interest in flying was that in 1963, a local friend in the police force, who had learnt to fly towards the end of the war, but never saw active service or combat, Vic Thomas; took me to my first ever air show at RAF Gaydon, near Warwick. This was one of the annual "Battle of Britain" shows around the country. I was impressed, and almost had my first flight there, as they were giving helicopter flights in a Westland Whirlwind, but the queue was too long and we gave up waiting.

On return to boarding School, I decided to write a letter to the station commander at RAF Gaydon thanking him for putting on such a good show and asking some intriguing questions about flying matters. This started a year long series of correspondence with a Group Captain Ruthven L Wade, who always replied and answered my questions. I had got hold of an Aerad Radio Navigation Chart and do remember asking him what "GM" 334 AOA2 was; was it something to do with Birmingham airport. That was of course the way in which an NDB (Non Directional Beacon) was depicted on the chart in those days; something I would learn more about in the future as I developed my flying career.

To cut a long story short, the letter correspondence eventually resulted in my Parents, Sister, and I being personally invited to attend the next "Battle of Britain" show as an official guest of the boss.

Unfortunately, there was a problem as the official show date was after I was to have returned to school as a boarder for the autumn term. My parents considered it would be unfair to take me away from school for this special occasion, and rang to decline in invitation. Group Captain Wade was understanding and instead invited us all for a special day out before I returned to school. This day out was in many ways better than the show itself as we were all given VIP attention from start to finish. I remember driving to RAF Gaydon in the Land Rover, reporting to the guard room at the main entrance with an official letter and being given instructions to carry on straight ahead past the first roundabout, on to the second, where we were to turn right and park outside the station commander's office. After being received by the Group Captain himself, we were given an official luncheon at the top table in the Officer's Mess during which my mother had a very poor steak. On being asked if all was well, she explained that it was not a steak at all and far too tough to eat. A command was given to replace it with a proper steak which duly arrived after we had all eaten and we had to wait while she eat her massive replacement and proper steak.

Following that experience (for my mother that is) we were shown around a Victor bomber servicing hangar, visited the control tower and radar approach room, taken for a drive along the main runway which I landed on myself about 10 years later; and had a flight in a Valiant Bomber flight simulator where we flew up to 10,000 feet, circled around and landed. I remember being told to keep re-trimming the control column; what a wonderful experience that was for a 12 year old! This extraordinary day out convinced me that I wanted to fly and helped foster my interest in aviation for life. What I did not know at the time was that Ruthven had told my father that I had no chance of flying in the RAF as a pilot, as I was already wearing spectacles and would not pass the very strict medical tests.

After this event, he was posted elsewhere and eventually rose in rank to become an Air Vice Marshall. Correspondence then ceased, but there was a finale to this friendship when in 1977, while I was a Britten Norman twin engined Islander pilot for the Rhine Army in West Germany, I briefly met him again and told him that I had indeed succeeded as a pilot and had learnt to fly as a civilian. I had spotted him as part of the VIP delegation to the Queen's silver jubilee celebrations with the British Army which were held on the Sennelager ranges. I approached a security guard and asked if I might have a word. When asked why my presence should be made known to the Air Vice Marshall, I said tell him "Gaydon 1964, Hugh Thompson". Being able, 13 years later, to tell him that his efforts on my behalf had not been entirely wasted must have helped to make his day; and I am sure he appreciated me taking the trouble to make myself known to him again, if only briefly.

After leaving Aymestrey, which you had to leave at the age of 13, it was hoped to send me to Bromsgrove School but I failed the so called "Common Entrance" exam, so I ended up going to Lucton School near Leominster; the same school my father had gone to 30 years earlier. It was here that my interest in aviation really took off literally, as I used to go down to the nearby Shobdon airfield almost every weekend Sunday afternoon. This old wartime airfield, which had been used for the training of glider pilots during the war, was re-established by a group of aviation enthusiasts as a flying club airfield after 1960, and happened to be just three miles from the school. I visited it regularly on Sunday afternoons when we all had to get out of the school grounds for 5 hours or so. I used to get the occasional flight in return for carrying out general chores in the hangar. I probably made a nuisance of myself as well!

I was told many years later that the Headmaster of the day, Keith Vivian, actually rang my father while I was boarding and informed him that I was taking flying lessons at Shobdon, (which was not entirely true as I was only going for flights if offered one) and was asked if he was happy for that activity to continue. Father replied that "If he wants to fly, let him fly". The result of that conversation was that the school had to change its insurance policy for boarders to cover the possibility of an accident while under the school's jurisdiction and responsibility. After an unfortunate closure in 1984 due to financial mismanagement, the School re-opened in 1990, and is now a very successful and thriving private public school; now admitting girls and currently having a lady headmistress. A good aerial photograph of the school is shown in the first of the colour pictures sections.

At the same time that I started at Lucton, my sister also started a new school and the two of us were photographed together in our new school uniforms. This was in September 1965. She was also sent to two boarding schools after about a year at the local day school. Sending us both away to school must have been an expensive choice but it did allow our parents to concentrate on developing and running the farm, which, luckily for me in the future, was expanded by a further 60 acres in 1967 when the next door "Little Down" Farm was purchased.

Lucton was a good independent private boarding school set in open countryside very close the Mortimer's Cross and a large area of woodland which was used for cross country running which I enjoyed very much. Unfortunately, I did not excel academically, had no real interest in any sports, and left with just 5 "O" levels after four years in 1969. However, I do remember two events very well. One was making a spectacle of myself in front of the headmaster on the public road just outside the school gates when, on my bicycle, I applied the brakes but only the front ones worked, and I fell straight off over the handle bars; badly spraining my arms. Also, I did not feel happy there to start with and wrote a letter home asking to be taken away. After I had written and posted it I had second thoughts, and, as a result, had to wait by the post box until the postman arrived so I could retrieve it.

My first serious aviation book which I had while at Lucton was "Flight Briefing for Pilots Volume One", written by Birch and Bramson. I still have it today. I studied it page by page and really thought I knew how to fly, without even leaving the ground. I got the wrong impression at that time that to turn; you applied aileron and rudder in the direction of the turn and then centred the controls when the turn was complete. In reality of course, you apply bank with the ailerons in order to turn by moving the lifting force of the wings away from the vertical, and maintain balance as required during a turn using the rudder. I remember my first ever visit Shobdon airfield when I walked there carrying an old suitcase of flight magazines and made a nuisance of myself talking to the then secretary of the Hereford Aero Club, retired Wing Commander Jimmy James. The club then consisted of a small garden shed by the hangar, a couple of chairs and a table with a public telephone box nearby, together with the one club aircraft; an Auster (G-AIJZ). In addition, there were several privately owned aircraft based there, including a Piper Tripacer (G-ARDU) and a Cessna Skymaster G-ATID which belonged to a wealthy local businessman, Sir Derek Bailey. Other aircraft included a Beagle Terrier G-ASMZ, which I eventually flew in on several occasions as a passenger while at the school. The club expanded while I was at Lucton School and held its first air show in 1967. I used the watch the Tripacer climbing out over the school and saw it dropping parachutists over the airfield many times, and brought myself a small air band radio which I used to listen to Air Traffic Control at the airfield; and to other aircraft on the airways.

During holiday times, I became interested in the local branch of the Royal Observer Corps at their nuclear bunker and look out post "Charlie One", at nearby Clows Top. Although formed during the Second World War to observe and report on aircraft movements, the organisation had taken on the role of monitoring potential nuclear blasts and radiation fallout using underground bunkers scattered across the United Kingdom. As the ROC was a branch of the Royal Air Force, I became a junior member and regularly attended meeting at the local pub during the school holidays and had a visit to RAF Colerne, where I had a special treat.

My very first flight, in an RAF Handley Page Hastings transport aircraft, was from RAF Colerne near Bath on the 11th September, 1966, when we flew around the new Severn road bridge the day after it was opened. My father had given me a letter granting permission for me to fly in a military aircraft but I had to declare that I was 16 years old to get on board; when in fact I was actually just 14 at the time! I distinctly remember seeing the sheep and cattle from the air and thinking they all looked like white maggots and toys. There was a postscript to this flight when in 1980 I flew with the very same pilot as a First Officer during my first commercial flying job. Captain Ken Halls checked his log book against my ticket, which I have always kept, and saw that he had indeed been the Captain of that flight when doing his RAF service. See the ticket below which has been re-produced. At Lucton, I tried to get a school attachment to the nearly "Alfa Three" post at Lyonshall, but there was a lack of interest from other school members and I eventually left the ROC. I remember my yellow ID card number was 114239. The ROC was eventually disbanded in the late 1970's and the underground observer posts were abandoned.

While at school I did however enjoy being in the Combined Cadet Force (CCF) and attended a three week army leadership at Thetford in Norfolk after my last term. I returned home from that course fitter than I have ever been since; grateful in the end, to have been put through hell for several weeks of intense training which including 24 hour exercises, my first helicopter flight in an RAF Whirlwind, learning to ride a motor bike and visiting the American Air Force Base at RAF Mildenhall where I remember watching a Boeing KC135 Stratotanker take off leaving a lot of smoke behind it.

It might be interesting for readers to learn that as I passed through two London railway stations on my way to Norfolk, I saw a book of flying pictures, (which I still have today) which I purchased and took with me wherever I went until I got back home.

I was at Lucton School from 1965 until 1969 when I left at the age of 17, intending to continue my education in a technical college at Kidderminster studying a science based subject. However, as we shall see, my love of flying took over and while working on the farm, I started to learn to fly in earnest, eventually getting my Private Pilots Licence in May of 1970 after completing nearly 47 hours of training which included 18 hours solo flying.

After I had learnt to drive, I used to let some of my school pals borrow my mini van on Sundays while I was at Shobdon. Barry Chamberlain, with whom I have kept in contact all my life, stayed on at Lucton for about another year or so after I had left, so he was able to make good use of my van. As far as I know, he, and some other boys used to go Ludlow regularly for a swim there, but they could have been up to mischief or visiting girl friends; but I shall probably never know? I had great trust in Barry and the car was always returned intact with some extra fuel in the tank. He did have a scare on one occasion when he came out of the swimming pool at Ludlow and found the van had disappeared, but his pals had moved it out of sight as a joke. I only found out about that while writing this book.

He later went on to have a career in the aviation industry involving avionics and flight recorders which was always of interest to me. As a result, I once got an invitation to a special private event at RAF Boscombe Down, where the Queen was due to celebrate 50 years of Test Flying. Princess Anne attended instead as Her Majesty had a cold on the day.

That air show was one of the best I have ever attended, performed in the most atrocious weather conditions with perfect timing and exhilarating displays including a live dummy ejection from a Meteor aircraft. One aircraft performing there was a Scottish Aviation Twin Pioneer, XT610, which I myself was to fly as G-BCWF 12 years later and on one occasion land there while working for British Aerospace.

Chapter Two.
The Early Shobdon Years.

My first actual flying lesson, in Auster Autocrat G-AIJZ, similar to the aircraft shown above, was in 1968 during the school holidays flying from Shobdon airfield. Note how basic the cockpit instruments are; just an airspeed indicator, altimeter, turn and slip indicator, engine rpm gauge, an oil pressure gauge, throttle and fuel on/off selector. The rather large but very stable P1 compass was on the floor. Consulting the first of my 23 small log books, I see that my first lesson was on the 16th August with Flt Lt Mike Sparrow of the Royal Air Force, who was an experienced military instructor at RAF Shawbury and the current part time Chief Flying Instructor at the aero club. I flew with him 10 times until he was posted to RAF Valley in Anglesey where he then flew the Folland Gnat; on one occasion doing a very low fly by along the taxiway at Shobdon. That I think was the nearest I ever came to being knocked over by a jet!

He was an excellent instructor and gave me a lot of confidence and encouragement to continue learning. Two events I remember well with him were that on one flight, we were rudely overtaken by a Cessna 182, which was carrying out quick 10 minute pleasure flights and rushed by our Auster just after we had landed. A robust exchange of words was exchanged with the other pilot which I remember, worried me at the time. The other event was taking my sister Janet for a flight above the clouds for the first time when she sat in the small bucket seat in the back of the other club Auster G-AJIM.

I then flew with two other instructors and was eventually sent "Solo" for the first time on the 27th January 1970 after flying a total of 13.5 Hours on 19 flights; a day when I was supposed to have been at the College in Kidderminster. As it was a good day, I had made arrangements to meet the instructor Mike Edwards at Shobdon at 10 am and had turned right for the airfield instead of left for the college at the road junction in the village. When Mike told me to stop on the runway and started getting out, he had great difficulty as I was holding the stick back as taught. When I got airborne I remember looking up and seeing a V bomber passing high overhead. On landing, I took the aircraft back to the hanger, put it away and secured the padlock as there was no one else about, but I am sure Mike watched me land successfully before departing. On returning home that day I was obviously elated and had to break the news to my mother who asked why I was back from college early, that I had in fact been flying and gone solo for the first time. Mike was a good instructor and just right for me but he was a rather arrogant man and could upset some students but he did not like rules and regulations and was a bit of a rebel.

Before flying solo you had to hold a Student Pilots Licence and have a current Class Three medical. The Licence, No 89625 was issued by the Board of Trade in those days. When I went for my first flying medical with an approved doctor in nearby Ludlow, he asked me if I wanted to fly for a career. On replying "Yes", he told me to forget it as my hearing was poor and eyesight not the world's best either. I asked if he could give me a private pilot's licence medical, which he said he could, so I accepted it with delight. Note that this was a gentle hint **NOT** to take up a career in flying; something I ignored due to my love of flying.

I remember, to this day, a lot about those early days. The propeller swinging start up procedure went like this: Brakes On, Switches Off, Petrol On and Throttle Closed. Then, Switches Off, Sucking In (four to six swings on the propeller) Throttle Set, Contact, selecting "On" the Right Magneto only which had an impulse to give a strong spark. If hot you sometimes had to open the throttle and with the switches off, had to blow out by turning the engine backwards for about 10 swings. The pre take off check list was **TTMMFFGGHH** which stands for **T**rim, **T**hrottle friction, **M**ixture rich, **M**agnetos on both, **F**uel On, **F**laps set, **G**yros and **G**auges including the oil pressure, **H**arness and **H**atches. All the flying was without any radio or intercom in those early days and use of the airfield signals square was always used prior to landing for airfield information. I could explain more but it gave me a very good start to my flying which was to be of great help in the years ahead.

After that great day, I started to fly more often to keep the continuity going. I continued on the Auster to start with, doing alternate dual then solo details but eventually had to change aircraft and completed my PPL training in the club Cessna 150 aircraft, mainly G-AWAW which had a long career and ended up in the Science Museum in London; but more about the reasons why later. Being a nose wheel aircraft it was a lot easier to take off and land but after my first solo flight in it I taxied in and was not sure how to stop the engine. In the Auster you had always had to swing the propeller to start it and switched off the two magnetos to stop the engine. In the Cessna there was an electric starter and you pulled out the red mixture knob to starve the engine of fuel rather than just switching off the ignition.

During one solo cross country in the Cessna 150, G-ATMM, shown in the picture above, with G-AWAW in the background, I had my first real scare. During the flight as I approached Worcester, I noticed the engine rpm falling slightly and simply increased the throttle to restore the power. This continued until I had full throttle but the engine was still losing power. I was contemplating a complete engine failure and thought I might have to land at the Racecourse there when I saw the knob "Carb Heat", next to the throttle. I pulled it out and the engine started to cough and splutter for several seconds until eventually recovering. I had learnt the hard way about carburettor icing. One reason why I was not aware of the risk was that the Auster and its Cirrus Minor engine did not suffer from icing problems and there was no provision for any carburettor ice removal; I had never had to worry about it until then.

While still a student I also took part in a navigational competition in rather windy conditions and whilst I did not win it, I was one of only a few to get 25 bonus points for accurately flying directly towards a mystery checkpoint and the letter "L" which had been placed on Romers Common, near to Bromyard. I also remember being helped out to the runway as, due to the stiff wind, I kept weather cocking into the wind as I taxied out to the runway and was helped out by an elderly gentlemen by the name of Bill Stokes who was one of the founder members of the Hereford Aero Club when it established itself at Shobdon in about 1961. See **Appendix Three** for the results. I also had my second scare, when flying in the circuit solo and landing downwind in a 5 knot tailwind due to the late afternoon sun as authorised by the instructor, I met a Cessna 172 coming the other way on the downwind leg of the circuit. He missed me by just a few feet and proceeded to land into the wind which is normal aviation practice having observed a good smoke indication of the wind direction. What he had not done is observe the "Signals Square" which had indicated an out of wind runway was being used. This was a good example of how a series of relatively small mistakes could have led to a disaster but as a student at the time I really did not expect to meet an aircraft in the circuit going the opposite way.

I finally qualified for my Private Pilots Licence in May of 1970 but not before I had made a serious error at Bristol Lulsgate airport during my qualifying cross country. After having had my qualifying form completed certifying that "the nature of the landing was good and the standard of airmanship high", I proceeded to line up and take off before being cleared not realising that a Vickers Viscount airliner was approaching to land on the other longer runway. I had been cleared to "Line Up" only. Profuse apologies were made and I was on my way. In those days, a lot of airfields had more than one runway in operation, the so called three triangular runway layout allowing aircraft to more or less land into wind but in recent times, only one long runway has remained and the other old runways have become taxiways and parking areas at many airfields.

After I had left Lucton School in the summer of 1969, I enrolled at the Kidderminster College of Further Education with the intention of continuing my studies, studying a science subject. However, my mind was elsewhere; in the clouds most of the time, although having girls around was interesting after Lucton, which in those days was just a boys school. I eventually left the college, and continued to work as a farm labourer at home, the only trouble being that whenever the weather was good for both farm work and flying, flying came first. As I was keen to learn, I often used to get telephone calls from Shobdon saying that someone was flying somewhere and did I want to come for a trip? I often used to cycle the 20 miles to the airfield, then be collected later by my Father after he had finished the farm work! One person I particularly remember was Andrew Gilliat who was the hatchery manager of Sun Valley Poultry Ltd. Whenever the weather was suitable for flying, he used to fly on his own all over the country on company business, and often asked me to accompany him.

My first passenger in the Cessna was my father but I was slightly nervous and was high on the approach saying so as I put more and more flap down. I then slowly built up my hours while working on the farm and flying whenever I could afford it or found a passenger to help pay for it. I continued flying the remaining club Auster occasionally, the other having been sold and actually "Looped" it once over my old school at a safe altitude of 4000 Feet, but it was later written off in a downwind forced landing after the throttle linkage had become detached during an approach. I also got my first telling off soon after I had my licence when I pulled the Cessna just out of the hangar and started it up blowing the dust and slipstream back into the hangar. I remembered that and since then have always made sure my aircraft was parked in a suitable place before starting up, with nothing in front or behind. It is no good getting strapped in, starting up and then finding you are boxed in and cannot get out of your parking place. On one occasion, I went outside to see an experienced instructor had just started up a Cessna 150 with the nose wheel tow bar still attached. Waiving my arms frantically to get him to cut the mixture and switch off, I got his attention and saw a very red face thanking me when I told him why!

As I have already said, the club Auster "JZ" was lost to us all when it suffered an engine failure during an approach and attempted a downwind landing in a light wind. This resulted in it nosing over on to its back after touching down. What had happened was that the engine was still running OK but the throttle linkage had come adrift for some reason. This left the club with a fleet of Cessna 150's, the reliable and faithful AW, together with G-AWFF and G-AWCP which was I believe loaned to the club by a local company. AW and CP had two distinctly different propellers and when I first flew CP I found I could not maintain height at the "usual" setting of 2200 rpm, more like 24-2500 was needed in the cruise. That was because one had a course pitch setting on the propeller which was ideal for long range and good economy but had a poor take off performance; whilst the other leapt off the ground quickly but used more fuel in the cruise. No two aircraft are ever the same, even if the same type, so you have to learn the individual characteristics of every one that you fly.

I am fourth from the right

During the late summer of 1970, I attended a gliding course at the Long Mynd near to Church Stretton but did not achieve a solo because I was always getting too close, not realising how far a glider will glide. I managed 18 five minute flights on the winch; something which helped me in later years. I continued gliding at Shobdon after I became a flying instructor now using aero tow launches; and did a little more winch launch gliding again in West Germany in 1977. Having had some gliding experience proved useful as a flying instructor in later years, but even now I only have just over 11 hours to my credit over a total of 41 flights.

After a period flying various Cessna 150 aircraft, hour building as they say, I was eventually able to start flying an Auster again. G-AIPW, which had been purchased by a family friend, became available. Initially, I had a difficulty landing the Auster again as I tended to round out too high but soon got the hang of it. With this aircraft, I once flew non radio to RAF Shawbury with an Air Training Corps cadet to an Open Day but got told off for not waiting for a green light to land. In fact, it was the ATC controller's fault as I had been directly overhead for about twenty minutes waiting for the Aldis lamp or Very pistol signal. An RAF officer who was waiting for me on the ground confirmed this for me and all was well. Also, I lost the tailwheel on one occasion and had to shut down on the runway and walk it back to the hangar with help from my passenger.

At about this time I also applied to join the Royal Air Force but was not sure about what to do with my life. I attended a selection process at RAF Stafford and effectively talked myself out of it as it was clear to the selection board that I wanted to fly; that would NOT have been possible in the air force due to my hearing and eyesight. I had big ideas that I would drop parachutists and tow gliders with Chipmunks, a popular tailwheel training aircraft at the time. They did say I might get the odd trip in a Hunter, Jaguar, or Phantom but I declined to take up an offer to be trained as an airframes and engine fitter. That probably turned out to be a big mistake, as years later when I found myself out of work and seeking a job, all that I had to my credit was a pilots licence and flying experience with no other skill or trade to fall back on. At one time when unemployed in the early 1990's, I could have got a job in Africa but they needed pilots with engineering skills as well as flying time. I might not have got all my early flying had I joined up but it would have helped later on as I was not able to get a commercial licence until 1979 due to the medical problems I had; primarily with my hearing.

I also flew to many different places and on a wall map had thought up a number of triangular cross country flights I could do. On one such flight I flew round London and got into trouble flying from Stansted to Southend when I got my frequencies mixed up 125.55 MHz and 128.95 MHz were similar on paper and I remember being told by Luton that I was already in their airspace when I called them. I said I was not but it turned out I was using an out of date map. On another occasion going into Gloucester, my radio failed but I could still receive so I proceeded to land after doing two go-arounds or overshoots as they were called then, due to being keyed up and anxious about getting into trouble. I was told off for not diverting elsewhere or returning to Shobdon but this experience proved useful on a later flight when the radio failed completely on my way back from the Channel Islands.

When I first learnt to fly a radio licence was not required while acting as a student but you had to do an R/T rating after you had qualified for your private pilots licence. This I did at the Staverton Flying School with "Woody" who was to become my boss at Shobdon some years later. I was nervous when I turned up for the test and thought you had to get into a Link Instrument trainer rather than using a specially designed console and switching unit. Today the radio licence forms part of the PPL training.

While building up hours, I was offered the chance to fly a single seat turbulent aircraft, (G-ARMZ), but it frightened me a bit and I flew it only a few times. However, I was to fly another example G-BLTC many times over 20 years later; and, having more experience by then, enjoyed flying it the next time.

Also, a new arrival on the club fleet at about this time was a Rallye Commodore aircraft G-AWOC, which I used to great effect taking passenger friends on cross country flights to many places. This particular aircraft met a sad end when, after routine servicing, it was taken out of the hangar and ground run. Unfortunately, the independent wheel brakes were not on, and it was facing towards the hangar doors. The engineer accidentally selected full throttle, and it hit the side of the hangar leaving a wing behind, and caused serious damage to a parked Cessna 182 aircraft. Unfortunately, "OC" was subsequently written off but the other aircraft was repaired. This aircraft is shown below on one of my first flights into my own airstrip at Milson.

Knowing that I was hoping to become a flying instructor at the club, the airfield landowner and club treasurer at Shobdon, David Corbett, kindly agreed to help me by giving me a very special rate for some of my flights when flying the club aircraft which I repaid by having a very low salary later on. One such long flight, in the famous "AW", was to and from Stansted airport in Essex, where the return was to be flown at night. This was an experience as both the CFI who was with me, and I, got totally lost. We eventually saw some barrage balloons which I recognized and an airfield in the distance which turned out to be Weston on the Green and Brize Norton near Oxford. Later, I was also persuaded against my better judgement to fly the Rallye solo one moonlit night, for the first time at night, on my own. I got airborne and soon realised that I had completely lost the airfield, so flew to the nearest town at Leominster and followed the road back to the airfield. Flying at 2000 feet, I then spotted a relatively small set of two lines of lights, which of course turned out to be the runway; lit by small individually battery powered lights. Needless to say I was glad to be back on the ground; my third serious scare. There was no visual approach aids in those days unlike the VASI or PAPI systems that are widely used today to help you make a safe landing.

I observed two incidents which I remember vividly at about this time in my flying life. One was a club member arriving in a Sipa 903 aircraft (G-AWLG) and being unable to land it. He had learnt to fly in a Cessna but had purchased this tailwheel aircraft and stupidly, did not get a proper check out or type conversion. He made numerous approaches with many bounces and go-arounds and eventually managed to get it down with a ground loop damaging a wing in the process. Some thought it was a funny event but in all seriousness, it could have led to a nasty accident or worse. I flew it myself later on and found it a very difficult aircraft to safely take off and land due to its very narrow undercarriage track. The other was a show off taking off in a Rallye (G-ATWE) from directly in front of the clubhouse on the grass parking area and having an engine failure just as he got airborne; he had not turned the fuel on! Suitably embarrassed, he rectified the problem and then took off normally using the runway and departed. These things you remember and recall as you get more experience flying; you learn from the mistakes of others. I was to fly that aircraft myself years later and land it at RAF Gaydon where my interest had developed.

In late 1971, during a gliding club competition at Shobdon, I got checked out in a Super Cub G-APZJ and for the first time flew home and landed on the farm at Milson. This was the start of another enterprise which will form the basis of a later chapter in this book, but it gave me the idea that one day I would create an airstrip of my own. I also did some instrument flying to obtain what is known in the UK as the IMC Rating which is a UK recognised qualification, allowing you to fly in cloud and down to a minimum visibility of 1800 Metres. This qualification could be called a mini Instrument Rating but it is only valid in UK airspace and does not allow you to fly IFR in Class A controlled airspace such as the Airways system. I did most of my training for the IMC Rating with an RAF Instructor, Flt Lt Alan Munro, who at that time was doing a ground tour of duty at Hereford and probably flew more then than when he was posted on a flying tour. He not only instructed but also did parachute dropping and glider towing as well. We remain close friends to this day but he had to eventually give up commercial flying due to a loss of hearing; probably caused by his many hours sitting in the Quick Reaction Alert (QRA) hangars in his Phantom during the cold war years in West Germany.

Finally for this chapter are several other events I recall. One was a serious social mistake of seeing a £1 note on the bar and thinking it had been dropped, I pocketed it. As short time later, I overheard an argument at the bar between a club customer and the barman about this £1 and duly owned up to having taken it; a serious embarrassment to me and something I learnt about; being honest, even it gets you into trouble. Also, the club arranged to trip to the Paris Air Show at Le Bourget in 1971 and about 50 of us flew out from Manchester on one of the last flights by a Dan Air Comet 4b. The weather there was very poor with low cloud and rain and I think we must have made about two or three approaches before landing; with lots of pilots criticising the Captain's efforts to make a safe approach. There was also an occasion when one of the club instructors played a rather nasty trick on the part time air traffic controller on duty one day. From inside the hangar he called up the tower on the Shobdon frequency 123.5 MHz and declared an emergency saying he was an American Aero Commander aircraft on Amber 25, the airway just to the west of Shobdon, flying at FL 100 (10,000 Feet) with an engine fire; and that he was diverting to Shobdon. Jenson Jones, who was in the tower got somewhat flustered and cleared him to land. When he called to say that he was downwind to land, calling again on finals, he could not see the aircraft and suggested he might actually be making an approach to Madley, a disused airfield to the west of Hereford. You could get away almost with murder in those early days, but I doubt whether this sort of thing would be tolerated today. Another trick was to fire a Very Pistol flare an hour or so after dark on a Friday or Saturday evening upsetting any courting couples who might be parked on remote parts of the airfield. Shobdon airfield was a much quieter place in the late 1960's and early 70's before it was developed.

In 1970, Shobdon Airfield was chosen by the British Aerobatic Team as the site to practise their aerobatic sequence and they used it extensively that summer during training prior to the World Championships which I think were held at Hullavington near Swindon. I sometimes used to help by swinging the prop on the Pitts Special and was eventually rewarded with a trip in their Zlin Trainer. I flew a complete aerobatic sequence with Mike Riley, one of the team members, who was a BA 747 Captain and part time aerobatics display pilot. I do not generally like aerobatics preferring to fly around on a nice day with good visibility over wonderful countryside and mountains but I must say that this trip was exhilarating; with very little "G" loading. If flown correctly, you do not have to pull vast amounts of "G" which is when you experience a greater force of gravity on your body. 2.5 "G" for example, is when you would weigh 2.5 time your actual weight.

I continued to fly from Shobdon on and off for many years and still fly from there today as an LAA coaching pilot and part time instructor. However, 40 years later, there are very few faces around that I remember from the earliest days apart from David Corbett, the airfield owner, who was so helpful and supportive in my early years there. While he was the treasurer of the aero club, he introduced a LIFETIME membership to the club for a one off payment of £100 to raise additional capital. I wish I had taken up that offer because today the annual membership fee is now about £120 a year. Sadly, I did not take up the offer as £100 then was a lot of money to find. As far as I know only a very few took advantage of this generous offer.

At the HEREFORDSHIRE AERO CLUB Shobdon Aerodrome

Of all the caricature sketches of the main club members shown above, drawn in 1973, only David Corbett and I are still active pilots and as far as I know, all the rest have sadly passed away apart from Andrew Gilliat who is still living in Shobdon.

Chapter Three.
Early Years as an Instructor at Shobdon.

By the end of 1971, I had obtained the 150 hours necessary to qualify for an assistant instructor's course at Rogers Aviation at Cranfield Airfield in Bedfordshire. By the time I enrolled on the two month course, I had obtained just over 200 hours. The course was run by a very famous ex RAF wartime pilot by the name of Ron Campbell who had written a number of good training manuals. I also took advantage of the Cranfield facility to do my full night rating qualification and thoroughly enjoyed my time there. The airfield had a standard military layout with three hard runways, a large grass landing area, a full set of navigational aids including VOR, NDB, and an ILS. I remember they had a good College of Aeronautics there with a museum containing all kinds of aero engines and jets together with a collection of aircraft including one of two surviving TSR2 aircraft which had been cancelled by the Labour government of the day. They were all ordered to be scraped but some wise person realised some should be saved for the future. I stayed in an annex to Mitchell Hall which was named in memory of the designer of the Supermarine Spitfire, RJ Mitchell.

One demonstration he used to show was that, even in a non aerobatic Cessna 172 with a +4.4/-1.76 "G" limit, you could happily do well flown barrel rolls whilst keeping water in an upright glass if you maintained the balance and a positive load. The standard of the instructional "patter" teaching and class room work was first class and I qualified as a new Assistant Flying Instructor (AFI) after 25 hours. "G" is the force of gravity acting on you.

I now started work at Shobdon full time as an instructor at the age of 19 and found myself passing the school where I had once been a boarder, twice a day, morning and night. As well as being an instructor I found myself doing the odd ferrying trip for servicing and maintenance tasks. I also became a glider tug pilot and started dropping parachutists; all for the good of Shobdon and the three clubs there.

Work at Shobdon for the Herefordshire Aero Club was varied and very interesting. To start with, I was just an assistant instructor, working under the supervision of the Chief Instructor; firstly Mick Barry, then later, the famous "Woody" from Gloucester. You could instruct in those days on a Private Pilots Licence and be paid for it. At the same time, I found myself being asked to carry out parachute dropping for the Herefordshire Parachute Club and a month or so later, started towing gliders as well, so I was kept very busy.

The parachute dropping was carried out using a Cessna 172 G-ARIV to begin with but shortly afterwards I started flying a wonderful aircraft, a Cessna 185 Tailwheel aircraft G-ARMJ which I enjoyed very much. I remember that although there is a mark on the trim wheel indicating the position for Take Off if empty, you had to wind it fully forward when loaded with 6 parachutists for take off and then fully nose up for the landing when they had all departed the aircraft. To help keep it straight on landing there was a tailwheel lock which engaged automatically when you held the control column back but you had to relax the back pressure if you wanted to unlock it for turns and taxying on the ground.

As part of a bet in the bar one night, I said I would jump out if a certain lady did so as well. She did, so I had to follow, and after training I made just ONE successful parachute jump over Shobdon airfield which was an experience not to be forgotten. I remember being the first to be despatched. After aligning myself with the airfield and spotting the Dropping Zone (DZ) I soon realised that I had been dropped too early. I could see that I was going to overshoot the landing area, so had to turn into wind and hold off against the wind all the way down. I was alarmed by how quickly the ground came up to meet me and landed with a bump. However, it had been a useful experience and I believe that any parachute pilot should make at least one parachute jump to understand what goes on behind him. It could be argued that in my entire flying career, I have made one more take off than landings since I got out during one flight!

Once I was asked to fly a parachute friend to Halfpenny Green from Shobdon and drop him over the airfield which I did early one morning. Apparently that was not an approved way to get from place to place and he and I got told off later. The parachute club was a good happy club with lots of social events, with young people and college students in abundance including pretty girls, and a good time was had by all. Unfortunately, the extraction of gravel from the airfield area which resulted in some large pools being created, and increased use of the airfield by other aircraft, including gliders and helicopters, meant that in the end, all parachute activity had to cease. They did for a while try using an off airfield dropping zone (DZ) but in the end, the club decided to move to a site in Gloucestershire, and the abandoned building became part of the new Tiger Helicopter's school in later years.

David Corbett decided to get a number of Cessna 182 and 206 aircraft which were made available to the parachute club and other users and I was duly checked out on these aircraft which were slightly more difficult to fly as they had variable pitch propellers, cowl flaps, and additional radio aids. On one occasion David started up one aircraft but found the main alternator circuit breaker kept tripping out. He asked me to come and have a look. I pointed out it was obvious why, ALL the various electrical switches which were of a rocker type in a line under the instrument panel were ON when he thought they were Off. A simple mistake so you should never assume anything, always check and double check if need be. Tony Mavro, the gliding instructor once visited me at my home airstrip at Milson and when he came to leave went through the motions to start up, placing the fuel to "Off" when he thought it was "On". I suggested that he do his checks again. This he did twice more before he noticed what he had done. Again, a simple mistake; so never assume, always check.

The glider towing was also very interesting. After two qualifying tows with an experienced glider pilot on tow with the new club Rallye, I found myself starting this aspect of my flying by towing gliders from a grass field at Usk near Monmouth, which had a slightly curved airfield runway. Later on, the club got a Beagle Terrier aircraft G-ARLP, and I was determined to be the first pilot to fly it when it became available. After being told by the engineer that it was ready, I got in, started it up, and off I went. It was similar to the other Austers I had flown by that time. On landing, David Corbett, the airfield owner and club treasurer, gave me a very severe ticking off for not having asked if I could fly it; "How did I know it was insured", he asked? It was, but I was not to know that, so I subsequently learnt to be more careful in future.

I did quite a lot of towing at Shobdon, a total of at least 199 in all over about five years. This included two long tows to Nympsfield in Gloucestershire on two occasions, but most were from Shobdon locally up to about 2-3,000 feet. When I checked out the one gliding instructor Anthony (Tony) Mavrogordato on the Terrier tug, I emphasised that no landing is complete until it has come to a complete stop; especially with a tailwheel aircraft. His first solo on type ended up with a really good "ground loop" in front of a watching crowd which resulted in a very red faced pilot! I reminded him again what I had said. "You cannot relax at all when landing a tailwheel type aircraft as it is directionally unstable and WILL eventually catch you out if you do not concentrate until it has stopped moving".

Apart from the Long Mynd Course most of my gliding experience has been from Shobdon. Although I now have just 11 hours in total, one flight not long after I had gone solo in the club Blanik glider, was for over 3 hours. After being towed to about 2000 feet, I had drifted down to about 1200 feet above ground level (agl) and was just about to return to land when I felt some lift just upwind of some cloud. Turning into the wind I found myself climbing rapidly and this continued all the way up to 15,000 feet when I decided to call it a day and pulled out the air brakes. I did not want to suffer from lack of oxygen, and in any case, I needed a pee by then! While I was airborne the club instructors had gone to lunch, which in those days was always taken at a nearby factory canteen on the other side of the airfield. On return the Blanik was nowhere to be seen and they all feared I had landed out, but I duly arrived overhead and landed much to everyone's surprise. This wave flight turned out to be a record for the club at that time but I was left with a degree of overconfidence. On my very next flight, which was to 1.5 hours, I went again to 11,000 feet but the cloud rolled in and after a quick descent found myself too far downwind of the airfield to make a safe return. I therefore decided to land out on Bircher Common which was about 5 miles away. Unfortunately, although the landing was perfect, I broke the canopy later when the strong wind ripped it out of my hands cracking it badly. Although repaired with glue, the crack remained as a reminder to all for many months that you should be careful in strong winds when opening the canopy. That ended my gliding days for over 10 years until I managed to do a few flights at Detmold in West Germany which included 3 short solo winch launch flights; much to my surprise and shock. I did not expect to be allowed to go solo but I handled the check flights very well.

My brief gliding days was a useful experience and I remember to this day the two main check mnemonics, **CBSITCB/CB** and **USTAL** which stand for **C**ontrols, **B**allast, **S**ecurity, **I**nstruments, **T**rim, **C**anopy, air **B**rakes, and finally, **C**able **B**reak for take off and **U**ndercarriage, **S**peed (which unlike an aircraft, you increase before landing to give a safety margin over the stalling speed and some residual inertial energy in case you suffer any wind shear or get low on the approach) **T**rim, **A**irbrakes, and **L**ookout for landing. I found you could use the airbrakes in a similar manner to the throttle of an aircraft to control your rate of descent. This knowledge proved useful in later years when doing conversions on the aircraft for glider pilots. I have always found that glider pilots have a better understanding and appreciation of the weather and the effects of the wind in particular; after all, in a glider, every approach is a forced landing and you cannot go around for another attempt. I hope to do more of this one day but anything to do with flying is expensive, so this book will have to be a best seller!

I also got checked out and did quite a lot of flying in a Motor Falke G-AXIW, similar to the aircraft shown, which was a motorised glider with one main wheel and two small outrigger wheels on the wings; just like the Monowheel Europa I was to fly extensively in later years. I often used to fly home to the Milson farm airstrip with it while I worked and flew from Shobdon.

G-AWAW was the main club aircraft of the day supplemented by G-AWCP which was later converted into a tail wheel aircraft, and G-AWFF which I had flown at Cranfield during my instructor's course. On fetching that aircraft, it was found to have a dead magneto when I got to Shobdon which was not a good start. "AW" had a very varied life and once got forced down by a downdraft in the lea of a hill south of Shobdon in strong winds and ended up in a cornfield. After studying my log books I see that I personally flew 588 Hrs, 25 minutes on this particular aircraft over 829 Flights between March 1970 and September 1977. This included at least 1550 Take offs and Landings.

Later, after the aircraft had been sold on, it was flown all the way to Australia in 1980 by a lady pilot Janette Schönburg on a trip to commemorate the 1930 flight of Amy Johnson before the war. It was flown VFR with a map and compass, long before the advent of Global Positioning Satellites (GPS) and "Sat Nav" which has now made long navigation flights too easy; if it works correctly? It came back in a British Airways 747 Jumbo and as I said earlier, ended up in the Science Museum in London. Janette and I were to fly together in later years as a Shorts SD360 Crew and we remain close friends. A photograph of its final resting place for many years is shown on the next page, together with a brief explanation and history. While writing the book, I learnt that it will soon be on the move again; to the Cessna 150/152 Club in the United States.

G-AWAW – Flight Lab exhibit, Science Museum

G-AWAW has been housed in the Science Museum in Kensington, London since May 1990. Having suffered storm damage the Cessna aircraft was purchased for use as an exhibit in the museum's Flight Lab. As in Australia, prior to transportation to England following the Amy Johnson Memorial Flight, the wings, tailplane, propeller and undercarriage were removed in order to transport the fuselage via elevators and corridors into it's present position.

With the aid of audio-visual effects G-AWAW is used to demonstrate the controls and instrumentation of a typical piston-engined training aircraft. Visitors are able to listen to an instructor's pre-flight brief whilst observing the responses of the aircraft controls.

So, after more than 20 years of work, mainly in training ab-initio pilots, and a flight of 12,000 miles to Australia, G-AWAW is now in a fitting resting place together with Amy Johnson's Gypsy Moth, 'Jason'.

Looking at my log books of the time, it is impossible to remember every flight but some events I do recall very well and are engrained on the memory for ever. I cannot be sure if they are in the correct order but are useful tips for any hopeful instructor who might be reading this book. Studying my log books as I have written this book has certainly brought back some memories, some good and some bad. There are even some flights I just cannot remember making

One flying instructor who used to work part time had the idea of pulling out the mixture to simulate an engine failure rather than closing the throttle which is normal practice. I tried it at about 300 feet just after take off but after the student had picked a suitable field and decided to climb away, the engine did NOT restart and I ended up having to land it in a sloping field just past the Milton Cross roads to the west of the airfield. I was red faced to state the obvious, but I remember the student thinking it was all part of the training. I left him with the aircraft as there were cattle in the field and walked back to the club where I walked into the office and gave Woody the keys of the aircraft telling him it was in a field. He flew it out later when the wind had dropped. Using the same aircraft, the other instructor tried the same trick some days later when carrying out a glide approach but when they got low on the approach and decided to restart the engine the same thing happened; and he ended up landing one field short of the runway. Luckily there was a farm gate available and the aircraft was simply pulled through the gate. All was well, and both he and I had got away with it. However, pulling out the mixture to fail an engine was banned thereafter. It turned out that there was a fault on that particular Cessna 150's carburettor. Normally, an engine which is rotating should restart if the mixture is inadvertently pulled out; instead of the carburettor heat for example.

On another occasion, I was doing a grass landing on the airfield next to the runway. As the grass was wet, the main wheels locked when the brakes were applied and the aircraft started to skid like skis towards the corn ahead. I said to the student, who I met again at Southend some 30 years later, "Stop Braking". He thought I had said "Stop by Breaking", so we just continued sliding into the corn which was not our intention. The skid marks were evident when we got out and started pushing the aircraft back on to the grass.

When flying one winter's afternoon at 4000 feet above the thick haze layer, whilst carrying out a straight and level training exercise with the radio turned down (we used to use a hand mike and speaker then rather than headsets), the club was trying to call me to say that the visibility was falling rapidly and Fog was forming. Being well above the haze and forming fog, I could still clearly see the airfield and had no concerns or worries, until that is, I started my descent to land. On entering the haze layer and forming fog during the approach I could hardly see the airfield and only just got back in before dense fog covered the airfield completely. I learnt about flying, and meteorology, on that day. The slant range visibility is always much less than when you are looking down through a haze or shallow fog layer, so be warned, you can get caught out!

I also had my first partial engine failure while doing a one hour circuit detail, I think in G-AWAW. Shortly after take off there was a loud bang followed by a reduction in the maximum rpm from about 2500 to just 1800. First thoughts was that I should land immediately in a suitable field but I soon realised that with about 10 degrees of flap down, I could remain in level flight, flying at an airspeed of about 70 mph. This was in fact flying at the safe low speed configuration that you use when flying below low cloud and/or in poor visibility. I therefore chose to fly a careful circuit over open countryside with shallow bank angle turns and landed back on the runway normally. One cylinder had cracked wide open which accounted for the bang and loss of power. Never rush a decision, always weigh up the options first. An ex RAF flight engineer who I have flown with in recent years told me a good saying, **"The bigger the problem, the slower the response"**.

One serious event occurred while I was an instructor at the club which had luck not intervened, could have been a fatal mistake. An elderly student, the local town milkman named Fred Smith was sent on a solo cross country at about 1500 hrs on a winter's afternoon and told to over fly Gloucester and return, about an hour's flight normally. Unfortunately, he got lost and did not return as darkness fell. West Drayton, the London Air Traffic Control Centre (LATCC) was informed and all airfields were told to try and find him and assist a landing. Unfortunately, he had not flown at night before so found himself in darkness with no lights and for some reason the radio was not working. After just over 4.5 Hours flying and virtually out of fuel, he spotted some runway lights which turned out to be Manchester where he made a successful landing, just in time; a guardian angel saved him. Where he had been for 3 hours and at what altitude he flew, we will never know but it was a good example on how mistakes can lead to near misses. The main fault was letting him go on a solo cross country so late in the day.

I did something similar as well. When I once went for my annual CAA medical in London at the CAA House in Kingsway, I left the medical centre at about 13.00 and looking at the weather decided to go to Elstree aerodrome just north of London to collect an Auster which had been ready for collection for some time. On the first attempt a month or so earlier, I found it had not been prepared as promised and the fuel tank was full of water! On arrival at the airfield at about 15.00 Hrs I booked out, and gave 10 pence to someone asking that they telephone the Upper Heyford airbase north of Oxford to tell them I would be passing through their Military Aerodrome Traffic Zone (MATZ) non radio in about 45 minutes. I got a propeller swing and was on my way, flying west north west at about 1500 feet but as you can already surmise, it got dark. After passing Pershore airfield where I could have landed, I found myself flying without a map and in the dark non radio but I do recall that I had got myself a small torch before departure. I arrived overhead Shobdon at about 18.30 and knowing where the runway was in a black hole south of the village made an approach which resulted in a perfect landing on the runway where I found the altimeter reading exactly zero on landing. Woody came out to me on the runway in his car and seeing who it was, gave me a severe dressing down for being so stupid. However, in the bar later over a few drinks he congratulated me on my wartime spirit of adventure and daring. I had got away with it but things could have turned out differently. I had at least done some night flying and had a night rating on my licence, but lack of preparation and desperation almost cost me dear, another lucky escape.

An interesting additional comment about MATZ zones is worthy of note. At about that time, the early 1970's, these new zones were added to the map in the shape of a frying pan on the map. They were intended to give additional protection to military aircraft at their home bases especially within the circuit area but were not mandatory for civil aircraft so you could pass through them without permission so long as you did not enter the actual aerodrome traffic zone (ATZ) which extends to 2 or 2.5 nautical miles depending on the length of the longest runway and is centred on the mid point of that runway. An elderly lady pilot, on landing her Hornet Moth at Shobdon, came over to me and asked what all these "Frying Pans" were, as they had recently appeared on the aeronautical charts. Telling her they were the new MATZ she replied that she took no notice of them at all and simply flew through them non radio. That lady was Marion Wilberforce, one of the wartime Air Transport Auxiliary (ATA) pilots who flew just about everything from Spitfires and Tiger Moths to Lancaster and B17 heavy bombers during the war. An interesting obituary was written about her in the Observer and Telegraph newspapers when she died some years later. The interesting thing to note was that they flew all kind of aircraft without any serious problems, yet today a commercial pilot is only allowed to fly a maximum of two current types at any one time, if working commercially!

You can never be sure what a student will get up to when sent solo. One of mine, Bryn Meredith, who still flies today on both fixed wing and helicopters, inadvertently landed at the wrong airfield on a cross country, a disused one called Lichfield, and simply took of again when he realised his mistake. I, on the other hand, once flew above some patches of low cloud on my return from East Midlands Airport where I had flown to do my upgrade test to become a full instructor, saw some hill ahead in the distance which I believed to be the Clee Hills, and flew on. When the ground below me became uncertain, I actually descended to look at the motorway road signs and seeing an airfield covered with radio masks, suddenly realised where I was; it was Snittersfield airfield near to Warwick, some 20-25 nautical miles off course! I must have flown through the Birmingham Control Zone without a clearance but once again, got away with it; and I was now supposed to be a full instructor? I had probably not checked the Directional Indicator (DI) against the compass and mistook Meon Hill south of Stratford to be the Brown Clee Hills in the distance. Even the most experienced pilots can get caught out, especially if the balance of their mind has been disturbed by a good (an enjoyable date?) or bad event (car crash of relative?) has recently taken place.

I would now like to recall the first overseas trip which I flew, in 19723, when I took my parents and sister to Guernsey in the Channel Islands. This trip was in the Cessna 172 which had been used by the parachute club. When checking it before departure I discovered a slow valve leak on one main wheel which worried me slightly, but just like a car wheel, it was slow to deflate and was not a problem. We flew first to Bournemouth Hurn where we cleared customs and then carried on to Guernsey via the French coast. After a day on the Island, we flew back but I was not prepared to be asked to leave the Jersey control zone not above 1000 feet via the Casquets Lighthouse to the west of the Island of Alderney which I had never heard of. I decided to fly northeast and said nothing which was just as well as the generator failed and I eventually lost all my electrics. As the ADF was not working I just held a steady heading knowing that in time the south coast would come into view. If carefully planned beforehand, the use of "Heading and Time" will suffice on most navigational trips.

As I was due to land at Hurn and had not got a clearance to enter their zone, I was concerned about getting into trouble and arrived overhead, looked at the windsock and decided to land on the into wind runway R/W 36, which was not the main runway and the one in use at the time. However, as I had filed a flight plan all was well; ATC had assumed that I had had a radio or electrical failure and watched me on primary radar as I approached. Air traffic control is there to help a pilot and if you follow correct procedures you will not get into trouble. I do not remember whether or not we got the problem solved, but we continued on our way back to Shobdon. These days, we also have radar transponders which can be used to communicate certain information such as a radio failure to ATC (code A7600) but in 1972 they were relatively new to light aircraft and not a mandatory requirement.

I also decided to train for a Twin rating while an instructor at Shobdon. Sun Valley Poultry Ltd had purchased a Piper Apache aircraft, G-ATMU, and it was made available to the club if required. This was a useful bit of extra knowledge to acquire, but was expensive, so I did not fly it very much. I used to get some friends of our family to pay for some of the flights I did. The flight test was at Weston super Mare and I flew down there with the instructor, Mike Gibbons and another pilot who had also done a twin rating to help with the costs. I was nervous during the test and remember being very slow to reduce the drag after the simulated engine failure by failing to raise the landing gear once a positive climb had been established. There is a "Blue Line" speed on the ASI of most light twin engined aircraft, which is the best rate of climb speed with the gear and landing flap up.

While working at Shobdon, I passed the 700 Hour mark which qualified me to apply for a commercial pilots licence. I therefore applied for a Class One medical but the CAA turned me down due mainly to the loss of hearing I had. They sent me to the Central Medical Establishment (CME) of the Royal Air Force where both my hearing and eyesight were closely examined. They confirmed what the first doctor in Ludlow had said in 1969 and told me I could **NOT** have a medical for a commercial pilots licence. I was bitterly disappointed about that decision as my mind was set on an aviation career, but I was given some hope for optimism when the CAA said "Come back in 5 Years". As I did not require a class one medical for PPL flying club instructing at that time, I simply carried on doing what I knew best; instructing, parachute dropping, glider towing, and generally flying around. I was not put off and lost none of my enthusiasm to fly.

One other piece of useful knowledge is the fact that one day I witnessed the destruction of a Cessna 150 G-ATML which had arrived for its regular 50 hour check from Gloucester in rather windy conditions. The regular pilot, a local postman from that area who used to do the trip for some free flying, parked it nose up to the hangar doors ready to be pulled in. As the doors were opened, there was a gust of wind which promptly, and unceremoniously, turned the aircraft upside down before anyone could react. That aircraft was written off due to a careless thoughtless action. Once again, something to remember in case it ever nearly happened to you? I also witnessed a friend of mine, Keith Jones, running out of fuel just after take off while parachute dropping with a Cessna 206, G-BATD. To minimise weight, the pilot was always being asked to fly with minimum fuel but he tried to fly one lift too many. He later became a commercial pilot and flight examiner, and I flew with him many times on the Shorts SD-360 aircraft some years later. He landed in the ploughed field past the end of the runway and turned it over as the nose wheel dug into the soft ground.

I will return to other events and recollections at Shobdon in a later chapter when I flew there between jobs or whilst carrying out coaching flights for the Popular Flying Association (PFA); an organisation which was later renamed the Light Aircraft Association (LAA). I still fly from there today, but I get the general impression that the current staff and flying instructors do not like having me around, which is a pity as I could be very useful to the club; especially with ground school teaching.

The Famous G-AWAW outside the Shobdon Hangar. (I am checking the Oil)

Chapter Four.
The Cardiff Years; Twice!
"Pegasus"

Although I was enjoying my flying from Shobdon, in early 1974, an opportunity came about which was to change the course of my life and lead to more responsibility and greater experiences. I cannot remember how I found out about the vacancy for the Chief Flying Instructor's (CFI) job at a small flying club at Cardiff Airport called the Pegasus School of Flying, but I accepted the chance of an interview and remember that a fellow club member, Keith Miles, offered to fly me down to Cardiff in the leased Robin Regent aircraft G-BAJY. I could see the job offered a challenge and the opportunity to start flying from an airfield with full air traffic control facilities, controlled airspace, and airline operations including jet aircraft.

With RAF St Athan close by as well, there was often military jet traffic in the circuit as well; mainly practice diversions from RAF Brawdy along the South Wales coast in Pembrokeshire. I decided to accept the job, but was sad to leave Shobdon. However, the club treasurer David Corbett said in his farewell message that I was moving on to "pastures greener" but would probably return one day.

I remember very well my drive down to Cardiff on my first day as I stopped and admired the view in the Monmouth area. The flying club was accommodated in part of an old style military building on the south side of Rhoose airfield, shared with the neighbouring Glamorgan Flying School; a friendly rival. The job as CFI had come about following the sudden departure of the previous instructor who had either resigned or retired. The club members were very pleased to have found a young and enthusiastic instructor who was, not only to live at the club, but ran it almost exclusively on this own; looking after the flying, club aircraft bookings, the bar, arranging social events, and generally running the show on behalf of the few so called directors. They were Bob Coles, an ex RAF Typhoon and Tempest fighter pilot, Frank Todd, who owned the nightclub complex on nearby Barry Island, Ray Browning a businessman (and the person who came to see me at Shobdon originally), and David

Fletcher, a Cardiff solicitor. Another director, who was determined to see the club make money and expand, Bob Watts, joined the team shortly after I arrived and remained a close friend for many years after I eventually left the club for the second time.

The club had just two PA-28 Piper Cherokee four seater aircraft, G-AXIP and G-AXIR when I first arrived, both four seater aircraft, which were then maintained by a company at Weston Super Mare on the other side of the Bristol Channel. I quickly decided that one should go and be replaced by a Cessna 150 for training, with the other Cherokee being used mainly by club members for touring trips etc. I tried to get the famous "AW "from Shobdon, but it was not for sale at the time and the club ended up with a Cessna 150 Aerobat G-AYRP. I also decided to change the maintenance arrangement but this decision was not entirely successful as there were some poor companies around, all keen to take your money, but never prepared to accept that a mistake had been made.

Both Cherokee aircraft had Hobbs meters in them which recorded aircraft engine running time using oil pressure. This was a most unsatisfactory system to me as it caused no end of argument and misunderstanding. As it recorded 10ths of an hour, i.e., 6 minute jumps, it was possible to someone to effectively pay for 12 minutes of someone else's flight! A click up one point just after start up and another click up, just before shutdown, was not fare. Also, whenever the aircraft was fetched or taken to the hangar, or across the airfield for re-fuelling, who was going to pay? I discontinued their use immediately and started making spot checks on people's accuracy and honesty by checking with Cardiff ATC who kept a log of all flights, take off and landing times included. I once returned back to the club after a day off to find much less fuel in the Cessna's tanks than I had expected. I could see from the booking out sheet that a PPL club member had been for a 45 minute flight but when I checked with ATC, found the aircraft had in fact been airborne for 1.5 hours! That member never flew from my club again. Three years later, I came across a German Cessna 172, D-ECIE, which had an airborne recording meter, which only recorded flying time (admittedly above 60 Knots). This was much fairer to all if an allowance for some taxying fuel is made in the hourly fee charged. This system is also a safer one for engine wear and maintenance because only airborne time needs to be recorded in the aircraft and engine log books, and there is NO rush to do your checks prior to departure, or taxy fast. Also, if you find yourself in a queue at the holding point, you do not have to worry about having to pay for it. That happened to me at Luton airport once where, for at least 25 minutes, I was kept waiting for a take off clearance. This was when I used the German aircraft to fly home during my army days (1976-7) but it cost me nothing to wait. I flew and gladly paid for 21 Hours, 35 minutes precisely; no more, no less. See picture in the first coloured section.

Consulting my logs books for reminders and hints, I am able to recall lots of events and incidents which will all help the reader learn a few more tips about flying. One of my first students from start to finish was a small Welshman from Tredegar named Dave Edwards. He completed his PPL with me but not before doing a final cross country of 2.5 hours all on one tank in the Cherokee. It returned virtually empty on one side and full on the other; no wonder he complained that it was flying one wing low. He had in fact not landed at either of the two airfields he had planned to visit and had to do it all again; after some re-training and a careful brief. The one remaining Cherokee appeared to run rich and we often leaned the mixture control in the cruise to reduce consumption. As a result, we eventually needed two new engine cylinders due to overheating. The problem had been in the priming system where a leak past the plunger had allowed raw fuel to be sucked into the two priming cylinders even when locked. That was one fault not found by our maintenance company at the time but they denied any liability, and the club had to pay for the repairs.

When the one aircraft went for its three yearly Certificate of Airworthiness renewal, it cost the club over £4000, so we decided to change our maintenance company and go to Exeter instead. The very next service for that same aircraft came to over £1500 after just 50 hours due to all manner of faults, but all liability for any bad workmanship was denied by the previous company at Weston. I distinctly remember being shown how a fuel drain valve had been forced into the wrong gascolator bowl fitting, requiring a complete replacement, at a cost to the club, of both parts. I have always been suspicious of maintenance companies so it is important to be around, if you can, while work is being done; at least check things over very carefully before accepting the aircraft after any work has been done during a check or inspection.

One airfield I used to visit regularly for cross country training was Dunkeswell in Devon. This was an ideal airfield to catch out a student if he did not do his altimeter checks correctly. As it was over 800 above mean sea level, if you did not get the airfield QFE setting over the radio or calculate the pressure setting difference of 28 millibars, then you could find yourself flying around the circuit at just

170 feet above the airfield ground level. As it was situated on top of a sharp hill, you appeared to be much higher when in the circuit itself. As an instructor, I found it difficult not to give a hint and keep quiet.

In December of 1974, one club member who had been learning to fly with the club, John Penny, decided to purchase a tailwheel Jodel D112 aircraft, G-AXTX, which had to be collected from Aberdeen in the north east of Scotland. Although not the best time of year for a long ferry flight, I was asked to fetch it and flew to Scotland for the first time via Bristol, Liverpool and Glasgow, to Aberdeen on a couple of Vickers Viscount aircraft.

As there was a young schoolboy member of the club, Mark Habberfield, who was as keen on flying as I was during my days at Lucton, John offered to pay for him to accompany me. This turned out to be a blessing as he was able to help me taxy in the strong winds we encountered by holding the one wing tip while taxying out to the various into wind runways that we used during the trip south.

After flying up by airline which was an experience by itself, I did an air test on the aircraft which was fine apart from a very old style radio fit which had crystals for a select number of frequencies. We therefore flew back almost non radio except for some common frequencies such as 122.1 MHz used for airfield tower communications and the international emergency frequency of 121.5 MHz. The trip south via Edinburgh (Turnhouse), Sunderland, Doncaster, Nottingham, Shobdon, and Weston super Mare was flown over two days in very windy but with excellent visibility conditions totalling just 8 hours of flying. It was a rough trip but all the landings were made directly into wind with no problems but taxying without a wingman would have been impossible; so Mark was a great help, and an extra pair of eyes as well. This aircraft together with another one owned by a fellow club member were later painted in a camouflage colour scheme with German Swastikas on the tail for air show purposes but it did not go down well with some people and the idea was abandoned after a year or so.

While flying one day on a circuit detail I became the vital "Linkman" between air traffic control and all arriving commercial aircraft when the Cardiff control tower suffered a complete electrical failure and the standby batteries were found to be almost flat. ATC found they could only talk to me on the ground close by the tower but not to any other aircraft; so I effectively relayed messages from ATC to/from arriving aircraft which included a Viscount, BAC1-11 jet, and an HS 125 Executive jet. A slightly unnerving experience, but I was able to help get those aircraft down without any serious delay. I was later thanked by the CAA manager at Cardiff, Mr Keith Mack; and an article was put in the local South Wales Echo newspaper which is re-produced as **Appendix Six** in the book. On another occasion while taxying out for take off I happened to look up, and saw a French registered Beech Baron just about to touch down with the undercarriage UP! I called "Gear" or something similar to which ATC replied say again; until the controller saw what was happening and uttered a swear word over the airways. Unfortunately, we were just too late to prevent an expensive mistake, but it does show how keeping one's ears and eyes open with an awareness of what is going on around you, can possibly prevent an accident. I did see an inspection cover open on a small jet once and said so allowing it to be correctly closed before take off. Better awareness and caution might have prevented me from almost being blown over in the Cessna one day while taxying back to the club. A Vickers Viscount was doing high speed engine runs on the servicing apron next to the flying club one day with the slipstream crossing the taxiway itself and I happened to pass it during one of the engine runs. ATC should have been advised of the engine run above idle but the engineer on board forgot to inform them

At Cardiff you could effectively fly all day and night but being in controlled airspace did mean that flying was severely limited when the visibility was either below 10 Kilometres or the cloud base was low. There were days when it would have been flyable at say Shobdon but aviation law rules sometimes prevented Visual Flight Rules (VFR) flying in the control zone around the airport when the weather was bad. However, being able to have a full ATC service, radar control and a full set of aerodrome facilities for night flying and instrument flying training was of course a bonus.

I returned back to the club after my two days off one week, usually a Monday and Tuesday after a hard weekends flying, to find my faithful Cessna 150 "RP" all cut up. The two wingtips, nose and tail had all been sliced up into pieces by a Glamorgan Flying Club Grumman Trainer which had gone amok after a break failure with an Air Training Corps cadet on board. A PPL club member who was to have gone for a flight had RP's engine running and that cut the

Grumman to pieces as well! A real mess, which was sorted out by the insurance companies but I did not get any compensation for the loss of business having to use just the one Cherokee for training. I think we did use one of the other clubs Glos Airtourers for a while for those students that wanted to try that aircraft. The Airtourer was in fact one of the easiest aircraft to land and take off, had just one central control column and I enjoyed flying it immensely. However, they did have two drawbacks; one was that with full flap so called "Dutch Roll" was a possibility rolling from side to side on approach caused by over controlling it, and with the fuel turned OFF, it was just possible to get airborne, as it would run for 5-10 minutes, just enough time for you to taxy out and do all your engine checks! Most training aircraft will not run long enough with the fuel off for it to be critical, but don't try it for your self, just in case you do manage to get airborne?

I encouraged early morning flying at the club by introducing a slightly lower rate for the 08.30 Hrs booking slot. This helped to get the flying hours up but also had the effect of getting me up early as well! On trial lessons, I often used to use the 4 seater Cherokee if any potential student wanted to take a family member or friend along for the trip. However, on one occasion, the gentlemen's lady friend or wife became petrified and tried to get out in the air. This was a genuine emergency and ATC let me land as quickly as possible. I have never before, or since, seen anyone so scared; her face was white and a real fear showed in her eyes.

Cross country and overseas touring flights were encouraged and any club member could book either aircraft for a day or more but they had to guarantee at least two hours flying to make it worth it for the club itself. I flew a few trips to France and Ireland in particular, and on one trip forgot to switch off the battery master switch. On returning to the aircraft, we were grounded until I got a small charge into the battery. After a swing start which is not recommended on a PA28, we were on our way, but the alternator, which requires a small current to be excited, rapidly charged the battery from zero to 60 amps when the circuit breaker would tip. After allowing the battery to cool, I then reset the circuit breaker (C/B) for the same effect to happen again and again but gradually the charge rate came down and eventually the battery was fully charged up. It could not have done either the alternator or the battery much good and a valuable lesson was learnt by all. Flying across the Irish Sea to the west of Strumble Head once, I became convinced while above cloud that the artificial horizon was faulty as I repeatedly wanted to bank the aircraft slightly. In fact, it was the cloud layer that sloped slightly, making me think something was wrong. You must trust your instruments when no visual contact with the ground is possible, even if in clear air. It was a weird sensation but in training manuals we are all warned such illusions can occur.

My flying at Cardiff was not confined exclusively to the club aircraft as I kept in touch with Shobdon and other places. As some members in the past had flown tailwheel aircraft, I had the loan of an Auster G-AJAB for a short while and got at least one member, Geoff Claxton, solo. He had learnt to fly many years earlier on a Tiger Moth and was keen to try his hand at tailwheel flying again. I also did the odd type rating or some night flying on other member's aircraft, one being a Rallye Club, G-BAOF, which a local farmer owned. He had in fact learnt to fly with me when I was at Shobdon.

One club member, Gwyn Jones, decided to buy himself an ex wartime Noorduyn Harvard, LN-MAA, which I was privileged to fly several times. It became G-BDAM (216) on the UK register and was eventually sold on but not before I had flown it P1 from the front cockpit; always with the owner on board, as he did not want me to fly away with it for obvious reasons. A good air to air shot was taken of this aircraft with me flying it from the club Cessna which is shown above. Another member, John Powell, got his hands on two De-Havilland Chipmunks, G-BCAH and G-BFAW on which I did quite a few hours flying, including some trips home to my airstrip at Milson.

He started off as a member of the other club but found lots of pilots taking advantage of this unique aircraft, so he and a friend came over to my club where he got a more friendly and helpful reception. After the Chipmunks had moved on, he purchased an old Percival Piston Provost, G-BGSB; which I was also lucky enough to fly solo on one occasion; at night! Unusually for an aircraft, it had compressed air brakes, which were applied using a handle on the control stick. That one solo flight ranks amongst one of my favourite flights. The Harvard and Piston Provost both had unusual engines; a Pratt and Witney Wasp R895 radial engine on the Harvard and an Alvis Leonides radial engines on the provost; both of which I was to have a long association with in later years on other aircraft, namely the DHC-2 Beaver and Scottish Aviation Twin Pioneer.

Later on, John and two other club members Densil Davis and Tom Jenkins formed a friendship and decided to purchase several aircraft from the United Sates and I went with them one at least two occasions to help fly them back. These adventures will form the basis of a separate chapter later on.

I also flew an Auster G-AGXV from a small private airstrip on the side of a mountain at Tredegar; an unusual and not particularly safe airstrip in the middle of the town. I did consider buying this aircraft some years later but on close examination felt it would be costly to maintain and decided not to go ahead. It has since been lovingly restored and still flies today.

The club gave me a very nice painting of this aircraft with Porthkerry Park, just to the east of Cardiff Rhoose airport, in the background as a present on my 23rd birthday. It was painted by Lynn Williams, one of the flying club members, and is shown as one of the colour prints in this book.

At Tredegar, you had to land one way uphill and take off the other, regardless of the wind there. There were plans at one time to make a new airfield close by on the site of an old quarry and I landed on the levelled site a few times in a Piper PA38 Tomahawk, but nothing came of it and the plans were abandoned. A British company, GKN Sankey as I recall, had a factory at Tredegar and on one occasion, never to be repeated, decided to fly their Britten Norman BN2a Islander twin engined aircraft into the airstrip. Careful planning had not revealed the extent of the slope and the pilot realised too late that he would not get out again. Having landed safely, the aircraft left by road on a large trailer some weeks later! All I can say about that is be careful when planning to fly to any unlicensed airfield or farm strip, there can be hidden hazards; one of which I will recall in a later tale.

When flying once with Mark Habberfield, the young lad who came to Scotland with me to fetch the Jodel, we were over the sea in the Portcawl/Port Talbot area and he asked if we could do some low flying over the sea and follow the coast back to the airfield. I was a little reluctant to go too low and remember looking at the fuel gauges which showed about 5-7 US gallons on each side. Enough, so I thought, so down we went, and we flew all the way back at about 50-100 feet; perfectly legal over open water. As we passed the Aberthaw power station on the coast I pulled up and climbed to about 1000 feet to position myself for landing on R/W 04 at Cardiff when the engine failed to respond on the approach. Looking at the fuel pressure gauge, I saw it had gone to zero so I quietly asked Mark to change the tank selector which was on his side of the aircraft, the pressure returned to normal, and the engine power was restored. After landing safely, I told him we had had a very close shave as we had actually run out of fuel. Just think what might have happened if the fuel had run out while at 50 feet over the water? This was another lucky escape for me which I did not forget in a hurry. Fuel gauges are NOT to be trusted and as you may know, a US gallon is less than the UK Imperial gallon measure so be warned.

While flying for the Pegasus School of Flying, I flew to Cranfield and did an instrument flying course with Rogers Aviation to remove my No Instrument Flying restriction. This allowed me to teach for the UK IMC rating which was mentioned in an earlier chapter. I enjoyed teaching I/F for short and, having an airfield with all the various aids enabled us to fly radar approaches down to both 2 miles and 0.5 miles respectively, as well as carry VDF letdowns which were a requirement of the rating at that time. This is when an approach is made using just the two way communications radio and utilising radio bearings known as QDM's. That stands for the "magnetic radio bearing in still air to home to the overhead". Careful use of the radio, with calls for bearings at frequent intervals made it possible to do an approach in bad weather to a suitably equipped airfield using an appropriate VDF procedure. This method of approach is very rarely used nowadays due to the advent of GPS, and other improved radio aids.

I once flew with a student to Bristol Lulsgate airport and started to make a VDF approach but was using the WRONG chart and procedure for R/W 09 when in fact the runway in use was 27, the opposite direction. A stupid mistake but I had not realized that at some airfields there were two or more VDF procedures available. Again, careful planning and some sensible questions beforehand might have prevented me making that error. However, I did once make a flight to Perranporth in Cornwall which was covered in cloud and made a DME Arc approach over the sea flying the exact 21 nautical mile range line towards the coast, using the Lands End VOR/DME beacon, knowing that as I pulled up over the coastline the airfield Runway would be dead ahead. It all worked out very nicely as the cloud base was about 200 feet over the airfield but around 500 feet over the sea. I remember being very pleased with myself.

In early 1976, I suddenly decided to leave the club and left my assistant, Steve Taylor who was an ex RAF trainee pilot, to run the show. He was fully qualified to take over as CFI, but was not as dedicated to the club as I was and eventually moved on. Although he was a failed RAF student pilot, he successfully re-joined some years later partly as a result of a report I was asked to make about his motivation and thinking. The reason I left was that I was getting fed up with doing everything. On one busy Sunday, when being pressured to do yet another hour in the circuit, having already done three trips; I just said "enough is enough". Bob Watts, the one forceful director, was always trying to get me to do more flying, even if the weather was not always suitable for the student concerned and

I had felt for some time that it was time to look elsewhere. The eventual destination was a surprise and shock as it happened quite unexpectedly. The next chapter in my book will reveal all. I did however return to the club about two years later and tried to get it going again but with hindsight, I think that was a mistake and I should have tried to get into commercial flying sooner.

After a short period flying out of Halfpenny Green in the autumn of 1977, at a club where the CFI was Mike Edwards, the instructor who had sent me solo back in 1970, I returned to Cardiff after my time away but the club was to suffer a severe setback when the Cessna 150 "RP" was lost in an accident. The student pilot, Paul Harp, was doing solo circuits when on the down wind leg the engine failed possibly due to Carburettor Icing or as a result of him pulling the mixture control out (we will never know exactly). He made a downwind landing on Porthkerry Park, a piece of open parkland just to the west of the town of Barry. He landed successfully but regrettably passed between two trees and removed both wings. The propeller, nose wheel and fuselage were undamaged and on retrieval to the airfield I was able to swing the propeller and the engine started. I saw the event happen and remember driving down a track into the park to find the aircraft. I remarked at the time that he would probably survive as the aircraft had a full "Sutton Harness" for doing aerobatics and I felt that even if he hit a brick wall he would walk away, which he did! I got Paul airborne again within just a few days using one of the other clubs Airtourers and went over the water where I let him unwind with some low flying and steep turns over the sea.

When I returned to the club for the second time, one of my students was an experienced school teacher named Merle Giles, who had started to learn with the other club but came over to me for a better deal. She and her partner Tom Jenkins who was learning with my club were both keen and went on to purchase a Cessna 172 G-ASUP and then later on, after an Atlantic ferry trip which I shall describe later, acquired a much better and faster Piper Arrow which was appropriately registered as G-MERL. Note that once a sequence of aircraft registration letters have been allocated to an aircraft, it is no longer available, even if that aircraft is subsequently withdrawn from use, destroyed, or sold abroad, so she was lucky to get her name on it. While doing her final qualifying cross country to Gloucester/Staverton and Shobdon during training, she got uncertain of her position but stated over the radio that she had recently passed over a large factory with the name "Chunky Chicken" on the side of its large Lorries. Someone at Shobdon recognised where that location was; it was at Craven Arms to the north east of Shobdon and they were able to give her directions over the radio to find Shobdon. As she was too late to complete the entire cross country on the day, I arranged for her to stay at my parent's farm at Milson. My father picked her up from Shobdon for me and took her back the next day, when she completed the flight successfully. She always remembered that day, as did I, and I was proud of the fact that she did not panic or take any chances.

One of my students was planning to emigrate to Canada and wanted to complete his PPL before he left. Although he was a good pilot in the practical sense, he could fly the aircraft very well; his ability to digest some of the technical subject material was not so good. I therefore stood and looked over his shoulder while he did the navigation and meteorological exam papers dropping the odd hint here and there! He passed obviously, but I made him promise to work hard to improve his knowledge when he got to Canada. About a year later he called into the club while on a visit home, and I asked him how he was getting on? "I purchased myself a Cherokee and now fly all over the States and Canada, flying VFR on the airways; and I have been all the way to California". He had learnt by experience and hard studying and was now doing things I would not have dreamt about at the time. You sometimes know deep down if someone has got the ability and capacity to learn. In another case, where an engineering student in the RAF at nearby St Athan, was suddenly being posted abroad, I worked hard to get him solo before he went. He did so after about 7 hours, but I had left out a lot of the necessary training you would normally cover. With hindsight, that was probably a mistake, but his solo was fine as he had no emergency or ATC problems to deal with. He later completed his training when his overseas posting ended.

Finally, in later years the shorter crosswind runway 04/22 was withdrawn as a runway and became a taxiway only; sometimes having aircraft parked on it. Once John Powell returned home in a Cessna 172 to find he had a 40 knot crosswind on either RW 30 or 12. He asked, perfectly sensibly, if he could land on the so called disused runway 22 directly into wind but his request was denied by ATC. He landed on it anyway and was threatened with legal action but nothing more was heard about it. It is worth noting that it is better to be on the ground wishing you were up there, rather than in the air wishing you were on the ground. ATC is really there to help an aviator in distress and this incident illustrated the kind of problems which can occur when airfields withdraw their secondary runways from service. Exeter, Bristol, East Midlands, Cardiff itself and Norwich, to name just a few; all have done so over the years which can cause problems in very strong winds; especially for light aircraft.

As far as the social side of the club was concerned, we had a clubhouse, bar, kitchen, bedroom for me, and an office; plus shared toilets between the two flying clubs. Club night was always a Friday and the club often had social events but again the directors wanted more and more all the time, which made a successful evening more difficult to achieve. I myself had a few girlfriends while at Cardiff including one, Ann Long, who was a student, trying to learn to fly. Regrettably she moved on before she had gone solo and I felt like a fish out of water when she ended the friendship. I was also sorry that she did not actually go solo or complete her training although she may have done so elsewhere. I arranged a date with a girl from the Welsh valleys once and had arranged to meet up at a certain red telephone box. Unfortunately for both of us, we both went to different phone boxes and cursed one another for not turning up. Another long term girlfriend, Mary Preece had a glass eye but I did not believe her until she tapped it with her finger!

During one club party on a Friday evening, the snows arrived and we all found ourselves marooned for several days. There was a funny side to it as some guests were there with someone other than their lawful wives, which was not easy to explain away! For food and drink we all went to the nearby British Airways engineering complex which was next door and where I had all my own meals while staying at the club. It was top quality food with a good and varied menu, changed on a weekly basis. After two days snowed in, I remember one of the club members, a Polish friend whose name I cannot remember, offered to go across the airfield to get help; I did not see him again for weeks. I also recall that on one occasion when there had been a reported inside job and payroll robbery in the club next door, Frank Todd's wife, Pat, had a large amount of money in her own handbag; the weekly takings from the night club on Barry Island. My own room in the club had a shower which was only 50 metres from the main runway; it was also very cold in the winter months. Being so close to the runway, I often witnessed unusual movements during the night. If it was the usual traffic then I slept soundly but if something different came in during the night, like Air Force Two carrying the United States Secretary of Sate Henry Kissinger, I was wide awake in an instant.

On days when it was too windy for club flying or when there was low cloud and/or poor visibility, I often found myself leaning against the window with a student waiting. As the engineering hangar was next to the club, I used to see various Viscount aircraft and BAC 1-11 aircraft on the flight servicing apron being made ready for an air test or ferry flight. On a number of occasions, I would go over and ask if I could come on a trip. One of my students, Ken Power was totally taken aback when I suggested we go and get on that jet! We flew to Birmingham at FL70 in less than 20 minutes standing behind the Captain and First Officer on the flight deck, saw a Viscount coming the other way 1000 feet below at the correct quadrantal flight level, and then took over 5 hours to return to Cardiff on the train; but it was worth it, especially for Ken. I also went on a few air tests when individual engines were shut down and restarted. Once, I could have gone to Gibraltar on the Gib-Air Viscount but on ringing British Airways about getting a return seat was not given an assurance I could get one, so did not take the chance.

The Cardiff flying club days were good experience and certainly broadened my outlook on life, including flying knowledge and although it was sad to leave Shobdon, which was near to my home, it was worth it in the long run. I made many new friends, one of which, Peter Bukowski became a long standing friend, as he had fishing and farming interests as well as flying, and has for many years had a long association with my parents. Peter claims to have had a unique experience when flying the Cessna 150 solo in that he said he once got sucked into a cumulus cloud and forcibly carried up to over 6000 feet but I suspect he was being a little too dramatic. However, you never really know what happens to your students and customers when they fly away on their own, so he may well have been telling the truth?

As I have said coming back to the club in late 1977 after my period away was probably a mistake and delayed my attempt to get into commercial flying for another year or so. The events described in this chapter may not have been in strict chronological order but are reflections based on my memory and log book records. I was to spend some additional time at Cardiff a few years later while temporarily based there flying for the Ordnance Survey carrying out aerial surveys, and renewed many friendships again but more about that aspect of my flying later on in the book. In later years the club house building where I used to live was completely demolished and the one remaining club had moved into the old British Airways office building after the engineering complex had moved to a new site on the other side of the airfield.

Most flying clubs give something back when a student pilot makes his or her "First Solo". Some give a signed certificate while others get a free drink at the bar. One club I know, the Shropshire Aero Club at Sleap airfield, used to give an engraved Tankard to the men and something else to the ladies but I had a much better gift which I hoped would provide some useful air safety hints for the future. All my students after they had completed their "First Solo" flights, and you can do only one, good or bad; got awarded a copy of Neil Williams's book "Airborne". This great book features a number of tales from his extensive flying career both in the military and as a test pilot with Handley Page Aviation, as well as stories from his aerobatic displays. I used to give each student a signed copy courtesy of the club. The book appears to be out of print now but I always thought it was a good book to give to someone learning to fly as it included a lot of useful flight safety hints; useful information for any prospective pilot! No doubt there is an equivalent example around today which would make a good gift for another solo pilot?

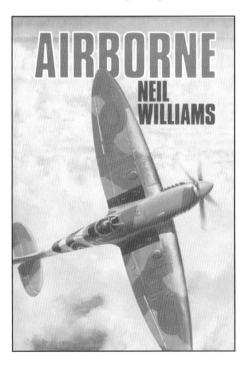

The Forward for the book illustrates WHY I thought it a good choice to give to student pilots after they had successfully carried out their "First Solo's".

"Flying stories have held a fascination from time immemorial, and the legend of Icarus intrigued mankind for centuries before the first uncertain steps into the air only three quarters of a century ago. This is a book of flying stories, but with a difference. All of these stories are true, covering the experiences of the author as a test pilot demonstration pilot, air show pilot, film pilot, jet charter and competition aerobatic pilot. The stories include aircraft from the early flying machines to modern military and civil jets. Here you will read of the exultation of a first solo in a Spitfire, the desolation of being lost over the ocean at night, short of fuel, in a jet bomber, the sickening fear of hurtling earthwards out of control, the humour of receiving a parking ticket after a forced landing, the shattering experience of crashing an aeroplane in front of a crowd of 80,000 people, and the unbelievable story of how the author crash landed an aeroplane after a wing folded in flight, which gained him the Queen's Commendation for Valuable Service in the Air. The pages abound with famous aircraft: Mosquito, Sopwith Pup, Hunter, Scimitar, Meteor, Yak, Heinkel, Falcon and many others. The Magic of flight is here to be shared; the tranquillity, the excitement, the terror, the humour, the adventure."

Not often does a book cover such a wide range of personal experiences; it will attract the attention of pilots from the airlines, the services, and the flying clubs. It will also admit the non-flyer to a new world, where he can share the thrill of flying aeroplanes which are already legendary. After Neil was killed while flying an old Spanish CASA 2.111 (German Heinkel He 111) to the UK, he flew into high ground; a party from the flying club went and attended his memorial service at the St Clement Danes RAF church located in the Strand, London. One reason for this was that his artist brother Lynn was an active member of the club and he asked us to attend.

A final thought about present day security arrangements. There were almost none in my days at the club, and you could easily move around the south side of the airport with no restrictions. Getting those flights in Viscounts and BAC 1-11 aircraft would be virtually impossible nowadays. The golden days of aviation are well and truly over I am sad to say. You cannot use your own initiative anymore! When I called at the old club a little while ago, you could not get access "Air Side" without a club membership pass and had to pass through a security gate giving proof of identity and showing your pilots licence; wearing a high visibility yellow jacket as well. I understand that there is in fact no flying club at Cardiff now partly due to the increased use of the airport by commercial traffic, and like a lot of other commercial airports, light aircraft have been effectively forced to move elsewhere.

The faithful Pegasus School of Flying's PA28 Cherokee is shown parked next to Auster G-AIPW at Milson Airstrip during one of the regular visits I made to my home while a flying instructor at Cardiff. The Cherokee was not the best aircraft for short grass fields but by arranging to arrive with about half tanks and with just two persons on board, it was not normally a problem.

Chapter Five.
My Army Experiences in Cyprus
And West Germany.

After a year and a half flying out of Cardiff and running the flying club there, I began to feel that I needed a change. I did not want to leave the many friends I had made but it was time to move on. One Friday evening after the usual club night had finished and the bar had been cleaned up, I sat down to watch some television and found myself watching a programme about a parachute course for army cadets at Netheravon in Wiltshire. It showed parachute drops being made from a Britten Norman Islander, De Havilland Rapide and a Cessna 206 aircraft and it gave me an idea; why not go and fly those aircraft? Although I had a twin rating by that time which I had done some years earlier at Shobdon on a Piper Apache G-ATMU, I felt it would be a good move to get more "twin" time in my log book. Twin flying is expensive, so I thought this might be a good idea.

As far as I can remember the following Monday which was my usual day off and happened to be a wet one, I decided to drive to the Army Air Corps and RAF airfield at Netheravon, and make enquiries for myself. Using my initiative, I arrived at the Guardroom on the main gate and asked if I could see someone at the parachute centre. I was duly told to keep going across the airfield, something you could do in those days before security became an issue, and was instructed to park outside the first hangar I came to on the right. Here I was met by an army Major, Gerald Stacy, who invited me in for a cut of army tea and a chat. He asked me what my interest was and I explained I had seen the TV programme the previous Friday and would like to come and fly his aircraft. He responded in a negative way stating that all his pilots were either ex-military, or airline pilots, who flew in their spare time, and that in any case, you had to have a minimum of 100 hours in command of twin engined aircraft to even be considered. Unfortunately, I had just over 9 hours in total at that time!

I was just about to bid my farewell and give thanks for the tea, when Gerald, said, "Hold on, there might be something of interest for you? We have a Beaver aircraft in Cyprus and are having trouble finding anyone to fly it. Would you be interested?" I said yes without hesitation and when he pointed out the De Havilland DHC-2 Beaver was not a twin, I told him it did not matter and that I might get the chance to fly the Islander aircraft next year (which is what happened). After we had discussed matters further, during which he explained that the job was unpaid but with all expenses and accommodation provided for, he said he would be in touch as soon as the necessary arrangements had been made. I then left elated that I had found myself another job and travelled home to tell them all the surprise news.

My mother could not believe it when I arrived home at the farm and said I was off to Cyprus in just over two weeks time. The club at Cardiff could not believe it either but wished me well. After a few telephone calls, postal telegraph messages and an appointment letter over the next week or so, I was on my way. However, just before I left for Cyprus, Gerald Stacy rang me and at the eleventh hour said that after all, I could go and fly the twin engined Islander for the Rhine Army Parachute Association (RAPA) in West Germany if I wanted to change my mind. I told him that as I had already accepted the job in Cyprus, had told friends and family what I was about to do, had read up details about Cyprus and the Beaver etc, that I would leave things as they were; hoping that I would go the Germany the following year, which I later did.

My parents took me to RAF Brize Norton in Oxfordshire and saw me off on the 20th January 1976. This was to be my first time away from the UK and home although I had been at Cardiff for about 18 months, so I was a little apprehensive about going abroad for the first time. In fact, when I spoke to one of the flying club members, John Penny, about my opportunity, he had said that I should take it, "You can always come home if you do not like it and you might regret it if you do not go". That gave me encouragement and I was looking forward to a new challenge when they left me at Brize Norton. The flight out to Cyprus was in a BAC/Vickers VC10, XR-806, which was named George Thompson, VC. This aircraft met a sad end 21 years later when it sat on its tail during an incorrect de-fuelling operation.

I was met at RAF Akrotiri in one of two British Sovereign Base Areas in Cyprus by a Major Nick Cooke, who was the commandant of the Joint Services Adventure Training Centre (JSATC) at Dhekelia on the eastern side of the island close to the closed off port and holiday town of Famagusta which had been (and still is) deserted since the Turkish invasion of Northern Cyprus in 1974 He drove me in an army mini van the 80 miles or so to where I would live for the next 9 months on what I recall was a very pleasant spring like day with a temperature in the mid 70's Fahrenheit, even in January. I was to be accommodated in an annex to the Officers Mess at the main army base where I was very well looked after.

Apparently, any civilian guest is entitled to the privileges of an Army Captain or Air Force Squadron leader, so I was more than pleased with how things turned out. The bar was effectively free for me, food was good, if not excellent, and the newspapers arrived about 4 days late from the UK.

The aircraft however, gave me a shock when I first saw it in the Army Air Corps hangar next to the two or three Sioux army helicopters they had there. It was not the standard issue army Beaver which I had seen at Middle Wallop, but an American registered, weather beaten and worn out looking machine, N7283; which had been rescued from Beirut in the Lebanon the previous year. The underside of the aircraft was covered in oil and sand caused by a massive oil leak from a split in the crankcase of the radial engine. They had been putting over a gallon an hour into the tank when using it for the parachute dropping that it had already done before I arrived.

Photographs show the cockpit of the Beaver N7283 and after I had decided to change the leaking engine at Larnaca Airport. I left the old engine in the sand.

I had changed the engine myself with help from an army maintenance manual, a torque wrench and a small crane.

My so called check out was with a Cyprus airways Greek Cypriot pilot who knew less about the aircraft than I did. However, due to my previous tailwheel experience on Austers, the Cessna 185 and other types, I had no problem handling it and the radial engine was not new to me as I had flown the Harvard with Gwyn Jones at Cardiff. I also had a 45 minute flight in one of the army helicopters, a Bell 47 Sioux aircraft, XT-807, and was shown where I could and could NOT fly. The base was on the disputed border between the Turkish north and Greek south and an infringement of the north could have led to a nasty diplomatic incident, or worse. I flew with the AAC base commander Major Peter Childes with whom I had to fly with again just over a month later after an incident had occurred.

After I had done some circuits of my own, the parachute flying started in earnest, flying off a 4000 foot sand and gravel airstrip known as Kingsfield. I had barely done 5 hours flying and about 20 lifts, when on landing, I hit the top of a motor car that passed in front of me just as I was making a short landing on the threshold of R/W 04. I had knocked the roof rack off the top of the local Greek Cypriot cobbler's car, but no damage was done to the aircraft, as shown in the photograph above.

I also thought the matter was closed; after all, he had driven in front of me and should have given way to an aircraft, so aviation law says? However, the threshold of the airstrip at one end happened to be the edge of the public road going from Dhekelia itself to the Pergamos Camp. The Greek driver of the car was obliged by law to report it to the Cypriot police, which he did. Repercussions followed just days later.

I was walking back to the officer's mess a few days later, when Major Childes pulled over and ordered me into his official car. He had just had a report from the Cypriot police who were treating the matter as a road traffic accident, and was told that I was to be prosecuted in the courts for quote **"Flying in such a manner as to be the cause of danger to persons and or property"**. I could not believe what I was hearing, more so when he said I was grounded until further notice. Luckily the aircraft had been taken to Larnaca airport a few days earlier for me to carry out an engine change which I did myself, with a little help from an army Beaver maintenance manual, a lifting crane and a torque wrench. I took the old leaking engine out, dumped it in the sand and replaced it with a newer engine off another worn out Beaver which was in even worse condition than N7283. As I was not an engineer, I chose to remove and replace the engines with their variable pitch propellers still attached. The only problem was that the starter motor was unserviceable so for some of my time in Cyprus we had to swing the propeller to start; which turned out not to be a problem at all, especially when cold. Eventually, a new starter motor was fitted but the maintenance arrangements for the aircraft left a lot to be desired. It was supposedly done by a Greek engineer named Andreas Ionides under FAA regulations but in reality nothing was done unless the Army Air Corps helicopter guys helped. However, all was well, and during the next nine months, I flew a total of 140 hours which included at least 465 separate lifts according to my log book records. This was not as much as I had hoped for but worth it all the same.

As far as the car incident was concerned, I was advised to plead guilty to the charge as I had hit the car even if not intentionally. I was obviously found guilty and was fined £100 Cypriot pounds, which was eventually paid by the army. After a one hour training flight with Major Childes, which I was ordered to do and went surprisingly well, I was airborne again. The army authorities had considered sending me back to the UK for a complete conversion course on to the Beaver with the Army Air Corps at Middle Wallop, which I would have liked to do just for the additional flying, but in the end, they got me to fly with the major who had been an army Beaver pilot in Aden some yeas earlier. A few days later, the following well written poem appeared in the officer's mess but exactly who wrote it was never revealed. It has amused me and many others over the years since.

Wings of Death!

MOD in their wisdom sent, a pilot for the regiment,
the one that came by name was Hugh
but there's one thing they did not do,
one small error in the halls of fame
as unfortunately they mislaid his brain.
He bumbles through the sky it seems, and oblivious to the tortured faces
Puts the Beaver through its paces.
Our CFI has had his fill of hurricane Hugh and his need to kill,
But hurricane Hugh will not relent, to kill more cars he is hell bent.
With hawk like eyes he scours the ground, until at last his victims found;
Nose dips earthwards and down he flies, a glint of fire in his steely eyes,
Swoops across his victim's path, no one can escape Hugh's wrath.
The tails flicks down, the wheels dig in
With eagle like talons piercing the skin;
But this is just a game he plays, I don't get bored is what he says,
God forbid is what we cry, For he wants the job of CFI!
Anon.

79

In the late spring of 1976, the parachute centre had its annual leave so I returned home to the UK in theory to fly a Cessna 172 back to Cyprus which the engineer Andreas had intended to purchase. However, that did not happen and over the next few weeks I did some further, mainly Auster flying, from both Shobdon and Cardiff as well as doing some familiarisation flights in the Army Islander at Netheravon with Gerald Stacey.

My time in Cyprus was in effect a glorified holiday with some free flying thrown in, but I enjoyed it; living in the Officers Mess, swimming daily in the Mediterranean sea, reading all the newspapers during afternoon tea in the lounge, having free drinks in the bar for which I just signed a chit (mess bill memo) and generally having a good time. My sister Janet came out to Cyprus for a 10 day holiday, all expenses paid indirectly by the army and we toured the southern half of the island in a car lent to us by an army officer.

I also had a religious type visit for one week to Israel and the Holy land which started with an emergency landing back at Larnaca Airport after a bomb scare in an Alidair Viscount aircraft G-AZNH, which was on lease to Cyprus Airways. I subsequently met the Captain of that flight in the flying club bar at Cardiff two years later; it's a small world in aviation.

I found that trip fascinating especially walking around on your own in the old city of Jerusalem; and seeing the various religious groups going about their daily rituals; Hindu's, Muslin's, Christian's, Jew's and Arab's alike. There weren't the security concerns and unrest that there is today in that part of the world. I also managed a float in the

Dead Sea which is 1385 Feet BELOW Sea level. Because it is so salty, you float on the water. I am shown reading a copy of the Daily Telegraph in the photograph on the previous page.

A few experiences and observations of my time in Cyprus are worthy of mention. One of the parachute displays we did was over the town of Larnaca where the Dropping Zone (DZ) was a football ground on the coast. For some reason, it did not work out as planned, possibly due to the wind and all the parachutists landed well out to sea. Rescue boats were on standby just in case so no harm was done, but it was an embarrassing moment for the army parachute school. The winds were very unpredictable in Cyprus due to the proximity of the sea so most of our parachute flying was done either first thing in the morning, or last thing in the evening. On the flying side, I often spent time at Larnaca Airport and happened to find myself trapped there during the hijack attempt on a Dutch DC-9 aircraft which was parked on the end of the runway demanding fuel. Luckily the hijackers were persuaded to give themselves up but it was a tense few hours with me listening in to the radio conversations and negotiations over my air band radio. I was once lucky enough to get a trip in a Cyprus Airways DC-9 which was doing a training flight and for 4 hours we flew an airways flight to/from Crete, circuits and landings at RAF Akrotiri, and an engine off approach back into Larnaca, all with me in the cockpit observing the proceedings. That flight had a lasting impression on my mind and I remember it well. Also, I had a look at an elderly Series 700 Viscount one day which was passing through the airport; it was on its way from Venezuela in South America, to Taiwan in the Far East with a very heavy but small block of titanium metal strapped down in the main cabin hold. The crew said that after delivery, they were going to continue across the Pacific to complete an entire circumnavigation of the earth. What a trip for someone to do.

On the non flying side, I was once asked by the American owner of the Beaver, Captain William H French, to look after a suitcase for him while he visited the Lebanon on business. Asking what it contained, he said $5000 (US Dollars). I did not believe it so he opened it to prove it! I simply hid it under my bed in my room in the mess and said nothing to anyone; otherwise I might have had my throat cut? I was once told to take the aircraft to Larnaca Airport by him, where on arrival; it was promptly loaded with Red Cross supplies to be flown to Beirut. I rightly refused to do this because, in the first place I was not allowed out of Cyprus without an army clearance and secondly, the aircraft had no navigational aids, useable radio, or paperwork suitable for an overseas flight. I suspected other ideas were being considered as well, such as possible arms smuggling but I saw no evidence of that.

My last flight in Cyprus was to fly the Beaver down to Larnaca with a long time girl friend of mine on board, who I had known while there. Patsy Aitken was one of the force's school teacher's, who had stayed in the mess with me. I parked it on the apron and said goodbye for the last time. Years later, the aircraft turned up in Canada as a floatplane, and I sent the current owner the story of it hitting the roof of the car while in Cyprus, hoping he might invite me over to fly it again. He did send me a nice photo of it as a floatplane but, unfortunately, with no offer to fly it again.

Finally, on one occasion I was in the officer's mess bar, wearing a tea shirt and shorts when a visiting high ranking officer entered. He was not amused by my appearance in an "officers" mess and ordered me out, until that is, my presence and reason for being there was explained to him. Needless to say the unpaid guest then got another free drink. I took a lot of good photographs while in Cyprus and kept sending them home for my parents to see. Two, which my Mother liked, are shown in the first selection of coloured pictures. One shows a Shepard boy tending his flock inside the Eastern British Sovereign Base Area and the other shows a donkey and its owner collecting salt off a dried up lake bed near to the town of Larnaca, close to the airport.

During the winter months after my return from "holiday" in Cyprus, I continued to instruct at both Shobdon and Cardiff and carried out some twin training on an Islander with the aircraft manufacturers Britten Norman, at Bembridge on the Isle of White. I also did two short flights from Manchester and paid half cheque/half cash for it, but several months later got a court summons for non payment of half the bill. The company pilot had obviously pocketed the cash but I was able to produce the cheque for the same amount and received a profuse apology and a small degree of compensation. After some delay due to maintenance problems, I eventually flew the RAPA Islander, G-AXHE, out to Bad Lippspringe near Paderborn and the Sennelager army ranges in early March 1977. I flew it out with one of their part time RAF pilot's, Ivor Gibbs, who was a Jaquar pilot in Germany at the time. I was not able to assume command until I had been checked out by Bruce Latton the chief RAF pilot responsible for administration of flying activities in Germany; as we were operating very close to the Iron Curtain and a "no fly" zone, so I had to be properly briefed. I was to meet both again years later, Bruce as CFI at the Oxford Air Training School when I went to work there as a ground instructor, and Ivor who was a ground instructor at an ATR turbo-prop training school which I visited once at Exeter in about 2008.

The Islander cockpit was a little more sophisticated than the Beaver but an easy aircraft to handle. G-AXHE was No 86 off the production line and I was to fly over 250 Hours on the aircraft in Germany flying out of Bad Lippespringe/Sennelager. The Islander flying in Germany was what I had originally been interested in a year earlier when I first visited Netheravon, but I am glad it worked out as it did because had I gone to Germany when given the chance, I would never have flown the Beaver or been to the sunny Mediterranean. I did not make any disastrous mistakes and spent several months flying the Islander almost daily out of the grass strip at Bad Lippspringe which was within the Sennelager ranges. However, I did not do as much twin flying as I had hoped because my contact was terminated early. This was when the military authorities decided to replace the civilian pilot with some grounded military officers following some severe defence cuts in the RAF when both the Belfast and Andover aircraft squadrons were suddenly withdrawn from use. It might be interesting for readers to know that a military pilot can legally fly a civil registered aircraft in the course of his duties <u>without</u> having a civil licence; so I had to go. The parachute centre did not like that ruling but orders were orders, and I returned home much earlier than intended. Subsequently the ruling was overturned and a fully employed civil pilot was taken on for parachute dropping work in future years.

First of all, I flew the aircraft back to the UK twice, once for an army parachute competition at Netheravon and Thruxton during which they allowed me to fly the aircraft home to Milson airstrip where unusually, I landed down the slope there due to a strong southerly wind. My Father witnessed the approach which he still talks about today, as it looked a little difficult to execute; downhill over trees! I later took our immediate neighbours, Brian and Wendy Orchard for a flight around the local area.

On the other occasion, I flew it back to Oxford for a propeller change but a delay kept me waiting a week during which the wife of an army officer and her two small mischievous boys had to stay with my parents on the farm for nearly a week. Those two flights home were claimed as my qualifying 300 nautical miles cross country flights for my commercial pilots licence about two years later. Early on during my time at the Rhine Army Parachute Association, we suffered a near disaster when one of the students reserve parachute opened inside the aircraft, and got caught by the slipstream pulling him out of the side door at a dangerous angle which damaged the door frame, took off part of the elevator and severely damaged the student's head; although I never learnt if he survived or recovered. He was a static line student so after his reserve parachute opened, he was then pulled out of the aircraft which in turn inflated the main static line parachute. The main parachute finally pulled the inflated reserve chute off the elevator. This was a very nasty incident, which happened in an instant of time. The jumpmaster had tried to stop it but saw the reserve handle come out to late. When I landed and pulled off the runway, the irony was that the next load of parachutists started to automatically climb on board, until I showed them what damage had been done to the aircraft. I did not appear to be affected at the time but later suffered delayed shock when I returned to the Officer's Mess and was asked about the incident. I suddenly went very pale, started shaking and was immediately put to bed with some sedatives. I suddenly could not remember where I was or anything about the near accident to the aircraft. Something similar happened to me many years later when I was a passenger in a car crash and when I was trapped in a lift, but more about those incidents in a later chapter.

We did not fly just from Bad Lippspringe but also from other German airfields and some of the military bases such as RAF Wildenrath. On one positioning flight back to base, I made a serious error of judgement thinking I would be able to fly under a rather active warm front which the met office had advised me about. Before the advent of the computer and internet, forecasts were given individually by meteorological forecasters in person. I set off from Wildenrath to fly back home and found myself flying lower and lower to stay out of the cloud as I flew through the industrial heartland of West Germany, the Rhur. As I found myself flying between large chimneys and just over power lines, I began to lose power without knowing it. Having constant speed propellers meant the engines sounded the same but in fact, the pitch was changing and the forward airspeed was reducing as my engine manifold pressures dropped due to carburettor icing. I eventually realised the problem, selected carb heat and the engines recovered allowing me to divert into Dusseldorf where they vectored me for an ILS to R/W 25 but the radio navigational equipment did not work and I had to get radar help. I certainly had a scare that day and learnt again about the perils of carburettor icing!

In all I managed 279 hours flying and flew at least 844 separate parachute lifts before the RAF and MOD compelled me to leave. I did get the opportunity to fly it again from Sibson airfield near Peterborough during a parachute competition, but lost interest in continuing to do that type of work. However, not all my flying while in Germany was on the Islander. For a time, we used a German registered Cessna 206 D-EGHK while the RAPA aircraft was grounded for maintenance and I duly checked out a young German girl, Monika Neumann to fly it while I was away in the UK. She had a German PPL and was somewhat nervous about doing some parachute dropping but in the end, got on with it and flew quite a few hours. I myself flew 13.5 hours on the aircraft which was a nice change.

She and I also shared the cost of flying the German Cessna 172 I have already mentioned earlier to and from the UK when I flew home for a break. I landed it at Milson and routed via Luton inbound and Southanpton outbound; a trip totalling 21Hrs, 35 minutes precisely! The most memorable part of the whole trip was the arrival back at Bad Lippspringe after dark, where I had expected some runways lights to be put out. Unfortunately, the airstrip was in total darkness due to a forgetful soldier who had not carried out my instructions and was getting drunk in the bar. As I knew the airstrip well by then and knowing that if I passed overhead a certain house at 200 feet on a magnetic heading of 300 Degrees I would be nicely aligned with the grass landing area, I made my approach and landed perfectly with no problems using just the landing light. This was a relief because I was deliberately arriving back LOW on fuel as the army had agreed to fill the tanks on return for free! The soldier in the bar, hearing the aircraft taxying in, came out to see me arrive but was too late to help; and he got a ticking off from me.

There is a funny yet serious sequel to this trip. When two of the German flying club pilots came to collect their aircraft a day or so later, I was in the Officers Mess at Sennelager and got a message to say they could not start it; and would I please go down to see them. I rode my bicycle down to the airstrip and saw they had the engine cowling off and were looking around the engine compartment. I immediately said, "Have you turned the Fuel On?" to which they replied, knowing their error immediately, "Oh No, we never turn the fuel off in Germany". Never assume always check is my motto as an instructor, and here is a good example why! It may have been their club policy not to turn the fuel off but you would have thought they would have checked it before calling me for help! I have always remembered the embarrassment on their faces and often tell the tale when discussing pre start and take off checks.

I also managed to get a little more gliding in Germany, namely at the Detmold army gliding club where they were brave enough to let me fly a single seat glider at least twice off a winch launch following a check flight. Not only did I do that, I also did a fair bit of flying on a Motor Falke during which I climbed from 1500 feet to over 6000 feet with the engine off in some good thermal activity, much to the amazement of the army passenger. I also had a flight in an army Scout helicopter from the RAPA parachute site to Detmold, and was lucky, if that is the right word, to get a very low level flight through some mountainous terrain in a German army Bell Huey, like the ones used in Vietnam. It scared me to death as the rotor blades were just inches from the rocks at times, but it was also exhilarating at the same time.

I would like to make two final comments about my time with the Army in Germany. Just like Cyprus, I was very well looked after and had an allowance of 400 Deutschmarks a month (in Cyprus I had been given £100 a month), good food and accommodation, and had made some nice but temporary friends. (You cannot keep in touch for ever with everyone you meet in a service environment.) In one German bar, I once talked to an American musician who asked me if I was deaf. On replying that I was slightly deaf and wondering **WHY** he had asked me, he told me that I had a slight speech impediment and did not pronounce my "S's" correctly in my speech. This is another indication that I have been lucky to have flown at all and makes it all the more surprising that my high tone deafness was not picked up as a child and possibly corrected at an early age.

The army years of 1976-7 were unusual as I was working as an unpaid civilian pilot with just a Private Pilots Licence. I doubt whether current regulations would permit this activity today, so I was lucky to have used my initiative after seeing that TV programme in the flying club at Cardiff. As a final comment, even the parachute club in Germany got it wrong one day. Doing a demonstration parachute jump on their own airfield during the Rhine Army Equestrian Championships, I dropped all 10 parachutists overhead but only one made it back to the field when he had realised they had dropped themselves in the wrong place and pulled his ripcord early. I did my low pass over the showground as instructed some ten minutes after the drop but could not see any of my colleagues. There were some embarrassed faces after that poor effort. A sudden wind shift was apparently to blame. It was while in Germany that I briefly met the RAF Group Captain mentioned earlier, then an Air Vice Marshall, who had given me encouragement to fly some 15 years earlier when he was the station commander at RAF Gaydon. I was glad that I had had the opportunity to inform him of my successful desire to become a pilot despite medical advice to the contrary.

Chapter Six.
My American Adventures!

When I returned to the Pegasus club at Cardiff for the second time, I became a little more adventurous and was trusted more by many of my friends. The club once tried to arrange an overseas trip to the USA to visit the Confederate Air Force at Midland Texas, where each year they have an annual air show flying ex wartime aircraft. However, like a lots of plans, potential party members started to drop out mainly due to the cost and in the end just four of us made the trip. The one name I cannot remember but Densil Davies and John Powell were the other two. We flew out from Gatwick using the "Standby" ticketing arrangement where you turned up on the off chance of travelling on the day. Luckily, we all got on the same flight and arrived in Houston where after getting our hire car and, doctoring the speedometer to avoid the mileage cost, (not guilty of that) we set off for Midland, Texas after first visiting the Johnson Space Centre where we were all surprised by the shear size of the Apollo Saturn Five moon rockets that were on display.

The air show itself was a worthwhile event to go to and luckily, we befriended an American and got entrance to the show free of any charge. After the show, we paid a short visit across the Rio Grande river border into Mexico where young children in the border town of Matamoras constantly harassed you for money. On the way back to Houston, we spotted a Boeing PT-17 Stearman which was making an approach to land at a private airstrip. We stopped, chatted up the pilot, and all ended up having a quick 15 minute trip in the open cockpit aircraft; the American equivalent of the British Tiger Moth which was used for basic training during the war years. On arrival back at Houston, John and the other person left to return home but Densil and I had agreed to say on, hire an aircraft, and fly across America to the Grand Canyon and back.

After visiting a local Federal Aviation Authority (FAA) office at Andrau Air Park to obtain our permanent American PPL's which were then issued on the basis of your current UK License, we hired what looked like a worn out Cessna 172, N20110, and after having a checkout with an instructor set off on our epic trip. The

US licences have a "restricted use" stamped on them, which basically means you have not passed their air law exam and prevents you from doing any commercial work such as crop dusting.

I remember the large amount of light aircraft traffic in the circuit and learnt very quickly that if you waited for the approach to be entirely clear, you might never get airborne. Also, there was no overhead joining procedure like the UK but instead, you just joined directly on the downwind leg at a 45 degree angle keeping a good lookout. There is also a widely used "Unicom" frequency, currently 122.7 MHz at uncontrolled airports, which is used to transmit your intentions at a lot of the smaller airstrips. This is similar to the Safety-Comm Frequency 135.475 MHz used in the UK today. (Please note that my recollections from now on are those relating to air law rules in force in the late 1970's so there may well be some changes today).

Densil and I set off heading west and I remember saying to him that it was no good just heading west until we got to the River Severn if we got lost and that we would have to navigate carefully. However, in the States, the visibility can be very good at times and there are an abundance of VOR beacons which you use on the airways. The "Victor" Airways, which are superimposed on the standard topographical charts can be used by VFR traffic up to 18000 Feet and you can fly on those airways at Odd or Even plus 500 feet levels with possible IFR traffic above or below you. You also have to use the local QNH or "Altimeter" setting which you can obtain while you fly across the country by listening in to the numerous ATIS broadcasts. You are also strongly advised to file a flight plan for every flight which you do before departure but you MUST then inform the regional Flight Service Station (FSS) to activate it once airborne. On one of the flights we did, across a largely deserted desert area, for some reason, this did not happen. As Andrau Air Park (now closed and converted into a golf course) was already at 800 Feet amsl, you could not be expected to set the altimeter to the QFE (height above the airfield or ground for landing. By the time we reached our second stop, at San Angelo, Texas, the elevation had already increased to 1919 Feet, so to set the QFE there, you would already have needed to wind off 60 millibars so it is not a viable option.

Continuing on the next day we made it to Gallop, New Mexico, where the elevation was now 6472 Feet and we eventually arrived at Grand Canyon airport the following day where the elevation had risen further to 6609 Feet amsl. We had also crossed over from Central Standard time to Mountain Standard local time which you have to be aware of if you are to get your timing and estimates right. In fact, all flying worldwide should be recorded in Greenwich Mean Time (GMT), now known as Universal Time Co-ordinated (UTC) to avoid any mistakes but it reads oddly in your log book to have been flying at say 0330 in the morning, so I recorded the actual local times in my own log book. We also learnt a lot about flying the aircraft in hot and high elevation conditions when the density of the air is less than at sea level. You do need a 9,000 foot runway if you are trying to take off from Grand Canyon airport in a temperature of 25 Degrees Celsius where, according to performance tables the International Standard Atmosphere (ISA) temperature should be just plus 2 Degrees. I remember the illuminated sign at the threshold of the runway stating the airfield elevation and actual temperature and informing us that our DENSITY Altitude, the altitude the aircraft THINKS it is at, was around 9200 Feet. The long runway is needed for even some light aircraft as the actual true airspeed on the approach and just after take off can be a lot higher than the indicated airspeed. Also, setting the fuel mixture control to the RICH position for take off, which is normal in the UK and sometimes written on checklists, would not have been helpful either as the aircraft's engine would have far too rich and probably would not have even started properly. You certainly learn a lot about flying very quickly in the United States where the attitude towards light aviation is completely different. Apart from some of the major airports, where there is a small charge to discourage you from using them, there are NO landing fees and often a courtesy car is available free of charge to take you to the nearest motel if staying overnight or visiting the local area.

After a one day stay at one of the great natural wonders of the world, the Grand Canyon gorge, where the Colorado River has for many centuries carved a pass through the desert, we flew on, but not before I had tried to walk down to the river itself from the rim of the Canyon. I gave myself a self imposed time limit of 2 hours to reach the bottom of the gorge which was just as well as it took me nearly 4 hours to climb back out. I did not reach the bottom and did not see the river itself but could just about hear it when I turned back. After a good nights rest, my leg muscles were stiff and I could hardly walk but it was an experience not to be missed. The flight back to Houston was flown on a different route, firstly over flying and landing to refuel at the world famous Winslow Crater like those on the moon which is shown on the next page.

90

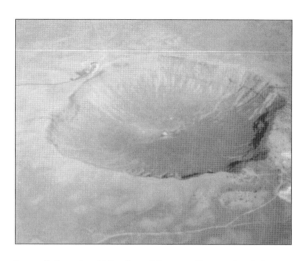

Over flying the Winslow Meteor Crater in Arizona.

The flight back was flown on a different route, firstly over flying and landing to refuel at the world famous Winslow Crater like those on the moon. The flight from there to an unusually named airfield called "Truth or Consequences" was one of the most interesting as we flew over the Plains of San Augustus and over the Mogollon Baldy Peak mountain area. It was also the flight where for some reason the flight plan was not activated just when it might have been useful. We also flew into darkness after passing the time zone boundary. However, all was well because you could activate the airfield and runway lighting automatically by clicking the microphone button on the required frequency several times. After landing at the completely deserted airfield, except for a barking dog and tying the aircraft down on a ready prepared parking slot with the chains provided, we then rang the local motel for free and a courtesy car came to collect us. I remember there was a very nice American bar girl there but I did not take advantage of the situation although she did seem keen on an Englishman that evening!

Two more days flying was involved before we got back to Houston where we found we had flown 25 hours over 6 days, without having any problems or any need to top up the oil. The aircraft was actually a good machine despite its appearance and it all cost just $25 an hour. This trip, my first to the United States, was a successful learning experience and I would thoroughly recommend it as a way to build to hours after getting your licence, learning about flying along the way.

It was a pity that only two club pilots actually went on this trip of a lifetime because there is so much to learn about flying in the United States. Obviously, the size of the country helps to make flying a more practical proposition than in the very much smaller United Kingdom, but the ATIITUDE towards flying and aviation in general is so very different. Densil and I thoroughly enjoyed the experience and our 25 shared hours of flying. Study the map shown below which was taken from an ordinary school atlas.

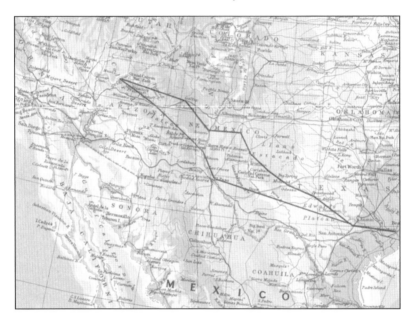

The route flown during our adventurous flying trip.

Densil and I returned to Gatwick after two weeks away. We had shared the flying with each of us doing a leg at a time. I still have the charts used on the trip, remember that the VOR beacons were all painted white so you could spot them more easily, and we saw remarkably little air traffic once we were away from the immediate airport areas. The vastness of the United States, where we had only flown in the states of Texas and New Mexico was a lot to comprehend but the country is geared up for using flying as a practical means of getting around. When I asked whey there were no landing fees, the response was that the FAA had enough money in the pot from the thousands of annual licence fees paid by the enormous numbers of light aircraft on the register. At the one motel stop, we overheard what could only be described as sounding like a murder in progress in a nearby room but we decided not to intervene! This trip wetted the appetite for flying tours but the next American adventure was to turn out a little differently and could have resulted in a disaster.

Early the following year, Densil and John decided to fly to America with the intention of purchasing an aircraft which they would fly back to the UK with me. We flew out to Chicago via New York where I remember we had to change airports and travel across New York City in a Yellow Cab taxi in a raging blizzard in very cold temperatures. At Chicago, we were met by an English national, Graham Miller, who had emigrated to the States a year so earlier, and he looked after us while we were there. After visiting a Packard Merlin engine factory where Rolls Royce Merlin engines were still being reconditioned, we collected a Rockwell 112 Commander N1388J and flew it across the central United States from Sheboygan, Missouri to Oklahoma City, a seven hour flight with just one stop and with two hours being flown at night. There, long range tanks were fitted while we had a day off in very cold but clear and dry conditions. Densil had a date with an American lady who failed to turn up and I was deposited for the day at a local "Flower House" for a day of adult entertainment; all legal in the USA! I do not remember what John got up to?

When we went to collect the aircraft which had had an extra long range tank installed, I made a close examination of the installation and found that if left alone, all the fuel would have drained out during the flight once the extra tank had been selected as the main feed. A serious error had been made in the pipe work which was quickly corrected. When we subsequently returned to Sheboygan, north of Chicago, John and Densil decided that they wanted to fly the aircraft back to the UK on their own. They told me to fly home by commercial airline. As I had very little funds of my own, as I was there at their behest, they all gave me the change they had which fell just short of the cheapest airfare I could find. I therefore had to borrow three United Sates dollars off the American government's welfare department, which I duly returned with a bankers draft on my return home. If I had not, I might well have been barred entry to the United States ever again. As it was, I was given a severe ticking off for not being adequately prepared to travel the world. My two friends, who were not experienced pilots, and the lack of any serious planning for a Trans-Atlantic ferry flight, caused them to end up getting lost as they flew up towards Greenland. On one flight they flew for 14 hours on just one flight after diverting up to Sondrestrom well above the Arctic Circle when they could not find Narsarsuaq on the southern tip of the Greenland peninsula. That airfield is at the end of a very long one way in, one way out fiord. It was a lucky thing that the ferry tank installation actually worked. They blamed the ADF for not working and wondered why the needle kept indicating a bearing to the left or right for a particular beacon but it was giving a true reading, and the problem was in fact the basic magnetic compass which had not been re-swung after the installation of the large metal ferry tank which was fitted in the cabin! In those days they did not have the benefit of the Global Positioning System (GPS) which makes the task of navigating across large uninhabited areas mush easier and safer but does also lower the basic navigational skills of the average pilot.

The final piece of this particular trip was that when I got back to Heathrow, I asked British Airways if they had a Viscount going to Cardiff for maintenance. As they did not on that particular day, I had to hitch a lift, but luckily for me, as I left the main Heathrow tunnel entrance, Keith Miles, who had taken me down to Cardiff for my interview back in 1974, happened to be passing by. He spotted me, stopped and gave me a lift all the way home; what luck!

The next American Adventure, in 1986, was a much more drawn out affair with a greater degree of planning before we went but even that one had its fair share of surprises. We actually flew an Atlantic ferry; the only one I have done, but there are many brave souls out there who regularly fly the Atlantic for a living and we met some of them during the course of our trip. This particular trip took place after I had qualified as a commercial pilot and I held a valid instrument rating, so I was much more confident and happy to take on such a trip in an area of the world where the weather can change very rapidly without any warning.

It all started back at Cardiff when John Powell teamed up with another flying club member, Tom Jenkins, to purchase two aircraft and fly them back to the UK. One was to be kept by Tom and his long time companion Merle Giles, and the other sold. Merle was a head school teacher who had learned to fly with me at the flying club. She wanted me to go along and keep a weary eye on the other two. This I gladly agreed to do. Tom and Merle had decided to buy a Piper Turbo Arrow retractable T tail aircraft, N2116N. Before leaving for the States I went to Oxford airport and had a look at one, also purchasing a copy of the Pilots Handling Notes which I think cost me £25. They had agreed a deal for the aircraft which was for sale at Eugene Airport, near to Portland Oregon, on the west coast of the United States.

On the basis of what they knew we eventually travelled to America and took delivery on this aircraft and another Rockwell 112 Commander which John had decided to buy. Unfortunately, on arriving in America, it was discovered NOT to have been a Turbo-Arrow after all but just an ordinary version without a supercharger for greater engine power. However, the misunderstanding was too late to put right and after consulting Merle back in Wales, it was decided to accept the aircraft which apart from this one omission was a nice aircraft and reasonably well equipped with a good set of workable radio aids.

After some dual training on the aircraft, John in the Rockwell and Tom and I in the Arrow set off across the entire United States in the most glorious weather which basically followed us all the way to Greenland. Using the normal topographical charts with the "Victor" airways marked on them, we both flew from VOR to VOR all the way to the Canadian border at Niagara Falls, which we saw from the air.

Problems started at this point, which were to make the rest of the entire flight home more interesting and challenging. In Canada there are less VOR beacons and more reliance is placed on the use of NDB's which use the normal radio wavelengths in the AM band. On our first trip across the central part of Canada, John said his ADF was not working, so he had to follow us visually in the Rockwell. This is what he endeavoured to do for the rest of the entire trip across the North Atlantic. The problem had not occurred up to that point as he had relied entirely on the VOR beacons which work in the VHF radio waveband. Also, I did buy some topographical charts for the first of our flights across the vastly wooded expanse of Canada but they were almost useless as the scenery was consistently the same, lakes and forests, lakes and forests, which just went on and on. It was much better to simply hold your heading, use your watch for sensible timing, look only for obvious landmarks such as a range of mountains or a coastline, and most importantly, make adjustments to the magnetic heading as the Earth's magnetic variation changed. As you got nearer to your destination, the line of sight VOR would be picked up, and even if you ended up to one side of your intended track, you could then home in to the destination like the spokes of a wheel converging to the centre. You also started to see signs of human habitation again after flying over a complete wilderness, sometimes for hours.

As we intended to fly the entire trip in VMC (Good weather) we did not buy any more topographical maps as most of the land areas we flew over was desolate featureless terrain which gradually changed from predominantly forest to become arid tundra with more and more evidence of ice and snow as we headed northwards. The only map we had was a small scale 1:1,000,000 scale area chart of the whole North Atlantic which I still have today. It turned out to be more than adequate for the entire trip with just a few Instrument approach charts for the main airports in case we got caught out. Our provision for emergencies was, to say the least, very poor with just some warm clothing, a large flask of water with some chocolate or something similar. The Canadian authorities are most reluctant to allow anyone to fly in these northern latitudes without adequate safety equipment, but somehow or other we got away with what we had. One aspect we had not considered was the length of daylight available which was almost 24 hours at that time of year, in mid May. This allowed us to keep flying, still with the good, almost cloudless skies and excellent visibility we had had since leaving the west coast.

The routing took both of us across the wilderness of Canada, across Hudson Bay to La Grande Riviere, shown in the next photograph, and onwards to Frobisher Bay where we then prepared for the sea crossing to Greenland. As we flew further north, the land became more and more barren and snow covered.

New House Farm, after it was extending in about 1962.

Family Photo on my 21st Birthday Party.

Part of Farm in 1981, taken from the Twin Pioneer.

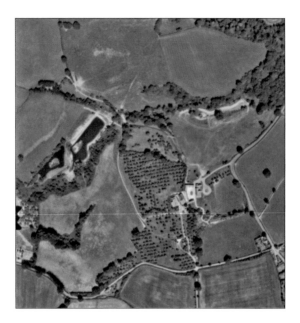

Part of Farm taken in 1999. (Spot Changes)

Aymestrey School.

Lucton School, from the Air.

Ready for a Day's Hunting on Minstral.

"Young" Commercial Pilot at 28.

Little Down Farm before ownership in 1967.

Little Down Farm when ownership ended in 2001.

On approach to Milson from the South.

Milson Airstrip and Helicopter Pad in 1999.

Airstrip Looking North in 2010.

Airstrip Looking South in 2010 (Note Windsock to Left)

That Famous Windsock Pole, taken in 2010.
House and Hangar buildings in the background.

Sheep Grazing on Airfield in 2001.
(Just prior to Sale).

The Pools, Father's Legacy.

Basic Instruments to Start with; in an Auster.

Auster Taking Off on my 21st Birthday "Fly In".

Chipmunk Taking off with Old Farm Buildings in Background.
1982 Fly In Event at Milson.

Pegasus School of Flying Badge.

Airborne Shot of Harvard LN-MAA, later G-BDAM.
(Taken from the Club Cessna 150.)

The painting of me flying G-AGXV, over Porthkerry Park.

At the Grand Canyon in 1978.

The Route We flew during our Flying Holiday.

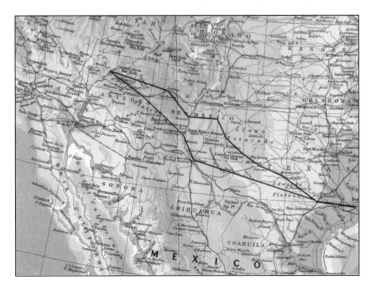

Kulasuk Photographs one showing the town at about 11 pm, and the Approach to the Runway with propeller blur on picture.

Beaver In Cyprus After Engine Change.

Taken after Final Beaver Flight.

Favourite Cyprus Photographs.

My Accommodation at Sennelager in Germany, and the View on
Easter Sunday Morning 1977.

German Cessna 172 (with passenger) at Little Down in 1977.
After flight Home from Bad Lippespringe.

We had one abortive flight when cloud forced both aircraft to turn back to Kuujjuaq. Flying in cloud at those high latitudes and temperatures can only lead to airframe icing and that was a risk we could not take.

The first sea crossing was just over 4 hours to Godthad/Nuuk on the west coast of Greenland. We saw the hills in the distance a good hour or so before they became mountains rising up to around 10,000 Feet. The vastness of what we were seeing made our destination airfield there look just like a small scratch on the surface. It is difficult to comprehend size and distance in this part of the world due to the lack of comparable human activities and hardware like towns, trees, roads and so on, so you have to be very careful. The clear air and excellent visibility also gives the impression that places are much closer than they actually are.

Due to fog on the eastern side of Greenland we found ourselves stuck at Godthab/Nuuk for nearly a week during which I was befriended by a local girl but not for what you might imagine went on; she was learning English and wanted to practise talking to an honourable Englishman? We also got a taste of Seal and Whale meat but it was not to our liking and it had an awful smell.

Eventually the weather cleared on the other side of the Greenland icecap and we were on our way again, flying in lose formation. The exact altitude of the icecap peaks is unknown and constantly changing so we elected to fly at 13,500 feet where you could just about define ice boulders well below you; that despite the almost unlimited visibility. In "Whiteout" conditions, you cannot see anything due to the lack of judgement of distance and the whiteness of the clouds above, blends in with the snow cover below! This is what happened to the Air New Zealand DC-10 which flew straight into Mount Erebus in the Antarctic in clear air after a change of flight plan co-ordinates which had been inserted into the inertial navigation system, caused the aircraft to fly unknowingly into the mountain. This is an experience not fully appreciated until it has happened to you yourself!

Outline of Atlantic Ferry Route flown in 1986.

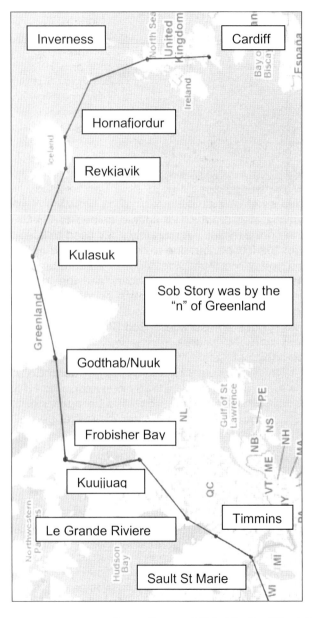

Inverness

Cardiff

Hornafjordur

Reykjavik

Kulasuk

Sob Story was by the "n" of Greenland

Godthab/Nuuk

Frobisher Bay

Kuujjuaq

Le Grande Riviere

Timmins

Sault St Marie

From Oregon USA (On the West Coast)

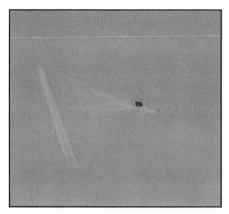

At one stage in the flight, we saw a speck of dirt on the windscreen which would not go away. After thinking that it could possibly be another aircraft or a UFO, it gradually grew bigger and bigger until it became recognisable as one of the Distant Early Warning Radar Stations (DEWS) on the ice cap known as "Sob Story". We had been flying towards it for over 45 minutes so the visibility must have been in excess of 90 nautical miles without knowing it. We passed almost directly over it, which of course helped to confirm we were flying in the right direction. Apparently, they used to keep track of all aircraft over the icecap, but due to their secrecy did not even talk to you even if you called them unless it was an emergency. The flight across the icecap was just over 3 hours and the trip of a lifetime. The photograph shows the radar station on the ice together with an "Ice Runway" to the left used by Hercules aircraft to keep the station supplied with goods and services. Sob Story certainly helped use to confirm we were on course and it was a sight I shall always remember. I think these stations have now been withdrawn?

We landed at Kulasuk on the eastern side of Greenland, and stayed there a daylight night before continuing on to Reykjavik in Iceland the very next day. With our meagre emergency supplies I would not have liked to do a forced landing in that part of the world. Once again, holding your heading, using your watch, and making adjustments for the changing magnetic variation was the order of the day, and the only way to fly this kind of route. Nowadays, everyone has the Global Positioning System (GPS) which enables you to fly direct great circle magnetic tracks between two fixed points where the magnetic reading is automatically calculated, so long range ferry trips are now much easier to accomplish safely if it works correctly?

The next sea crossing to Iceland was uneventful until we got close to the mainland of Iceland itself. Then, for the first time in the entire flight we were forced to fly into cloud and fly on our own separate navigation. Tom and I had no problems, but John, having no ADF, had to rely on radar help and for a short time just after we had landed at Reykjavik, we really thought he had flown into a mountain while in cloud as he suddenly lost contact with ATC. Tom and I had a few anxious moments before he eventually landed safely.

After a two day stop in Reykjavik, due to the weather, we both transited along the coast to a gravel runway airfield at Hornafjordur on the south eastern side of Iceland. The idea was that we would reduce the flying time for the last and longest leg across the sea from Iceland to Scotland which for extra safety would be flown via the Faroe Islands where we could have landed if necessary.

The picture shows Tom and the aircraft there.

The take off from Hornafjordur was interesting in that we had a 20-30 Knot crosswind to contend with and a gravel surface runway. I remember deliberately starting the take off run at an angle into the wind and effectively sliding over the gravel surface as we accelerated. As all departures from Iceland had to be filed as IFR flights, the two aircraft were not able to depart together so John left first and arranged to secretly meet up at 10,000 Feet (Flight Level 100 when set to 1013 millibars) on a particular VOR bearing and DME distance later on. This we did but I must say it is not easy to spot another light aircraft and for a time we thought we might not meet up again. The last part of the trip was flown in fine weather above cloud but over the Faroe Islands which was covered in cloud, we found ourselves in an area of sink and for a time thought the engine was losing power. In my mind, I also thought the oil pressure was falling slightly but all was well, as we were in the downwind side of wave sink off the mountains of the Faroes which required us to have to raise the nose, and lose airspeed, to maintain altitude.

On arrival at Inverness rather than Wick or Stornaway which we could have used, there was still enough fuel in the tank to allow us to fly all the way to Cardiff had we wished to do so. The whole trip had taken just under three weeks due to our week's stay in Greenland, but was flown almost entirely in VMC conditions with one aircraft following the other in a loose formation. Once back in the UK, John continued on his own and Tom and I flew an airways flight from Inverness to Cardiff as we had all the necessary radio equipment and I had an Instrument Rating. At no time did we ever land with less than half tanks of fuel but our preparations for any emergencies had been poor without any really adequate cold weather clothing for example. The realisation that in the northern latitudes in May, the daylight hours are almost 24 hours was not appreciated before we set off but this allowed us to fly whenever the weather was suitable.

Total flight time for the Piper Arrow during the ferry flight was nearly 60 hours but the flight was one of the most enjoyable experiences I have had in my entire flying career. It is also one I would not want to do again unless I had all the right emergency equipment. One of my friends at the flying club in Cardiff, Keith Abbott, who has ferried a few aircraft across the Atlantic while building up his hours, actually had to ditch in the sea following a partial engine failure but was rescued by a Spanish warship near to the Azores group of islands. Apart from a legal claim against him for losing the aircraft which did not succeed, he was more concerned about having lost his own portable GPS receiver. Since then, Tom and Merle have enjoyed flying their aircraft all over Europe for over 20 years so it was a worthwhile investment, even if it was not what they thought they were buying originally. It is still flying today from its home at Cardiff Airport but Merle has now sadly died.

I was to return to the United States again about twenty years later when employed by Air Contractors, an Irish registered airline who, due to Irish aviation law and regulations, had to do all their flying training on the type of aircraft's flight simulator (if there was one); and the only one available worldwide was in New York city. There is more about that visit and a trip to Washington DC later in the book.

Chapter Seven.
Commercial at Last.

In the autumn of 1978 when I was still instructing at Cardiff, I made an appointment to see the Civil Aviation Authority (CAA) to try and get them to allow me to have a Class One medical which is a requirement for any kind of commercial flying work in the United Kingdom and worldwide. I travelled to London and went to the very same office in Kingsway, London that I had visited back in 1973 when they had first refused me a commercial medical due to my hearing and eyesight problems. When I saw the Chief Medical Officer, he asked me why I was there and what he could do for me? I replied that he had said "Come back in five years" which is what I was doing. When he knew that for the past 5 or more years I had been flying almost continuously and now had over 4000 hours with no accidents attributable to any medical problem, he eventually decided to allow me a Class One medical, based on <u>experience</u> gained. I was therefore able to consider the necessary ground and flying training needed for a CPL/IR (Commercial Pilots Licence and Instrument Rating). Two of the letters relevant to that consultation period are shown as **Appendix Four**.

I decided to take time off flying to study and became unemployed while supposedly seeking work. I spent about 3-6 months doing an excellent correspondence course with a ground school company called Avigation in London. I studied all the various subjects at home, including air law, navigation, flight instruments, flight planning, theory of flight, meteorology, plotting and performance; all of which I had studied before for my flying instructors rating but this was in much greater detail. I virtually re-wrote the entire course in my own hand writing and still have the notes today, all written with ink using a fountain pen. I found one part of the meteorology course difficult to understand but the penny dropped when I realised that what determines whether the airmass is stable or unstable is in fact the actual Environmental Lapse Rate (ELR). The adiabatic lapse rate at the lower levels is 3 Degrees Celsius per 1000 feet when the air is dry or unsaturated and about 1.5 Degrees Celsius per 1000 feet when wet or saturated. If a parcel of air when it rises remains warmer than it's surrounding, then it continues to rise and is therefore classed as being "Unstable", but if it becomes cooler the vertical movement ceases, when it is classed as being "Stable" air. You might have to get your books out to confirm if I am correct?

I then decided to do it all again at Oxford on an eight week full time brush up course during which they concentrated on getting applicants up to speed to pass the written exams. I personally find myself to be very particular but slow and I had to speed up to meet the examination time limits. I also did what is called the "Performance A" exam but did not really understand it too well (no one does) but luckily I passed ALL my exams at the first attempt. I was particularly pleased with the separate plotting exam you had to do then as I only answered four out of the five questions and in theory could only get 84%. I was actually was awarded 85% so the marker must have been impressed! To help with the cost of my ground school I applied for an educational grant from the local county council but was turned down on the grounds that aviation was not a qualifying subject. However, when I appealed and explained that flying was another form of transport like any other public service, I was awarded a sizeable figure of around £600 which was a lot in 1979 so it was worth being persistent.

With the theory out of the way, I then enrolled at the Oxford Air Training School to train for the coveted and important full Instrument Rating. To qualify for commercial work this has to be done on twin engined aircraft which is expensive. After about 16 hours in a ground simulator, I then carried out just over 30 hours intense training over two months, firstly on a PA28 Cherokee to get the basic CPL and then on the Piper PA34 Seneca which was an ideal twin engined aircraft for I/R work. When doing the navigational test for the CPL test, you had to plan a three legged triangular flight, fly the first leg visually, simulate becoming IMC (in cloud) on the second when you have to establish a radio fix using the VHF radio by obtaining radio bearing, usually using true bearings or QTE's , and then divert to another airfield accurately afterwards. As luck would have it on one occasion during the training, after I had obtained the fix, the instructor removed the "Hood" which obscured the outside and asked me where I was. Looking outside, I happened to be passing a farmyard on the A345 road between Swindon and Marlborough where I had put some cattle after I found then on that road one day some moths earlier. I was therefore able to give him a very accurate position fix as being about 5 miles due south of Marlborough passing over the village of Oare! What better accuracy can you get than that, although I never gave the clue away? As a qualified instructor, you were exempt from doing the general handling flight test which was a relief financially.

During the I/R training part of the course, flown with an experience pilot named Wally Forster, the most memorable event was when making an approach to land on the ILS at London Stansted, which was nowhere near as busy as it is today, I FAILED to set the altimeter to the QFE setting, the height above the landing threshold of the runway or the airfield elevation and descended dangerously low almost flying through the tree tops. Wally did NOT intervene until I started the Go-around or overshoot as it was called then, but then opened the little hatch on the screens and asked me to look outside. Horror greeted me, something I will never ever forget. In later years the rules were changed and QFE is no longer used for commercial aviation approaches. You now use the actual altitude above sea level setting, the QNH, and ad a safety margin above the airfield elevation to give you a decision altitude below which you must not descend unless a visual reference has been established.

When I came to do the test, I obtained only a partial pass as I failed the ADF/NDB approach part of the flight. This section had to be done again but due to nerves I messed it up again, and had just one more chance before I would have had to do the whole lot again, with the corresponding additional expense. The advice I was given after the second failure was to have a complete rest, take time off away from flying and come back in a week. This I did and I passed with flying colours. Interestingly, the weather on the day of the final test was very bad with real low cloud, rain and poor visibility so the entire flight was flown for real with no screen or hood in place. I think that helped as I saw a practical reason for doing an ADF approach and was ironically more relaxed.

The whole training package had cost me about £5000 which I had obtained with a loan from my local bank. I remember going to see the manager and putting all my hand written notes from the Avigation course on his desk to prove that I was serious. You also had to have done a long night cross country with two 65 nautical mile legs before you could apply for the CPL licence. I did that flight using the Herefordshire Aero Clubs Cessna 152 G-BHAC which they allowed me to use free of charge as a gesture of thanks for all the instructing I had done there on a part time basis after I had left Cardiff. I also took Merle Giles along with me as my passenger, the lady teacher who I mentioned in the previous chapter.

At about the time I started studying for the commercial licence at home, I began to take a greater interest in horse riding again. I had ridden as a child before going away to boarding school but now had more time to enjoy exploring the local countryside and took to Foxhunting in an enthusiastic way. My Father had for many years had an interest in horses and there were now plenty to ride at home. Having your own land and plenty of Hay made the horses less expensive to own and both my Father and I enjoyed a long association with the Ludlow Hunt.

I enjoyed the chance to ride around different parts of the countryside and enjoyed the thrill of the chase, but liked to see the Fox get away. They weren't fools and often another fox would take over the running to keep the chase going. On one occasion, on a hillside, I watched the Hounds following the scent up one side while the fox cunningly passed them going the other way just yards apart. Once I got my first commercial job, I used to drive home in the early hours after flying to find the horse all saddled up ready for a day out in the hills; thanks to my father for being the stable boy.

You also used to meet some interesting people and once in woods near to Bircher Common where I had landed a glider back in 1973 found myself talking to the sister of the gliding instructor who did the ground loop in the Beagle Terrier when I sent him solo. Small World! I am a countryman at heart and feel strongly that whether you ride to hounds should be a personal choice rather than a matter of government legislation, so I broadly support the right to hunt if you wish to do so but if you do not like that kind of activity then persuade others not to indulge in it, and it would gradually fade away? As a result of the ban in the UK, foxhunting is now more popular than ever.

When I subsequently changed jobs, I found myself having long periods at home so I was able to ride even more. During those years, I developed a very close friendship with a close neighbour and was often accused by other members of the hunt of riding off into the sunset with my lover; which for a while was actually true! On one occasion, she bid me farewell at the door in her night gown but locked herself out of the house. I had to get a ladder, climb back in through the bathroom widow and let her back in; all in a hurry before her husband returned. However, that relationship ended amicably and we are still friends, no harm done, some 25 years later. Unfortunately, when I again changed jobs and found myself away from home it was not practical to keep the horses and they were sold around about 1986-7 but that turned out to be a mistake as I was made redundant again in 1991 and found myself having all the time in the world to continue riding. I have not been on a horse since. My father had intended to spend an entire season hunting one year but just before the very first day, he went to feed his pheasants on the farm and hooked the reins of the bridle over a fence while doing so. The horse was startled by some birds and took off at high speed subsequently galloping into barbed wire and tearing her one leg apart. That was the end of riding for him for a while and he eventually gave it up as his own health started to falter.

After getting my fully pledged and paid for CPL/IR, I now had to find a job. After considering a job flying in Southern Ireland which I turned down due to their tax laws, I was eventually offered a job as a First Officer but it had taken a few months to find one. I was to become a pilot with Express Air Services, a company based at Bournemouth Hurn airport who operated a fleet of Handley Page Dart Herald turbo-prop aircraft. They operated freight services to and from the Channel Islands, a mail service to Liverpool, and a few passenger routes out of Jersey into France, Belgium, Holland, and the UK, namely Swansea in South Wales.

The photograph above shows Handley Page Dart Herald G-BFRK parked on the freight apron at Bournemouth. It was later re-registered to become G-GNSY, before being scrapped in 1994.

After a well run ground school which was held in Jersey with hotel accommodation provided, I did 15 hours of training on the aircraft mainly in France operating out of Dinard and Rennes. While doing this, the other trainee pilot and I, were asked to go and refuel the aircraft but we inadvertently selected defuel on the selector and had what appeared to be gallons of precious Avtur or Jet A1 fuel spill all over the apron! An embarrassing mistake which was easy to make but hopefully you learn from these errors. The instrumentation was somewhat basic by today's standards and included two "Tune to

Max" ADF receivers, and a large weather radar receiver in the central console. The picture below shows my side of the aircraft which was where I sat as the second pilot.

I then had the chance to be based either in Jersey flying passenger routes which with hindsight I wish I had accepted but chose instead to be based a Bournemouth flying in the freight role which I found to be very boring and not what I had hoped commercial flying would be? Had I stayed in Jersey I might have found myself an early wife and may have had a good time with the girls there but I wanted to be able to get home fairly regularly so that I could ride the farm horses and go hunting. Whilst at home I once visited Shobdon and the CFI let me take a Cessna 150 G-AZZR for a short flight. As I had been flying the much larger Herald for 6 months or so, it frightened me to death and I remember my legs starting to shake; it was also a crosswind which did not help matters! I felt very much like a British Airways pilot who came to Shobdon once for a checkout in the Rallye but he kept trying to land it 10-15 feet up as his main type was flying a Boeing 747, and in the end had to give up trying. I took his family for a local flight instead.

I found the line training to be hard work, especially the paperwork to start with. For a while I could not get used to the idea that there was no column on the flight plan for the heading; you just flew the magnetic track from point to point bearing my mind the effects of any wind drift. Due to the speed of the aircraft and the relatively short sectors, it felt like I was still doing the after take off checks when we were already making our approach. However, I had a compassionate and experienced training Captain, Ken Halls, with me to start with who I learnt later was the pilot who flew me on my first ever flight back in 1966 from RAF Colerne. It is a small world in aviation. I did find the monotony of the regular flights to the same places BOH-JER-GCI-BOH and later BOH-BRS-LPL-BRS-BOH almost unbearable and decided I did not like the job. The pay was not brilliant and duty pay was one penny a minute, about £15 a day. After I had been made redundant after about 9 months on a last in, first out basis, I was actually glad to leave. By the time I had paid for my farmhouse accommodation near to Ringwood, I had barely enough money left to repay the interest on the bank mortgage, and felt I was getting nowhere.

However, the flying experience gained on a larger aircraft in an airline environment was useful. On one occasion flying up the A25 airway to Liverpool from Bristol, I was trying to manually tune the ADF to pick up the Knighton NDB Beacon on 404.5 KHz whose ident I think was KNI, when I found myself getting a "GO" ident. After landing, I tried to look up where GO was in the UK en route manuals but could find no such place. When I looked at the European supplement I found that GO was the local NDB for Gothenburg in Sweden, frequency 403 KHz; with a daylight promulgated range of just 15 nautical miles. Picking it up so far away was a very good example of skywave interference which can reduce the accuracy of the ADF in the aircraft at night very considerably. Treat all NDB's with more caution at night and be sure to correctly identify the Morse code of the beacon you are trying to receive. Today ADF tuning is more automated without the need to use a "Tune to Max" controller. I also learnt where NOT to look when making a cross wind approach to an instrument runway in very bad weather. Because the aircraft is angled off the centreline, the runway will not be directly over the nose when you reach minima, but out to one side of the aircraft. Also, there is a tendency to immediately turn towards it when the lights are seen which allows the wind to blow you off the centreline making the landing approach a near disaster.

On one flight along the same airway, now renamed N864, I experienced the roughest flight I have ever had. All attempts to do any paperwork were abandoned and you had to physically move your arm towards any switch or lever with the other arm. I think I also felt sick as I was not doing the actual flying and your vision was impaired as well due to the severe turbulence.

Along with a number of other commercial pilots, I was made redundant (for the first time) after the summer season as work declined and although appearing to be upset by it, I was actually glad to be moving on. I had flown a total of just 355 hours on the type but it was a start to my commercial flying career. However, as the company was later re-structured with new investment and another owner, their Herald aircraft started to appear all over the place, so a variety of routes would have come about eventually had I stayed. They once acquired another Herald from Southend which had just a few landings left on the airframe, they were limited to 122,000 and intended to use it as a spares source but on examining the paperwork found that an error had been made and it had in fact got another 5000 to go. That was a cheap buy, but does illustrate how paperwork errors can cost a lot of money, remember, never assume always check is my motto! The company was later renamed Channel Express and went from strength to strength over the years changing aircraft, firstly in favour of the Fokker Friendship, and then replacing those aircraft with Boeing 737 Freighters later.

G-BEZB, one of the Dart Herald aircraft I flew during my time with Express Air Services, as Channel Express was called at the time

After leaving, I was fortunate to find myself another most unusual job almost straight away; one which allowed me to very quickly pay off my bank loan. There is a lot more about that new aspect of my flying career coming in the next chapter.

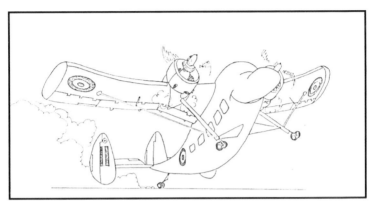

After I was made redundant from Express Air Services, David Corbett at Shobdon very quickly found me the ideal job, one which I consider was the most interesting and varied occupation I have had in my flying career. In 1980, a company named Flight One Ltd, had moved to Shobdon from Gloucester airport and brought with them four large and ugly looking Scottish Aviation Twin Pioneers Registrations, G-AYFA, G-AZHJ, G-BBVF and G-BCWF; which was the nicest of them all. They each had two large Alvis Leonides radial engines and were basically been converted from their military role for use as survey aircraft, with two camera hatches located in the belly of the fuselage. Within days of losing my job at Bournemouth, I found myself flying one of these monsters and was quickly sent away to the holiday seaside resort Blackpool in Lancashire, with all expenses paid. It was to be a blessing in disguise as I very quickly paid off my existing bank loan and was now flying as a Captain in an unusual commercial job.

As they were such an unusual tailwheel aircraft, a bit like the famous Dakota, training could not be done in the normal way as there were no approved examiners able to fly it. One of the more experienced company pilots, Derek Goddard was given authority by the CAA to check me out on type. As I had already got plenty of tailwheel experience, it was not too much of a challenge despite being nearly 14 feet up when sat in the cockpit on the ground. After just three hours training including a bit of night flying to qualify for the rating, I was on my own. Although it is possible to do a wheeler landing requiring a longer ground run, I personally always did a three point landing every time and had no problems with a direct 90 degree crosswind either, but I did sometimes find it a handful when the wind was about 45 degrees off the nose. The best way to do a crosswind landing was to land it one wing down. If set up on the last stages of the approach, I found the inertia and sideslip of the 12-14000 pounds of weight just kept the aircraft stable and nicely compensating for the wind drift as you first landed on the into wind main wheel.

Standing in front of the Company Twin Pioneer Fleet of Four.

One unusual aspect of this type of aircraft's performance was that in the civilian role take off flap could NOT be used for taking off. The reason was that if an engine failed with that flap setting selected, it would almost certainly become uncontrollable. In its military role, where it was specifically designed to get in and out of 150 metre long jungle strips and desert clearings, the possible loss of an engine did not concern them too much; but under CAA regulations, that was a major concern.

All four aircraft were different in various ways. HJ for example had much larger generators, was heavier, and for a while you always had to put 150 lbs of weight, usually sand bags, in the tail when flying it solo. However, some people, including myself, always wondered why when the other three did not require ballast, this one aircraft did? It turned out that the Weight and Balance schedule had been calculated wrongly some years previously and was incorrect.

The "Twin Pin", as it as affectionately called, was the first aircraft I had encountered where the weight distribution had both forward (-) and aft (+) moments with a nominal Centre of Gravity (C of G) datum about half way down the cabin area. All four aircraft had been modified for air survey work and had two camera hatches which had to be closed for take off and landing but open on task, when the cameras were in use. Although it did not happen to me, on one occasion when one of the aircraft returned from a 5 hour survey task, an engineer pointed out that the hatches were still open. "No, we closed them before landing", was the response until they all realised that in fact the whole job had been done with the hatch closed. Unluckily for that crew, the camera sight was through a separate aperture, so the error was not noticed and the flight was wasted.

My work with the Ordnance Survey started at Blackpool where we all had a £21.35 a day living allowance and stayed in local holiday let Bed and Breakfast costing about £12 a day. As survey flying could only take place during better than CAVOK weather with excellent visibility and clear skies being a mandatory requirement, there were days or even weeks at a time when we all went into the office, at about 8 am, and almost immediately decided to meet again the next day. All the crews were then able to do what they liked for the rest of the day. I got to know Blackpool so well that it became boring, with Fish and Chip shops and slot machines permanently engraved on the memory. On the various fair grounds, there were various prizes to be won but some were still on show after 6 months as it was an almost impossible task to actually win it in a competition. There were some nice girls around though. Once, when the weather was really bad for the whole weekend, Geoff Manning and I spent the entire weekend in the bar at Blackpool Flying Club, coming out less than sober on the Monday morning. We had to run the engines about once a week to ensure the aircraft were serviceable but once when we did go to fly, the starter motor failed and the flight was cancelled. The company boss complained about it at the time as he was penalised with a contractual clause but you cannot check for such an event, as if it is going to fail, it will fail. After a month there, where, according to my log book, we did not do one actual survey flight, it was decided to position to Cardiff where we all hoped for better luck.

While at Cardiff, staying in a Bed and Breakfast accommodation in nearby Barry, I was able to renew my association with the Cardiff flying clubs and was able to continue instructing when not required for survey duties. One weekend in July when it was too cloudy for photography work, I decided to have a "Fly In" at my home airstrip which was a great success. I also spent time at Shobdon as that was where the Twin Pins were taken for servicing, and on one very early morning was able to take both my parents on a short air test flight up the river Wye valley prior to going back to Cardiff. Afterwards, they decided to go fishing and caught 3 Salmon in quick succession; a day always to be remembered.

We did manage to do some revenue work from Cardiff including a long flight on the day that Prince Charles and Lady Diana Spencer got married, but on one flight flew all the way to Norfolk, found the target area covered in cloud, so proceeded to a site in North Wales, only to find that target obscured as well. As the camera has to run for a short time prior to any work being done, I suggested we take some pictures as we flew over **MY HOME** and farm. Those photos, which covered the entire farm except for one small portion on the north western boundary were the only shots taken on a five hour flight; and I got the photographs for free! It was interesting to compare that photo, with one taken 14 years earlier, and then compare it again with another one taken recently in the year 2009. One of these photos was shown in the first chapter. You can find at least 150 landscape and constructional changes over a relatively small area, and does illustrate how the countryside is constantly changing over the years; with hedges pushed out, new buildings constructed, road changes, pools and lakes made, woodlands planted and so on. During this period I had to return to Oxford to renew my instrument rating as it was a requirement to have a valid rating to fly into controlled airspace while doing aerial survey work, usually at about 5000 feet. We did return to Blackpool towards the end of the contract which was interesting but there were long periods with no activity at all which were then usually followed by an intense short period of concentrated flying when the weather co-operated. Finally, the Blackpool flying club bar experience was embarrassingly repeated one day when the forecast was bad; some of the crew, (not including myself as I was instructing at the flying club), went into a pub for a few drinks in Barry only to come out to find perfect flying conditions had developed but we had to cancel any planned flying for that day as they were all well over the limit.

Just before the Ordnance Survey contact finished we found ourselves doing another different type of survey in Southern Ireland, operating out of Dublin, where we had to tow a trailing magnetometer behind the aircraft over a large part of Ireland flying as near as possible to 600 feet above ground level; following flight lines drawn on a 6 inches to One mile Irish map. This period of flying, which was the most intense I have ever done, amounted to 89 hours flying in just 13 days. The flight line profile which I have kept is shown below. The task was completed successfully but was not without its little dramas and some further comment about it is worth mentioning.

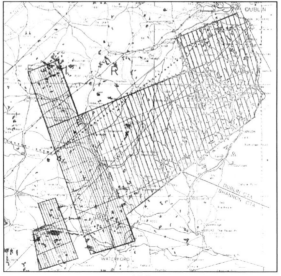

To begin with, I decided to route to Dublin via RAF Valley in Anglesey where according to my little "Red Book", an en route flight supplement provided by the military, I could get C, H, and I. (Customs, Health and Immigration clearance). On landing to clear customs, it became obvious that a customs clearance for a commercial business flight, especially one carrying sensitive surveying equipment, was not immediately possible, so HM Revenues and Customs had to send an officer to the airfield from the nearby Holyhead Docks and Seaport. Because we left the UK there, it was agreed that we would re-enter the UK at the same airfield, which we did 3 weeks later.

As it was not possible to fly when there was low cloud around, I was always reluctant to depart Dublin until I definitely saw a split between the actual air temperature and dew point on the few METAR weather reports you could get from parts of Ireland; notably, Cork and Shannon. I was criticised for delaying a departure several times until I agreed to go one day, only to find the target area covered in low cloud and mist. My caution was vindicated and they accepted my decisions from then on. On one flight as we passed over the peak in a range of hills, the survey operator in the back said he had "Lost the Signal". For a moment I went red in the face as I thought we had left the trailing magnet behind on the hilltop but it was just a joke. Geoff Manning was also my fellow crew member on that trip to Ireland, and he map read my flying directly over the nose with the large scale 19th century maps made when the British Army was the controlling authority of all of Ireland. So little had changed out in the country side, so that the stone walls, roads, isolated buildings, and field layout, were still almost the same, 100 years later! On one flight, one of the track lies past directly through the Baldonnel military airfield just west of Dublin. Due to our low level, I was not able to call them until virtually overhead and simply said I was about to cross their runway. Once on a flight line and making a recording the entire run had to be completed or re-flown, so I could not hesitate or abandon the run. They did however, know I was in the area as I had spoken to them during an earlier run which was being flown a little further to the east or west but I cannot remember which.

As our party was a fairly large one, we had the entire top floor of the Leofric Hotel, between Dublin airport and the City centre to ourselves but one night it became very noisy due to a party. On complaining the next morning, we were told that during the night a drunken Irishman had fallen to his death off one of the balconies.

After we returned from Ireland, I was sent back to Blackpool to complete the OS contract and then in formation, flew the 3 Twin Pioneers back to Shobdon in formation, that flight being recorded on film for an article later written in the Air Pictorial Magazine. Some of those photos are re-produced in the photographic collection as part of this book.

Once, when there was no avgas fuel available at Shobdon, I flew one of the aircraft to Wellesbourne to pick up fuel and uplifted 349 Imperial gallons, when the total useable capacity was just 364 gallons. In some ways it was not a good idea because we used about 150 gallons to fly there and back in 1.5 hours of flying. When we were later based back at Gloucester, I was invited to take the nicest aircraft, WF to the Badminton air day where I landed on the very smooth grass strip there and was given 500 litres of fuel free. I remember that on that occasion I took with me a very nice girl who I got to know well when at Shobdon in the early 1980's, Debbie Wright. She was slightly disabled and apparently suffered from some form of epilepsy but she and I got on well for a few years. Sadly she died young in 2001, at the age of just 34. I did not know about this until I happened to notice her name engraved on her parent's gravestone in Leominster cemetery one day while walking my dogs in the area. That was a great shock to me and I was really upset about it as I thought at one time we might have married. She and I had flown around Europe in a Cessna 172 G-CLUX on a flying holiday in 1984 during which we visited Alan Munro, the RAF pilot friend who was then based in Germany on a NATO assignment. A more detailed report of this trip is shown as **Appendix Five**. A photo of Debbie is shown in the colour photographs standing next to a Cessna 172 G-CLUX at Schiphol Airport, Amsterdam.

We did at least get a months rest after that intense period of flying, until that is, another contract was awarded, this time with British Aerospace from Warton in Lancashire. This contract was to do some flight trials for the development of some kind of new anti-tank missile and was to take place over a fairly long period of time. It was interesting work but classified, so I cannot give too many details about the work itself but I can tell you about the flying side; and some of the fun we had over the next year or so.

To begin with, HJ with the larger generators was required most of the time but at the very beginning of the one contract I had an engine fire indication just after take off from Shobdon and shut it down, returning to land on one engine. There was no actual fire but it was a shock at the time because when land flap is selected on one

116

engine, a landing becomes mandatory! What had happened was that the exhaust had ruptured and hot gases were blowing onto the fire wires inside the engine compartment. Some of the early flying down to as low as 200 feet agl with an official CAA clearance to do so, was done from the British Aerospace facility at Samlesbury in Lancashire, an airfield now rarely used for flying.

Once initial trials work was completed, in early 1982, the year of the Falklands War, we had to fly to West Germany where our development work was to be compared with that of another German company. After first flying out there from Manchester with British Airways in a Trident airliner, we all stayed on the 42nd floor of a hotel in Frankfurt where I distinctly remember feeling giddy looking out of the widows and experienced some nasty static electricity shocks off the door handles; due to the type of carpets fitted. I met a German Air Force C-160 Transall pilot who was to fly directly underneath me repeatedly during the subsequent trials which were held in an army danger area at Mengen in southern Germany near to Stuttgart. After some discussion, we agreed who would fly underneath the other; otherwise it could have proven fatal for all concerned.

About a week later we flew from Warton to Mengen via Southend and Stuttgart and flew an airways flight there, flying at FL100. I had to be sure that we would either be above cloud all the way or below the freezing level to avoid the possibility of getting airframe icing. The aircraft only had heated pitot tubes so any ice encounter could have been very unpleasant. The only comment about the flight was that when I first called German air traffic control, they asked if I was a "Helicopter" as we were flying so slowly, at just 100 Knots. The final short leg of the flight to Mengen airfield was interesting as we arrived in a raging snow storm and had very little if any visual reference on the approach to land. You could see trees and buildings in the far distance but could not determine where the snow covered ground ended and the grey/white sky started. You had no horizon as such; but I made a very gentle arrival which I was very proud of! This is commonly known as "Whiteout" conditions.

The trials in Germany went well. I did not hit the Transall and we eventually returned off airways flying across France VFR at a very low altitude against a strong headwind. On several flights out of Mengen to the two trials areas, I had noticed for several days large Cumulo-Nimbus type cloud build ups to the south and thought it would not be nice to be flying in that type of weather. It finally dawned on me what the clouds were; they were the snow covered Alps way to the south. I also rang my close girlfriend at the time from

Germany to learn she had had a car accident, but had to hear about it all again on my return home from my father who came to her rescue; as our relationship was a secret and discrete one!

The next part of the development work was flown from Shobdon using the RAE site at Pershore as a target point. On this occasion we repeatedly had to fly the same track line over the ground time and time again which must have started to annoy a public house near to Worcester which we regularly flew over during the five day period. However, around this time, two of the Twin Pioneers were effectively mated together during severe gales at Shobdon and the one, G-BBVF, was written off later becoming an exhibit at the Museum of Flight at East Fortune, near Edinburgh. It was taken there by road in pieces, a bit like the way one of the Concorde's got there some 20 years later after they were retired. The other, HJ, was flown by me to East Midlands Airport with a damaged nose where it was repaired by Hunting Aviation, so the Bae Trials from Warton had to be delayed by over two months. I remember that the ILS did not work as the aerial had been knocked off the nose.

There were other contracts with British Aerospace as well, and one was flown from Hatfield using G-BCWF, the best aircraft of the fleet which was also the best handling aircraft. This work was to develop a gyro stabilised infra red camera platform which can effectively see in the dark or through cloud. I remember repeatedly flying from Hatfield in very poor visibility, and flying up and down a long stretch of the railway system in the area. The local ATC controller could not understand how I knew where I was in such poor conditions but he did not know I could "see in the dark" through an infra-red TV picture in the cockpit. This system subsequently found its way into the navigational systems of today's Tornado and Harrier jump jets. WF was allocated to the Hatfield development team for some time and spent a lot of time based at Cranfield where it spent an awfully long period in one of the hangars there, until that is, it had a surprise outing.

I got a telephone call one day and was told to go the Cranfield and fly the aircraft to Prestwick in Scotland for the day. On arrival, I was met by a smartly dressed Gentleman, who said he was coming with me. A most enjoyable flight both ways was had in the most wonderful of weather conditions with light winds, excellent visibility and almost clear skies. We flew across the entire Lake District at 3000 feet and it was a flight to remember. We had lunch in the British Aerospace canteen and then returned to Hatfield. What I did not know until we got back was that in his small suitcase, he apparently had thousands of miniature detonators for some kind of missile system which they did not want to send by train or commercial air transport as they were too sensitive. Knowing the forecast was good they decided to use a "Twin Pin" for the journey, hence the very short notice. That was over five hours of pure enjoyment for both me and my VIP passenger.

As the Warton development work progressed, it was then necessary to fly in snow covered areas and it was hoped that this could be done in Scotland. In January 1983, I travelled up to RAF Leuchars, near to St Andrews and flew as a passenger in an RAF Wessex Helicopter, where I sat in the open door with my feet over the side, looking for a suitable area in the Cairngorm Mountains of Scotland but due to the often rapidly changing weather conditions in that part of the world, it was decided to fly all the way to Norway. It was partly the advice of the RAF helicopter pilot which convinced us all that Scotland was not a good place to do the trial flights we needed.

We flew therefore to Oslo/Gardermoen in Norway routing via airways and Groningen in Holland. The idea of going to Norway, which was cold, was to find some snow but in an unseasonable winter that particular year, we found very little of the stuff and had to fly further north to find any substantial snow covered ground. However, we succeeded in out task and flew home, this time via Rotterdam with one 7 hour flight en route, after two weeks away. An internal news report on this trip is shown as part of **Appendix Ten.**

During the course of my flying with Flight One Ltd, which lasted for over 5 years, I used to fly to Prestwick regularly, on one occasion to celebrate the 50th Anniversary of the Scottish Aviation factory there where all the Twin Pioneers were built. That trip was an excellent couple of days during which I took a flying friend with me who lived locally near to my home at Milson. His name was Christopher Chruckshank and being a good photographer, he took some excellent pictures of the trip. My flying was not without its faults however and I once got airborne with the pitot covers still on and had to fly a short flight from Shobdon with no airspeed. The chief engineer, Jock Kay, happened to be on board and found it rather amusing but I did make an excellent landing, probably because I was concentrating more. On another trip up north to either Prestwick or Warton when we were flying out of Gloucester (Staverton) again, having left Shobdon by then, I lost all my charts, bag, and flight details as I climbed up to 3000 feet just after taking off. They had all fallen away from the cockpit area and had made their way down the cabin to the back of the aircraft. You will not believe this but I decided to level out, trimmed the aircraft very slightly nose down to compensate for my movements and then proceeded to get out of my seat and quickly made two or three quick dashes down to the back to pick up all my missing items; checking each time I came back to the front that the aircraft was still at 3000 feet and everything was OK. The Twin Pioneer was an exceptionally stable platform due to its size and weight which is why it was used for trials work and survey duties; so I felt pretty confident that it would remain in level flight for just a few moments at a time. There was therefore once, a Scottish Aviation Twin Pioneer flying over Gloucestershire at 3000 feet with NO pilot at the controls, albeit only for a very short time! It probably wasn't the best thing to do and I should have landed back at Staverton but I got away with it.

Another job involved flying around a lot of government and aerospace establishments at night to do a heat loss survey, particularly over central London itself. We flew out of Luton airport on that occasion, and it all worked out very well with all the targets surveyed satisfactorily. I do remember getting back to Luton at about midnight and on calling at one of the hotels in the area, being asked for £40 a night, even though it was past midnight. I declined to accept and drove further into Luton town where we found an excellent Bed and Breakfast house who not only charged us only £25 each but also gave us all an excellent hearty breakfast the next morning. On a survey flight over the Scottish Highlands once at about 15000 feet, the navigation tracker who used to tell me which way to make small adjustments of heading when on task, felt I was acting strangely and found my oxygen pipe had come adrift behind my seat. I was therefore starting to feel the effects of Hypoxia or a lack of oxygen. This was quickly rectified but I do remember having the most terrible headache for a day or so afterwards.

As the Hatfield and Warton develop flying continued, I eventually found myself based at Bournemouth Hurn again flying regularly from the British Aerospace side of the airfield. This flying involved a considerable amount of flying in the SAME area for quite some time and was to lead to a newspaper article in the Bournemouth Evening Echo one evening on the 29th March 1984. We had been repeatedly flying round Stoney Cross airfield north east of Ringwood in Hampshire where on the disused airfield there, there was a Land Rover vehicle and trailer with a revolving series of special reflective mirrors inside it designed to replicate various types of military armoured vehicles. The flights we were doing had a radar system on board which trying to distinguish the different type of radar returns for the development of some kind of anti-tank missile. We flew a total of over 40 hours in the Stoney Cross and Bovington tank ranges on the south coast over about a month. I can do no better than to reprint the entire article on the following page, which readers should find amusing.

Moaning Monster Mystery.

A mystery plane is angering New Forest villagers by shattering their rural peace. Residents of the tiny hamlet of Fritham, near Bramshaw are intensely annoyed by the twin engined plane with a Triple-Fin tail which drones incessantly overhead during the afternoons. No one seems to know where it comes from or why it persists in circling Fritham for hours on end, but regular afternoon sessions have been going on for some months now.

The plane has been tagged the Moaning Monster and the Scourge of Fritham by the local community. Bramshaw postmaster Mr Derrick Roberts suggests that a ground to air missile would be an apt way of ridding the area of the nerve shedding nuisance. "It flies monotonously to and fro in tight circles at a height of less than 1000 feet. Its engines are hideously audible, enough to drive one mad", he said.

The plane circles Fritham, Bramble Hill, Minstead, and Stoney Cross in three minute trips for up to two hours at a time. "Would it be unreasonable to suggest that some other area might be burdened with this noise nuisance for a while?" asked mystified and angry Fritham resident Mr Desmond Polack. The matter was raised at the annual parish meeting where people were urged to write in force to the Civil Aviation Authority at Uxbridge and to the local MP, Mr Patrick McNair Wilson.

A protest letter has already been sent to the flight controllers at Hurn Airport, towards which the plane seems to head after its forest trips. Mr Peter Course, deputy director of Hurn airport confirmed to the Echo that the plane was using the airport, and suggested it had permission from the Civil Aviation Authority to do survey work in areas including Stoney Cross. He thought the survey was being done for British Aerospace, and advised the Echo to contact them.

But Mr Norman Barfield, spokesman for British Aerospace said the aircraft nothing to do with their company which has no interest in the Forest area and noted that it was in the process of closing down its Hurn production line. The Ordnance Survey headquarters in Southampton also said that the aircraft was not connected with them and that they would have been the only Government agency which would have been interested in such a survey.

There were other varied jobs including one flying out over the North Sea to try and find a small trawler which was to lay a deliberate patch of oil on the sea which we were then to survey with some oil sensing equipment. As you might imagine, it was not easy to find over an open expanse of sea, but the trawler Captain suggested we descend to a low level over the water and he would try and find us on his own ship's radar which sends out a narrow search band just above the water line. He soon spotted a very fast moving object which of course was our aircraft doing about 100 Knots. This worked a treat, he gave us a heading to fly and we soon found the ship which looked very small in an empty ocean.

We did a low level survey over parts of the English Channel once which required the aircraft to fly precise tracks similar to the job we had done in Ireland. In the days before the invention and use of GPS, a special, DME type, triangulation fix equipment was put on board the aircraft which interrogated and calculated our position using four UHF beacon transmitters, three on the English coast and two in France. This system was called "Syledis", and operated in a way similar to today's Global Positioning System (GPS). However, it provided me with an instrument in the cockpit, a bit like an ILS, and I was able to fly an accurate course line for hours at a time at just 200 feet above the sea; some of it in cloud; or sea fog to be more correct. That job was another intense period of flying, this time totalling 54 hours in just 8 days and I needed a well earned rest afterwards. We had flown out of Lydd airport in Kent which is right on the south coast.

Captain Hugh Thompson at the controls of a Twin Pioneer.

One memorable trip was when I had to take one of the aircraft to Oxford Kidlington for some radio work to be done. Knowing that Edwin Shackleton, an aviation historian, was trying to get a world record for the number of aircraft types he has flown in, I telephoned him at his home in Bristol one day and told him to be at Staverton airport at 7am the next day. He obviously turned up and we had a great day out with two short trips to and from Oxford. He brought me my lunch and took some very nice photographs, one of which is shown on the previous page. It is interesting to know that, as I write this book, he is STILL trying to better his own record and an article on his many adventures was published recently in the Daily Telegraph newspaper.

In mid 1986, I had had enough of this flying as we were having longer and longer periods with NO activity at all followed by a brief busy period. I therefore decided to leave the company and gave notice to leave. I wish now I had not done this because the company decided to cease trading a month later in any case and had I stayed just that little longer, I would have got a small redundancy payment for my five years of continuous employment. However, my flying with Flight One ended with me having one very interesting flight over central London in broad daylight during which I remember, we flew up and down "The Mall" passing over Buckingham Palace a few times.

Finally, although it did not happen to me, one of the company pilots flew a Twin Pin for the entire flight with the cross feed fuel valve open. As he slowed up to come into land, the aircraft started rolling over as the tanks were full on one side and empty on the other. It was normally standard practise to fly with ALL the fuel tanks selected but with just the booster pumps for the required tanks on. With the cross feed valve open and a slightly stronger fuel pump pressure from one side, both engines were fed from that side only. All he could do was to fly away for another hour or so with a different fuel pump on until the wing tank on the fuller side had been depleted of some fuel allowing lateral control to be retained during the approach. Personally, I managed to fly 800 hours on this unusual and unique aircraft. Today, in 2010, there is just one aircraft still capable of flying and that is WF, now re-registered as G-ARPS and flying as part of the "Classic Flight" collection of aircraft based at Coventry Airport. HJ also ended up there as a hoped for restoration project but it is now probably being used as a spares source.

There are other worthy stories I could tell about my Twin Pioneer days but I feel I have given you enough excitement for one chapter and so I have decided that we should move on. It was an enjoyable part of my flying career and certainly had plenty of variation and variety. I had managed to fly a total of 800 hours on the four aircraft over a period of five years but the job was blighted by intense periods of flying followed by very long periods with little or no work at all.

Being originally trained on tailwheel aircraft and having had previous round engine (radials) time on the Beaver and the Harvard, I found the Twin Pioneer surprisingly easy to fly and class it in my own mind as a mini Dakota. The fact that you were nearly 14 feet above the ground when on the ground did not deter me and I found landing into the wind or with a direct cross wind no problem as you could set up a gentle sideslip into the known wind by lowering the into wind wing. The inertia of the aircraft; its basic weight was around 10,500 to 11000 Lbs, always kept the approach stable.

A very good cockpit photograph of the aircraft during my time with Flight One is shown on the previous page. My worst ever landing in a Twin Pioneer was at Bristol Filton airfield when the very wide runway there deceived me and I tried to land it about 25 feet up. The runway at Filton is about 300 feet wide as it was originally built for the Bristol Brabazon airliner in the early 1950's.

Chapter Nine.
The Twin Otter Years

After I left Flight One Ltd, I decided to try some freelance work and found myself working for the one remaining flying club at Cardiff flying the popular Piper PA38 Tomahawk which was a good training aircraft. It had good all round visibility, handled nicely but was poorly and cheaply constructed in my view. Stalls and spins, if you dared to do any, made the T tail shake and that was a bit unnerving but I enjoyed flying it. On one training flight, which was a revision detail before the students final flight test, I switched off the alternator while we were taxying out but the student did not notice it on either the ammeter discharge or the "Alt" warning light and we flew the entire 45 minute flight on the battery alone. It was only when we made our final landing and he dipped his head, he was a tall person, did he notice the orange light which had been on throughout the flight. You can always be checking and re-checking yet still miss vital detail. To conserve the battery for the radio I turned off the rotating beacon and other electrics during the flight.

I also got a check out on the Piper PA23 Aztec G-JASP, on which I then did some survey work with Landsurcon, a company base at Gloucester. Once again, Geoff Manning was my navigation and sight tracker for the survey work we did. One trip which was particularly memorable was a trip to survey Gatwick Airport from 5000 feet. Air traffic control was reluctant to let us in the airspace but the British Airport Authority insisted the photography detail be allowed and we did it with no problems at all. I could see all the airline type aircraft, Jumbo's included, approaching to land or taking off and simply slotted in behind them prior to a run over the airport. I only did about 20 hours on this aircraft and expected to do more but the company went out of business, so that was the end of that little bit of enjoyable flying.

I also examined the possibility of starting up a flying club at Haverfordwest in South Wales and did some instructing there but it was a non starter for me as the airport owners, the local council, did NOT allow any flying at weekends or after 6pm in the evening. That restriction was ridiculous for a flying club offering flights as a pleasurable activity, so despite being a nice area to fly in, I did not stop there long. At the same time, I was starting to look for a new opportunity and had noticed that a turbo-prop DHC-6 Twin Otter aircraft had arrived on the commercial side of Cardiff airport and was starting to do a daily night flight to Liverpool with the Mail. I made some enquiries and ended up being offered a two year contract based at Cardiff flying the night mail flight. This was an ideal choice as it would also allow me to continue my association with the flying club, maintaining my contacts with friends in the area and I started to make efforts to buy a house near to the airport once I had completed my training.

After a self study ground school, I did my type rating training at Southend, where my employer, Hubbardair Ltd was based and after about 10 hours line training over three nights found myself being let lose at Cardiff as a P1 Captain flying the nightly trip to Liverpool (LPL). This was going to be an interesting job as it was all flown IFR at night in all but the worse of weather conditions, and as I settled in to what I hoped would be a two year deal, I found myself enjoying it. Fog and/or forecasts of fog were the only time you usually cancelled.

My very first trip to Liverpool had its excitement when on the descent towards the Wallasey VOR at about an IAS of 160 Knots, the stall warner went off and remained on until after we had landed when I was able to find the circuit breaker and disable it. The C/B was somewhere in several rows behind my seat and I could not even consider an attempt to find it and fly the aircraft at the same time. As it was a new type on my licence, I had an increment of 100 feet added to any Minimum Descent Height or Decision Height for the first 50 hours. Once I had settled down and felt happy flying the route I began to take members and friends from the flying club for a night experience trip, but that was in the days before security concerns required anyone going airside to have a passenger boarding card and handling agent. This treat became a regular occurrence when the weather was suitable and there was little chance of a diversion elsewhere.

During a period of particularly cold weather when most of the UK was closed down due to heavy snow, I continued to operate normally. When the air becomes very cold icing on the airframe is less likely than when it is just below freezing as the absolute humidity is less and the ice particles tend to bounce off the wings rather than adhere to the surface. However, when flying in more normal temperatures one week, with temperatures between 0 to say -5 Degrees, and I was getting some icing on the wings, I started to see an "Ice" light come on, on the Central Warning Panel (CWP). I thought this was normal as the port wing always appeared to be free of any ice and the pneumatic rubber boots on the wing appeared to work correctly. When, after landing at LPL one night, someone came over to me when I had got on the apron and shut down and said that my other wing was covered in ice, I realised that the reason WHY the orange warning light was coming on was that the boot connection in the starboard wing, which I did not look at during any of the flights, had come adrift. Never Assume always check I have always said, yet on that occasion I did not do what I preach.

I remember taxying out one night but decided to abandon the flight before getting airborne as I did not feel right about the weather, fog and very low cloud was forecast and I did not want to take any risks. When I had a CAA Flight Ops inspector turn up one night, I had to tell him we were not going due to a bad forecast, even though he tried to persuade me that Dublin was an acceptable alternate, on the other side of the Irish Sea. He had to come and fly with me on another night but complemented me for not being pressured into going on his first attempt to fly with me. If in doubt do not go; safety has to be the overriding concern even if there are commercial pressures trying to convince you otherwise. Sometimes when the Liverpool weather was doubtful, we used to fly the mail to East Midlands Airport instead, which was always a change. LPL was slowly being swamped with pink paper; these were the load sheet copies we all had to leave behind, supposedly with a responsible person in case of an accident but no one really bothered in the post office or understood the importance of having a loading record retained on the ground.

I did a total of 63 round trips to LPL before the company cancelled the contract and I had to move on. This happened just before I was to exchange contracts on a small house in Rhoose village and I was able to cancel it but not before I had lost money on solicitor's fees and the necessary house search costs. With hindsight of course, I should have kept the house and let it as houses in that area rapidly grew in value after British Airways decided to move their main maintenance base to Cardiff.

I was compelled to move to Southend in Essex where I continued flying the same aircraft, G-BGMD and another aircraft G-BFGP which was awful to handle as it felt as if it had been bent and was never in balance. I flew the routine 5 sectors a night mail route to from SEN to STN-EMA-LPL-STN and back to SEN. You could also fly it for up to 5 nights a week then so it was hard work. However, after a week I had found what I hoped would be a better job, flying for Loganair in Scotland and left Hubbardair; but I was to return one month later. I then continued flying the same route and another one to Brussels for about another 6 months before the company made me redundant.

The Loganair job had much better prospects and I moved to Glasgow with high hopes but after getting on line fairly quickly after going to places like the Isle of Islay, the Isle of Skye, and Barra where uniquely, you landed on the sandy beach after the tide went out, I was to make a serious error of judgement which regrettably cost me my job when the chief pilot found out about it. They did offer me an alternative position on the Fokker F-27 Friendship which they operated out of Manchester but I declined the punishment offer and decided to return to Hubbardair. During the line training, we had a nasty incident when landing at Broadford on the Isle of Skye when on touching down, the aircraft swung violently to the left. The nose wheel steering handle behind the control column had moved fully to the left and I had not noticed it. It should remain centred when the nose leg is fully extended but a fault had allowed it to caster in flight. We got away with it, but only just.

After flying 4 sectors of a 5 sector duty period, I changed aircraft at Glasgow and prepared to fly to Inverness for a night stop with passengers but on the apron had a propeller fault with the new aircraft which was quickly rectified. It made me late and I rushed the departure. In an effort to make up time I elected to fly direct to Inverness rather than following the advisory route but found myself constantly wondering off the VOR radial. I thought it was strong winds but the problem persisted, and I eventually ended up approaching Inverness in the dark from the NORTH when I should have been coming from the south. I had made sure that I was above the safety altitude over Scotland, which was 5500 feet (Ben Nevis is 4500 feet high) and only descended when the DME range from Inverness allowed me to do so according to the approach charts I had. I eventually landed and then worked out that both my gyro stabilised magnetic indicators had failed and were giving erroneous readings. Had I studied the aircraft's technical log before the rushed departure, I might have been given a hint. Engineers had swapped the two instruments and asked for further observations as one had been reported as being faulty. By changing them from side to side they had in fact failed BOTH units. My bad airmanship error was to not seek assistance from ATC and **I left the basic magnetic compass, which is completely independent of any other system, OUT of my instrument flying scan**. After a further week flying the night mail flights to LPL, from Glasgow now, instead of Cardiff, I was called into the office and given the bad news. I left immediately which was a great disappointment to me as I had enjoyed my month's flying in Scotland and I was just beginning to understand what the Scottish girls were saying to me; with my poor hearing making it difficult to understand them at times.

Interestingly, when I subsequently went for an interview for a job with Brymon Airways later on, I was asked about this error and explained it. They had wondered why I had only been with Loganair for a month. The one interviewer, Captain Peter Rolf, then left the room and came back with a company memorandum warning crews about a possible failure of the gyro magnetic compass which could happen <u>without</u> giving any warning; the same fault had happened to him and he thanked me for being honest about it.

After Hubbardair ceased trading, I got a job with National Airways and after a good ground school training, did all my type rating training, I/R test and line training on the Beech C-90 aircraft in just a few days. I was pushed through the training quickly by one of the training pilots and was complemented on how well I was doing at the time. However, I felt rushed, found the idea of flying at a much higher level at around FL180 (18,000 Feet) difficult to get used to and was really not happy about the job. However, the company themselves gave me the sack for not being good enough but it was a blessing as two of the pilots on my course were dead within a month due to overwork, long hours, insufficient training and possible bad management generally. It was all single pilot operations, one flew into a petrol station at Southend just after take off and the other died after making a missed approach at East Midlands after losing control during the go-around. National Airways did not last long and eventually they had their Air Operators Certificate (AOC) withdrawn by the CAA. Suddenly finding yourself flying a high performance aircraft at well above 10,000 feet was not easy to get used to, especially planning of the descent into an airport which required careful attention and good mental arithmetic.

After my brief experiences with National Airways and the high performance Beech, I quickly found myself a new job flying for South East Air Ltd, but this one did not to last as long as I had hoped as they too went bust, with assets of just £78 to their name; a bit of office stationary left behind at Biggin Hill. However, while it lasted, I was based at London's main airport, Heathrow and used to fly four nights a week to Maastrict in Holland, a round trip of about four hours a night. Flying out of Heathrow was an honour and I enjoyed it immensely mixing with Jumbo Jets and Concorde, which used to depart at about the same time as myself at 10 pm. The worse part of the whole night was that I had to go to the Customs hall on arrival, which was located in the centre of the airport. This could take up to two hours waiting for transport to get to and from the building through the service tunnel from the freight apron. I did eventually get Customs to agree to accept a monthly general declaration for the pilot, but the job ended the very next week so I was not able to take advantage of that well earned concession.

I once had an oil pressure failure on my way back from Maastrict and had to shut down the one engine, but safely completed the approach into Heathrow over central London on the one remaining engine, and was able to easily taxi to the apron after landing safely. It felt nice to be making approaches over the capital at about 4am in the morning, flying up the Thames estuary and feeling important, as you were usually the ONLY aircraft flying into the airport at that early hour. I had nice accommodation at Burnham Beeches just north of Slough which was a large forested area but always went home on the Friday morning to rest and had the weekends off, often riding my horses or hunting.

However I did have one major excitement (with a degree of hindsight), when, on the night of the great storm and hurricane on the 15/16th October 1987 which Michael Fish, the TV forecaster, had famously said was **not** on its way, I went to work as normal but did not like the feel of the weather at all. It was blowing a gale with heavy rain but the big difference to normal, was the temperature, it felt like a tropical storm and I remember thinking there was a lot of potential energy around. Whilst it was still technically within limits at that time and I could have gone, I was not happy. However, when checking the aircraft I found a slight leak of fuel from the gascolator bowl on the right engine. After getting a BA engineer to confirm the leak, I cancelled the flight and drove home to bed BEFORE the worse of the hurricane stuck. I learnt about the disastrous night's events the next day when I woke up at about 1pm. The irony of the whole episode was that after the storm had passed, the fuel leak appeared to have disappeared and the aircraft itself did not escape unscathed as the nose was ripped off by a very large industrial wheelie bin which was blown across the apron hitting the aircraft. I got away with that one but two of the other company aircraft were not so lucky and had a very rough night's flying.

On one of at least 77 round trips I flew out of Heathrow during the course of the autumn and winter of 1987, I had to divert to Dusseldorf in Germany due to fog at Maastrict. As I had to stay in hotel accommodation for a day stop and wanted to get the aircraft back to Heathrow for the next evening, I calculated the required "spilt duty" rest after being told the return load would be brought to the airfield. When I came back on duty, I was then told to first fly to Maastrict to pick up the load which meant an extra sector/flight. This put me technically out of hours and as I was concerned enough about it, I decided to write a letter of explanation to the CAA but nothing more was heard about it. The CAA do not mind a genuine mistake or inadvertent breach of the regulations but take a very stern view if anyone deliberately or intentionally tries to bend the rules for commercial or other reasons. They too make mistakes as well sometimes.

I also used to fly the well known and regular SEN-STN-EMA-LPL-STN-SEN route as well but almost got into a lot of trouble with the CAA once when, without my knowledge, South East Air had gone out of business but I had not been told the whole truth of what was going on. Earlier in the day, I had been told that the flight that night would be flown on a Jersey European Airway's call sign, JY 498/499 and wondered why? On arrival at EMA, I was "ramp checked" by a CAA flight ops inspector who asked me who I was flying for? When I said South East Air he told me their AOC had been withdrawn, and asked if I had a base and Line check with JEA? I was technically using illegal paper work but I pointed out to the inspector that regardless of who I was flying for, the aircraft, which happened to be G-BGMD again, was still operated in the same way from a pilot's point of view. I had my fuel carnet taken from me, and had to file fresh flight plans before I could continue to LPL. I also took a chance by buying £175 of fuel on my own credit card but I was allowed to fly on to complete my very last flight for a mystery employer. The next day I drove to Gatwick and was paid all my costs plus a £100 fee for my services by BAC Charter Ltd who had hurriedly arranged the flight the day before after the company had gone bust! I doubt whether the CAA would have allowed that flight to happen today.

Luckily for me, I had already been making enquires about a new job flying for Brymon Airways based near my home at Birmingham airport. Although I had just written a letter to turn them down as South East Air had also promised me a job at BHX, they knew the company was finished and that I would soon be back on the phone! Brymon Airways had leased one of their Twin Otters to them and was owed a lot of money which they did not get. I myself lost about £2500 but luckily I was back in full time work within a week, at last with a proper commercial airline flying passenger routes around the country. So began a stable period in my flying career which was to last nearly three years before I was made redundant yet again.

A new base check and I/R was flown with the chief Pilot Harry Gee from Plymouth during which I left the flap at 10 degrees after take off until I was nearing the end of the flight but he knew you could be nervous during a test and forgave me. The Birmingham flight was a possible four round trips a day on a shuttle service to/from London's Gatwick airport. The routine schedule apart from any leave or sickness was two afternoons, two mornings, and two days off. With the company's blessing, I used to stay at the Birmingham airport hotel between the last afternoon and the first morning flight. We also used to fly to Plymouth via Exeter on the Saturday and occasionally did other flights such as a flight to Cork in Ireland from time to time. Over a three year period, as you might imagine, I did have a number of incidents and events which are worth recalling in this book.

First of all, the flights were all IFR but if the weather was CAVOK any morning, we used to try a VFR flight to LGW at 3000 Feet via the Compton VOR. You could be lucky and arrive very early at Gatwick but on the other hand you could be held off while inbound Atlantic IFR traffic got priority. I once landed with just 20 minutes of fuel left after holding at Detling VOR for over an hour but my mistake was saying so to the passenger who was sitting in the Co-Pilots seat on that occasion. He reported me to the company for landing short of fuel and for not knowing where Biggin Hill was! That was the nominated alternate and he had wondered why I was getting the charts out for Biggin Hill towards the end of the flight. As it turned out I had done nothing wrong and in any case, the weather was perfect so I could have asked to land earlier or gone elsewhere; or even of landed at a grass strip just west of Gatwick if the need had arisen. However, VFR flights were not without risk as you do not have full ATC protection from other traffic.

On one flight back to Birmingham, I was flying at 3000 Feet and after passing Compton VOR had to pass through the Abingdon MATZ. I called them up and got clearance but seeing a Bulldog aircraft doing aerobatics over the airfield decided to put my landing lights on. Unfortunately, the RAF Pilot considered my contravention of his airspace as an Airmiss, or Airprox as a close encounter is now called. This caused a lot of form filling but I felt I was well clear of him with no risk. It does however illustrate the problems of flying off airways and under your own navigation. On another early morning trip from Birmingham, I had a partial radio failure and could only receive. As I had only just got airborne, and was visual with the surface, I decided to return and put Mode A7600 on the radar transponder. ATC picked that squawk up immediately and asked if I could receive. I responded by selecting the "Ident" Button as confirmation and they talked me round the circuit to a safe landing.

You were almost always late arriving at Gatwick on the first morning flight due to ATC delays and long holds often at the Willow Holding pattern where you could have Jumbos above and below you. You then spent the rest of the day trying to catch up. On one occasion, I found myself waiting for lost baggage and after a while asked the handling agent to look around. It was actually already on the apron in a baggage trolley that had been left unattended. When rushed, you could make mistakes and on one start up, actually started with the propeller tie still attached. The ground handler was also rushing and signalled me to start before he had checked the two engines. The Prop tie simply broke away and flew over the top of the fuselage; an embarrassment to the viewing passengers but no damage was done. While flying back to BHX one day and passing over Luton Airport at FL80, I suffered a **LIGHTNING** strike which entered the aircraft through the nose making a burn hole, and exited out through the tail light which was destroyed. What do you say to a load of startled passengers; well, I assured them all was well, and that "Lightning never strikes twice". The aircraft had to be grounded on arrival at BHX until it was checked over and all the magnetic instruments had been re-calibrated.

Passengers were not always co-operative. Once, while we were taxying out for take at BHX I got a report from ATC to return to the apron. This I did only to find that it was to pick up a late airline pilot passenger who was positioning for duty at Gatwick. He used his initiative to call the tower and call me back. He got to work on time but got into trouble and I was told never to return to the apron unless summoned by the handling agent once you had left the stand. Another American passenger wanted to get off the flight when he realised that it was being flown by just one pilot, which was legal up to the beginning of 1990; after which two crew members were required on all commercial flights over a weight limit of 12500 Lbs or 5700 Kilograms (Kgs). On a flight to Cork which was up to 2 hours long depending on the wind, a lady passenger asked to go to the loo just after getting airborne and had to relieve herself at the back of the plane peeing into paper towels. On I think that same flight I was given the option of making a non standard approach direct on to a right base leg for runway 36 to save some time but as I descended through broken cloud did not feel happy about my position and climbed back up to the safety altitude, proceeded to the Cork VOR, and then did the full and proper approach procedure. You must never attempt to cut corners unless there is absolutely no doubt you know where you are and that the weather will not catch you out; only a guarantied certainty in daylight. At night NEVER declare visual as there may be low cloud or fog you have not seen.

I also had a partial engine failure on a trip to Gatwick when I found that once I had retarded the throttle slightly, I could not regain the power lost. I therefore did not touch that engine again until on final approach to land, but I did manage to give a correct diagnosis to the engineers who were able to pinpoint the faulty part and send up the appropriate replacement. I got a nice letter of thanks for that as it saved the company of lot of unnecessary expense.

Concorde often provided a bit of entertainment when on the second flight of the day, you often passed the Woodley NDB beacon just west of Heathrow at about the time the BA flight was leaving for New York. On good days, I was sometimes able to tell passengers that if they looked out of the port/left side of the cabin they would see Concorde passing underneath them. As it did so, they would all rush to the other side windows to see it again as it continued its climb away from us. In fact, on one flight when I was not flying, the Concorde failed to level off as instructed and actually had an Airprox with the Twin Otter which featured later in a BBC Horizon Television programme about the growth in air traffic in UK airspace. The Concorde can be seen in the middle of the picture on this page which, due to a camera fault, is in fact two or more pictures, one showing the old house at the Little Down farm and a pile of bricks.

The funniest thing that ever happened was one morning when the stewardess, Louise Thompson (no relation), overslept and turned up late for the 07.20 departure. When I rang and woke her up, she asked if I could take out the £10 cash float, the drinks selection which included whiskeys gins and vodka etc, and other items for her; and that she would go directly to the aircraft. This I did, but to make it easier to carry, I put all the items into a black plastic waste bag and simply left it for her at the back of the plane. I also had my own flight crew bag as well. When she got on in a rush, she thought it was the previous days rubbish and threw it out. Just as we started up, I saw a black bag on the concrete apron and asked the despatch officer to check it but I will never know if he found himself a small treasure trove, or whether it was actually thrown away? When we got airborne,, she came to the flight deck and asked where was the money and drinks? "In the gash (rubbish)

bag", I said, which caused very red faced girl to regret getting up late. Never assume, always check is what I always say!

Another good example of why you should check and check again was that on one day I turned up for the afternoon flights to find the aircraft was out parked out on the taxiway with a flat NOSE tyre. I was told to prepare for the next flight as normal as the company was flying up a spare wheel from Plymouth with an engineer to fit it. The only problem was that when they arrived, they had a MAIN tyre instead. I did the flights using the other aircraft while the correct replacement was sent by road instead. I sometimes used to do a walk round during the turn around at Gatwick especially if we were not running late. I once looked in the rear hold and saw the strap of a small bag protruding from behind part of the fuselage structure. I climbed in to find it was a now missing passenger bag for someone who had been on the aircraft TWO DAYS before. The pilot is ultimately responsible for his aircraft and all that goes on around it but you cannot be expected to do everyone else's job for them. The handling agents at Gatwick and Birmingham had missed it repeatedly during about 20 loading and unloading sessions.

My worse error was making a radar approach to a visual final for short R/W 24 at BHX in very poor anti-cyclonic gloom in summer directly into the sun. I mistook a row of lights at a nearby car factory for being the runway and when the ATC controller spotted me, he said, why not land on R/W 33 which was at almost 90 degrees to my actual low position. I instinctively made a very tight turn which not only startled the passengers and the visiting stewardess but it caused my stall warning system to go off. I made an excellent landing however and apologised for the tight turn but it was not a good airmanship or professional thing to do and I got into serious trouble over it, even having to have a flight check with the chief pilot which went remarkably well. I should have made a go-around in a sensible way and re-positioned to land again. There was a contributory reason for what I did, as my mind was thinking about other family matters. On that day, the planning committee of the local council was deciding for the second time whether or not to grant permission for me to build my hoped for house on the farm, having already refused permission at an earlier hearing. Never fly if your mind is disturbed. When I got stuck in a failed lift at BHX on one occasion, it had dropped about 10 feet below the floor level and had shaken me up (shock set in), I cancelled the flight and got someone else to fly it. When suffering from an incident like that, you can suffer a short term memory loss, which can be dangerous.

After the 1st January 1990, the aircraft had to be flown with two crew members on the flight deck, which meant we were now always one passenger seat short, and the aircraft was becoming less viable from a financial point of view. The Twin Otter was therefore taken off the route and subsequently replaced for a short time by a Shorts SD-330 which was leased from Gill Airways in Newcastle. Although still a Brymon employee, I, and another BHX Captain, Ian George, were type rated on the Shorts aircraft and we flew it for several months as First Officers on Gill Air's AOC. However, the route was starting to carry fewer passengers partly due to the opening of the M 40 motorway and the route was abandoned at the end of September of that year. The relatively short route from BHX to LGW meant that by the time you had travelled to the airport, checked in, gone through increased security, waited for your baggage at the other end and finally travelled to your intended destination, you could well have driven the distance by road with time to spare. I was then made redundant yet again and my flying days came to an end with Brymon Airways. The UK is not a big enough country for some of the shorter routes.

Shortly before the Twin Otter was withdrawn from use and sold abroad, I had seen an advert for a Twin Otter Captain in the Seychelles, the idyllic holiday islands in the middle of the Indian Ocean. I thought it might be a very nice change and made enquiries. The company Air Seychelles invited me to  come for an interview, not to their offices at London Gatwick but all the way to the islands themselves. Their view was that it was best if you came to see exactly what was on offer rather than be disappointed so I duly flew out free of any charge on the company Boeing 707 which few regular twice weekly services from the UK. I stayed on the islands for four days during which I flew to all the islands except the famous Bird Island and thoroughly enjoyed myself. See the photos section of the book and the picture above. I was keen to take the job but found that living there on a full time basis would be too expensive, so regrettably I turned them down.

That was probably the biggest mistake I ever made as just a month later, I was given notice that the job at BHX was to end; so I had missed my chance to go to paradise! However, when I flew back home on the same fight, I did see the Egyptian Pyramids from 30,000 feet as we flew over Cairo in the cockpit, something which sadly is not allowed anymore, even if you know the person concerned. I was also thinking of getting married at the time and wanted to get my house built on the farm. On one of the island airstrips, Turtles from the beach had to be moved off the runway before a landing and take off could be made. Many years later two of the Shorts SD 360 aircraft were sold from BAC Express to Air Seychelles and I had the hope that a job there might come about, but sadly that did not happen.

In a letter to Brymon Airways saying why I had decided to stay with them, I had said that I was staying put for **"Security of employment and long term prospects"**. Little did I know that I would be losing my job a few months later, and that despite going back to school to do my full Airline Transport Pilots Licence examinations, I would find myself out of work for over 7 years due to the deepening recession and the first 1991 Gulf War which gave air travel a severe jolt with significant cutbacks worldwide.

Brymon Airways made all the Birmingham crew redundant at the end of 1990 to save money yet all their aircraft were re-sprayed at least twice in the next 18 months; firstly when the airline amalgamated with Birmingham European and secondly, after that arrangement failed to work, they were then painted in British Airways colours. They were not amused when I pointed out that they could have kept us all employed for a fraction of those combined costs.

My Twin Otter years were most enjoyable but all good things have to come to an end. I had flown a total of 2170 Hours on various aircraft with four different employers. I had managed to take most of my family members on a flight including one night flight with my father during which it was a very clear night and you could see all the way round London and the M-25 motorway, and up the M1 to Birmingham. I also took my mother on a flight to the Isle of White and back in G-BGMD, one of the Twin Otters which I flew with all the companies I worked with. It appeared to follow me wherever I went, but it was eventually sold to New Zealand; and sadly, I did not follow her. I was now to have a long period out of full time flying during which I tried to make my marriage work despite being out of work, and did my best to develop my farm and airstrip which forms the basis of the next Chapter.

Chapter 10.
My Legacy, Milson Airstrip.

In the summer of 1967, my father had the opportunity to purchase a small farm which became available on his own land's western boundary. The farm had been let to a tenant farmer who had lost interest, failed to pay the rent to the Landlord, and was shortly to be evicted. The owners had decided that it was in such a run down state that they would sell it at an auction which was to be held in the Royal Oak Hotel in nearby Tenbury Wells. I remember that we had had a look at the place and decided it was worth a small bid as it was in a very bad and derelict condition. The land had not been touched for years and the house and building were in an almost derelict condition with no electricity or running water system in place. One of the aerial photographs taken at about that time is shown in the selection of prints in the book. Sixty seven acres of land was therefore up for grabs by anyone keen enough to take it on. One wealthy landlord in the area had told my parents that he would not bid against them if they agreed to sell the one seven acre field on the opposite side of the public road which adjoined his own land. At the auction, my father's maximum bid was about £9000 and after it was exceeded he left the sale disappointed thinking he had lost the chance but later in the evening, got a call from the auctioneers to say he could have it after all for his bid price as all the later offers turned out to be unsubstantiated. My father thus became the proud owner of the Little Down Farm, Milson which now meant that he had a total of over 160 acres of ground, sixty of which needed some urgent care and attention.

The farm consisted of many very small fields, most of which were not suitable for modern farm machinery and action was taken to remove a number of hedges and an old apple orchard. Without realising it at the time, this left a fairly level area of ground roughly half a mile in total length. When I began learning to fly seriously in 1969-70, I said that if we pushed out just one tree at the southern end by the road, and flattened an old stony cart track which crossed the now bigger field, we would have created ourselves an Airstrip. Milson Airstrip was born in mind but it was not until 1971 that I first landed on the farm in a Piper Cub, G-APZJ. About 6 months later, after I had become a flying instructor and the Herefordshire Aero Club had got its Rallye; I then started to fly into the airstrip fairly regularly. I used it as a practise forced landing area when the field surface, wind and weather were suitable on training flights.

The Little Down Farm **BEFORE** our Ownership began.

The photo shows me at the airstrip with the Rallye G-AWOC in 1973. In the picture are my Auntie's children, Andrew, Rachael, and Rebecca; who were all about to have their first flight.

One day a commercial traveller, Gerald Donnelly, who was a temporary member of the aero club while an oil pipeline was being constructed across the area, incidentally actually passing just south of the airstrip, told me he had seen a derelict windsock pole on the side of the new M5 motorway which happened to cross the old military airfield at Moreton Valence in Gloucestershire. I decided to have a look at it, decided I wanted it, and tried to find a legal owner from whom I could purchase it. However, no one in the immediate vicinity wanted to know about it and I was eventually told to go and see someone I had already been in contact with. With my uncle Jim, (mother's younger brother) and using a Ford transit van loaned to me by a flying club member, we travelled down to Gloucestershire and basically nicked it!

140

It was very hard work dismantling about two metric tons of steel piping and balance weights and it took us a considerable amount of time and physical effort to retrieve it. However, we succeeded and after Keith Miles had accidentally arranged for two metal beams to be "dropped off the back of a lorry"; it was duly erected on site just to the east of the airstrip and has remained there to this very day. It was a complete windsock unit of World War Two vintage and had a proper swivel device on the top with a weather vane attached to it. Milson, and the Little Down Farm now looked more like an airstrip but it took a while for the prominent windsock to become an accepted part of the local landscape. I purchased the first of many Windsocks to put on the pole and was proud of my find.

An explanation of how I came to regularly fly the Auster G-AIPW is worthwhile. In about 1971, a local timber merchant from nearby Eardiston in the Teme valley, Mr Phillip Cadman, purchased the aircraft off Shobdon Aviation with the intention of learning to fly but never managed it as he always had far too much to say, wouldn't listen to good advice from his instructor, and I certainly did not feel he was mature enough to send solo, which was a pity as he was a very keen aviator with an interest in old aircraft.

As he knew my father and the Milson airstrip was near to his home, he asked if he might construct a hangar building on the site of the old farm buildings and started to do so but unfortunately never fully completed it. It can clearly be seen in the photograph of the

141

Chipmunk taking off on page 145. He managed to get the main framework completed and put an asbestos roof on it but never completed the walls and no doors were ever put on the front end of the building. The Auster and for a short time, a Tiger Moth, were kept there for many years until they were both sold. Jim Buckingham, who is mentioned elsewhere in the book, purchased the Auster in an un-airworthy state after Phil's demise for just £400 and actually flew it out which I thought was a bit of a risk. I was offered it but just could not afford it; with hindsight, that was a mistake as it would be a collector's item today if properly maintained.

There are two particularly good photographs of this aircraft, one above, and the other on page 144 (reproduced in colour in the first section of coloured pictures). G-AIPW was rebuilt, had another engine fitted and eventually found its way into the personal collection of King Hussein of Jordon. It is now on display in his museum in Amman, Jordon. Ironically the Piston Provost I once flew at Cardiff is also displayed there. The Tiger Moth which lived at Milson for a while was G-ANJK which had been owned by the Montgomeryshire Ultra Light Aircraft Group but a friend of mine, Dave Williams had acquired it for safe keeping following a an internal dispute about its ownership. I had one flight in it with Dave but found it difficult to keep in trim and balance, so it was a god aircraft to start on during the war years. It subsequently went to live on a farm in South Wales where Dave hopes one day to restore to a fully airworthy condition.

Unfortunately for Phil, his life ended tragically with a family dispute in which he first stated to his friends that he was going to commit suicide. He came to see my father and said he could have the unfinished hangar building, some ladders, and a concrete mixer, so we all thought he was planning something drastic. That indeed was the case as a week or so later he shot and killed his estranged wife's lover and had intended to shoot himself but was apprehended by the police in time. After being committed to stand trial for murder and sent to Winson Green prison in Birmingham he subsequently managed to hang himself on the very day my sister Janet called to see him. She was invited in to the Prison Governor's office to be told the tragic and shocking news. Worst still, she was then given all his personal possessions and asked to take them back to his mothers home; which was an unpleasant burden for her and was probably the wrong thing for a non family member to have been asked to do.

His daughter later tried to get some money off my father for the buildings materials which he had left on the farm but did not pursue the claim once it had been explained to her that he had effectively given it all away. I personally liked Phil Cadman very much. He was an eccentric but likeable character who always knew every bodies business, ran a successful timber yard for many years making larch lap fencing materials, and once tried to evade the customs man by putting a diesel tank within a tank on his lorry!

On the 8th July 1973, as I approached my 21st Birthday, I had my first "Fly In" at the airstrip which turned out to be a very special occasion which was very well supported by the flying club members. I was not sure how successful it would be and remember waiting for aircraft to arrive but we had at least 14 aircraft land. These included myself of course, in the Auster G-AIPW during which I made eight local flights for friends and relatives and a Chipmunk, Beagle Terrier, Two PA28 Cherokees, a few Cessna 150's, a Motor Falke, and the Rallye Commodore. Andrew Gilliat was also brave enough to fly in the company Piper Apache G-ATMU, which was the first twin to land there. I was more than pleased with the turnout which put Milson on the map for the first time.

One local farmer had his first close up look at an aircraft and wondered how it moved on the ground as the wheels were not attached to the engine; it had to be explained to him that it was pulled through the air by the propeller. Other local people had also never seen an aircraft before at close quarters so it was an interesting day for the Milson parish and other local villages in the area.

Auster G-AIPW Taking off from Milson in 1973.

The airstrip continued to be used during the 1970's on an occasional basis in the summer and when the grass was short enough. Father grew the grass crop for Hay and kept livestock off the airstrip field as much as possible. During my time with the Army in Germany, I flew the twin engined Islander home but because of a strong southerly wind decided to land downhill over some trees but into the wind. This was the first time I had landed the other way and I must say it looked a bit short. My Father watched me land and often talks about it in conversations over 30 years later.

Milson airstrip is about 500 metres long if you include the upslope at the northern end but the published length for safety purposes is given as 450 metres. Normally any aircraft landing there will land uphill heading north and take off the opposite way but in very strong northerly winds it is possible to take off uphill. Likewise, you can sometimes land towards the south if the wind is a strong one from that direction, like I did in the twin engined Islander in 1977. The prevailing wind is however westerly and although the windsock might show a stiff wind, it is often virtually calm in the lee of the high hedge and trees to the west, so you have to be prepared for some turbulence and wind shear at times. There is a 2 degree overall slope on the strip with a 40 foot difference between the southern and northern ends. It is 500 feet amsl at the northern end.

144

When I returned from my army days away and started flying from Shobdon and Cardiff again the airstrip was used more frequently and weather permitting I tried to have a fly in every year, some being more successful than others. The main requirement for a successful day was always LIGHT WINDS so I tried to plan these events at short notice when I was sure all the requirements including a grass cut surface were in place. I think I only got it badly wrong once and had to stop people coming as the cross wind became far too strong on the day. I used to watch the weather closely and if the grass was short enough, the field dry, and the winds forecast to be light with a high cloud base and good visibility, I would ring round a day or two before hand asking friends to spread the word. It usually worked except for one occasion when the food arrangement failed to materialize on the day.

We had a particularly good fly in event in 1982 when about 50 aircraft attended, including many form the flying club at Cardiff and elsewhere. That year, it included Jim Buckingham in his Miles Gemini G-AKKB which gave a very spirited low level display. He later went on to become the aviation fuel manager for the Total Oil Company and now provides all the fuel requirements at Shobdon airfield and elsewhere.

The old house and farm buildings can be clearly seen in this shot of a Cardiff Chipmunk, G-BFAW, taking off in 1982. The aircraft in the background is another visiting Turbulent belonging to Eddie Clapham.

On one fly in, a Jet Provost flew round and appeared to be making an approach but instead did a very fast low level fly by which was a great excitement at the time. I never ever met the owner of the Jet Provost but did manage to thank him for his brief visit. One pilot flying up to the airstrip from Cardiff got lost or temporarily uncertain of his position but was within radio range to talk to myself on the ground. When I asked him what he could see, he said he had over flown a town with a cathedral, railway and river and we all thought it was Hereford. However, when he then said he could see some tall radio masts, we deduced that he was approaching Droitwich and that Hereford had in fact been Worcester. Consulting a map I told him to turn on to a heading of about 300 Degrees and put on his landing light. I picked him up immediately even though he was about 30 miles away and told him to keep coming. A lot of my visitors over the years had difficulty finding he airstrip because grass field strips do NOT necessarily look like airfields. Also, sometimes they have navigated so accurately that they cannot spot the field because they are actually directly over the top and cannot see it. These days if GPS is used, the "Distance to Go" is the best clue; get down to about 0.5 nautical miles and you are almost there!

Sometime during those years the local electricity board wanted to lay a high voltage line directly across the airstrip linking the village of Milson with Coreley but when I told them of my future hopes they agreed to re-route it well to the south of the field. This was to benefit a local neighbour, who incidentally became a persistent complainer, when he wanted to have the electricity connected. He found that as a result of my influence, the main power lines past directly past his farm buildings. When I wanted the power myself in 1988, it cost me over £10,000 to get it connected as the electricity board had to put cables up all the way from the Upper Down Farm, about a mile away.

In 1988, my Parents gave me the Little Down Farm by "Deed of Gift" and I started to develop the site with aviation rather than farming in mind. At that time you did **NOT** require any planning consent for the construction of agricultural buildings so I had one large hangar type building built on a levelled site at the northern end where the old farm buildings had been located. I also had a Bore Hole sunk to get a reliable water supply and had the electricity connected, both of which cost me about £15000; with the new building costing another £30,000. I took a photo of the bore hole being drilled with the old farmhouse in the background, which was to prove crucial evidence when I came to apply for planning consent for a replacement farm house a year or so later. I very soon started to fill the "hangar" with aircraft; these included a Currie Wot G-ASBA and a Rollason Condor G-AYFD, which is still in residence today. I also had a Piper J3 Cub G-BGXA there for a while which I was able to fly, but the owner deviously got me to pay his insurance and have free hangarage, so I had a bad deal. He eventually left one day without saying anything and never came back claiming later that he had found some damage due to what is commonly called "hangar rash". We also had a nice silver painted Turbulent G-BTLC there as well. During the years I was unemployed, the owner of this aircraft, Graham Smith, kindly allowed me to fly it fairly regularly. However, on one flight I nearly destroyed it while landing at Bosbury airstrip south of Bromyard where a good friend and regular visitor to the airstrip, Hamish Moffatt kept his De-Havilland Moth G-AADR.

He was a welcome visitor and often used to fly in often to visit a family relative in the area. It was a great honour to have this aircraft visit the airstrip on a regular basis as it is one of the oldest airworthy aircraft on the UK civil register having been constructed in 1929. He once nearly lost control of it at the northern end when preparing to take off as he only had a tail skid to steer it with on the ground; and NO brakes. However, he switched off the ignition in time and gently went over the edge of the embankment settling nicely on its belly in the long grass. Unbelievably, no damage was done and a handful of people later helped to lift it back on the airstrip and its wheels!

My bad landing at Bosbury in the Turbulent was caused by several factors. Firstly, the airstrip had a pronounced uphill slope from East to West, well in excess of what I had been used to at other places. Secondly, although I was landing into a brisk wind I was also landing DIRECTLY into the Sun which more or less blinded me as I started to round out for the landing. That, coupled with a trace of oil on the windscreen, caused me to land heavily and bounce. I was not able to do a go-around due to the slope and trees ahead and had to let the aircraft land heavily again. This unfortunately bent the undercarriage attachment bolts, all of which had to be replaced. Luckily for me, Graham had attached the undercarriage legs to the main spar with removable bolts and spacers. These bolts took the full force of the heavy landing rather than the main wooden spar of the wing and saved the aircraft. I paid for the replacement bolts!

All was well with the airstrip until about 1990 when a new resident of Milson came to live nearby, at a smallholding where one of my girlfriends used to live. He already knew the airstrip existed yet decided to buy the adjacent property and almost immediately made a complaint about the airstrip activities to the local council. This person, who, out of ignorance to the reader, will remain anonymous, has caused no end of trouble ever since, both for me, my father and his shooting interests, in addition to today's current owner and has been known to cause trouble over other matters as well. I was actually flying a Taylorcraft aircraft G-BREY into the airstrip when he was viewing the property and he waved to me; but when I mentioned that fact to him later, he said that he was in fact shaking his fist at me; so why did he buy the place? He was to cause me and Dana, my future wife, a lot of heartache and considerable expense over the next 10 years or so; harassment which unfortunately still continues today but to a lesser extent, I am glad to say. I did once grab him by the collar and tie when we had a confrontation but I later went and apologized to him!

The official complaint he made to the local council resulted in an enforcement notice requiring me to apply for a retrospective planning consent for an airstrip which had already been in existence with supporting evidence (my own log books and a visiting aircraft book) for 18 years. With hindsight, I made a mistake to comply as quickly as I did, because in 1991, a new planning law came into force which would have given me automatic consent due with NO conditions due to the length of time it had already existed. However, trying to be helpful and co-operative I applied for consent and after a site meeting and lots of correspondence, got planning consent. However, it was only for ten aircraft to be based there, just 8 flights a day with one visitor allowed and, to try and placate the neighbour, a stupid condition preventing any take offs between 2 and 5 pm on Sunday afternoons from April to September inclusive; so the local community could have peace and quite on a Sunday afternoon. That takes no account of noisy lawn mowers, farm tractors and other aircraft from elsewhere who continued to pass overhead. I did successfully argue that you could not stop an aircraft from landing as that posed a valid flight safety risk; after all, as he saying goes, "Take off's are optional, all landings are mandatory". I was also allowed to have one "Fly In" weekend a year. This was later increased to two a year to allow for a second attempt if the weather was bad on the first occasion. A summary of the planning history is given in the last of the **appendices**; number eleven.

I did have strong local support for the first planning application and had 89 supporter letters with just 13 objections, mainly from new people to the area. After twelve months, I made another application to regularise the use based on experience gained and got a partial victory in that the number of flight including visitors was raised to 10 with two fly in weekends allowed each year. This application was initially refused and had to go to the Planning Inspectorate on appeal but I won most of what I was seeking to achieve. Some local people feared it was to be developed into an international airport but the reality is that for up to 2/3rds of the year it is not useable by fixed wing aircraft or microlights due to strong winds and more importantly in winter, WET ground. During the one planning application a sensational front page article was published in the well read local paper the Shropshire Star claiming there was a fear of a disastrous collision between the local school bus on the public road and aircraft coming in to land on the airstrip.

It was also agreed that the Sunday Take of restriction would to be removed in return for a LEGAL agreement requiring all aircraft to fly away after taking off rather than remaining in the immediate area, air safety permitting. I was happy with that but when it was pointed out to me that it would apply to the whole farm rather than just the airstrip field, I objected as it would have taken away my "28 Day" rule allowing me to use other parts of the farm if the need arose. A lot of expense was needlessly wasted on this legal agreement as it was unenforceable in any case but the sad fact is that the Sunday restriction still remains to this day. It is however not much of a handicap unless someone lands and had hoped to fly on almost immediately. As for the number of flights each day, it is possible for it to be exceeded but this very rarely happens and is never intentionally done, so that is not a problem either. Some microlight owners came to the airstrip and put up another smaller hangar which caused another complaint but on that occasion it was allowed without the need for another planning application as it made use of the supports of an existing building and site area.

In about 1995, I formally invited RAF Shawbury to use the airstrip for occasional helicopter training flights. This offer was accepted and about two years later the new Defence Helicopter Flying School (DHFS) at RAF Shawbury started using the airstrip field on a fairly regular basis, much to the annoyance of the main objector. That was after I had had my first free helicopter flight which is given annually to all the landowners who allow there fields to be used. I had a total of two flights in a Gazelle and Squirrel.

However, military aircraft are EXEMPT from planning laws as they fly for the government and the nation, so technically nothing can be done about it. However the RAF/MOD does not deliberately try and annoy anyone but their training flights have to take place somewhere. It was said in an official letter to the council that if a particular flight did not visit Milson airstrip, it would have had to go somewhere else, so NIMBY (Not in my back yard) is not an option!

That said, the DHFS have over 70 Field landing sites which they can use with the permission of the landowner and they try to distribute the possible annoyance from helicopter noise evenly. Ironically, I have always said myself that it is the lack of a regular use which causes the problem, as a regular activity eventually becomes part of the surroundings, and is not noticed after a time.

A good example of this is that I once went by road to Otherton Airfield near Stafford where there is a restriction preventing any take offs before 10 am on a Sunday, yet yards away there is the constant noise of almost continuous road traffic on the M6 motorway making normal speech difficult. The locals there cannot hear the motorway noise yet they complain about the odd microlight or aircraft. Odd, don't you think, or is it based on jealousy while someone else is enjoying themselves? When the planning matters about Milson were being discussed some local people said why could you not go and fly at nearby Shobdon yet if you go to Shobdon, some residents there could say why do you not go and fly somewhere else? My own view is that the more airstrips there are, the less intense will be the use in your own area as there will be more places that aircraft can fly to on a nice day. For some reason people like to complain about aircraft if I visit a friend by air but if I go there by road, in a car or lorry, by motor bike, on horseback, cycle, or walk, those modes of transport are acceptable. No one seems to realise that an aircraft is another means of transport, not just a way of making noise.

The longest continuous resident at Milson has been a Rollason Condor, G-AYFD, which was once flown by the Duke of

Edinburgh. The owner, Brian Manning, has been a regular air racing pilot for many years but when I flew with him once in a race practise, it scared me to death flying so close to other aircraft at low level. I once flew it back from Leicester for him when he had to leave to there due to bad weather. It is a good British built aircraft but is a little slow yet he still won the Schneider Trophy Race once.

Brian once wanted to go flying but there were thunderstorms in the vicinity some distance away. I advised him not to do so despite there being a calm surface wind. He took off but very quickly returned as the storm closed in and he was forced to make a go-around through the trees when he suddenly found himself trying to land with a very strong tailwind when there had been a headwind present on the airstrip just a minute of so before. It was funny to watch but in realty it was a good example that you must treat thunderstorms and large cumulonimbus clouds with respect. Brian has been at Milson airstrip since 1988 and is still there today.

I once had to write to the owner of an aircraft who had made an unauthorized low fly by of the strip threatening to report him to the CAA for dangerous flying. This aircraft and its owner, who I have never met, had come from Halfpenny Green and he claimed he had been checking the strip to see if it was safe to land. He had not telephoned beforehand and flew low over the main objector's house who promptly made another complaint to the local council. This is WHY you must seek the permission of a private airstrip owner before going there to find out about the do's and don'ts of making a visit. My letter had the desired effect and I never saw him again.

To help encourage any visiting helicopters, civil or military, to land further from his property, I put down a large metal helicopter landing pad which cost me £1500 but I had to get a formal planning consent for that as well after my neighbour objected yet again. That pad is still there and forms a noticeable part of the local terrain on Google maps and can be clearly seen as a white letter "H" on the aerial photograph shown above on this page.

DHFS Squirrel and Griffin helicopters still use the airstrip on an occasional basis but due to cost restraints do not use it as much now as they used to in the past. The occasional Chinook, Puma, or Merlin helicopter now uses it as former students at Shawbury go elsewhere in their military careers. I strongly support their continued use of the airstrip and hope it continues for years to come. The local objector is known to be one of the worse people the RAF have to deal with, so he has lost all credibility, even when making a genuine complaint. He did have other supporters once but in the main, most people now accept that the RAF and DHFS do have an important and vital job to carry out; training our helicopter pilots on behalf of our nation and government.

Unfortunately, due to being made redundant again in 1991, 7 long years out of work, a divorce, (I had spent too much time dealing with the airstrip problems and not shown enough affection for my wife, Dana), I had to sell the farm and airstrip and move on. However, my farewell "Fly In" event, held on the 24thJune 2001 was a great success with 85 aircraft from all over the country attending in excellent weather conditions. One of my most cherished photographs is an aerial shot of the airstrip showing at least 50 aircraft and microlights all lined up down one side of the airstrip. It was taken by a flying instructor who happened to be passing on a navigational flight from Sleap airfield, near Shrewsbury. This treasured "Legacy" photo is also shown on the page after next. A careful count will reveal **50** aircraft, helicopters and microlights present. As I have said, it was taken by a passing aircraft which did NOT actually land at the fly in but kindly sent me the picture later, and was taken at just the right time when the maximum number of aircraft were present; presenting a nice line up with no gaps.

Regrettably, Milson Airstrip has had a few incidents and accidents over the last 40 years but that is to be expected at a small rather tight airstrip. Once, one of the club members flew up from Cardiff in the PA28 Cherokee and had a dilemma about whether to take off uphill into a 10 knot headwind, or try going the other way downhill, downwind. I said I would demonstrate the best solution by trying a take off both ways. I nearly crashed as I barely got over the hedge taking off uphill with the stall warner ringing in my ears whereas I had no trouble taking off downhill with the slight tailwind. On balance, the slope is probably more of an advantage provided there are no obstacles to climb over immediately after getting airborne.

During one of the earlier fly in events, the pilot of a Cessna 150 tried to take advantage of the steep slope at the northern end intending I think to get airborne quicker than anyone else. The only problem was that he lost control as he turned too fast at the top and ended up in the roof of one of the old farm buildings. The tail of the aircraft with its registration letters, G-BAXV, was clearly visible for all to see for many months until it was taken away, pointed vertically upwards; a good example of how not to attempt a take off.

Once a Kitfox owner flew in and despite several attempts to take off when he tried to leave, firstly into a fairly strong northerly wind, which should not have been a problem for a STOL performance aircraft, he crashed. After two attempts uphill, he then decided to try a downwind downhill take off but abandoned it too late and ended up in the small brook at the southern end of the strip. I witnessed the accident and fearing the worst, telephoned the police stating that an aircraft had crashed at Milson Airstrip. I then stupidly rang off and went to the aid of the pilot and passenger who, it turned out, were shaken but unharmed. As the emergency services were not able to get any more details they assumed a major air disaster had occurred and sent four fire engines, several police cars and a helicopter from nearby Halfpenny Green. I got a severe ticking off for over reacting but more seriously, for not staying by the phone until matters were clarified.

A microlight owner who kept his three axis Phantom at Milson once flew an air test after a long period on the ground, but failed to round out sufficiently on landing and left his wheels behind. It looked funny at the time as the wheel spats both broke off and were thrown some distance away, but it could have been worst. Finally for this depressing page, the very first arrival on my final fly in day which is illustrated below and over the page, failed to round out and left his undercarriage behind. The Jodel, G-ASXY, was pulled off the strip but I have cropped the photo to remove it from view. It turned out that neither pilot, both friends of mine, knew who was actually to do the landing, a clear case of miss-understanding one another in the air. Luckily there were no other incidents during the fly in and we had at least 85 visiting aircraft and probably about 200 movements during the course of the day. Aviators from across the country came to pay their respect to me for my efforts in developing the airstrip over the previous 30 years. I was more than pleased.

My "Legacy" Photograph showing 50 Microlights,
Aircraft, and Helicopters.

This final event took place the day after an unfortunate fatal flight which had taken off from Milson the day before. The Mistral microlight suffered an engine failure while on a local flight and for some reason, the pilot entered a spin from which he was not able to recover, and sadly he and his passenger were killed. To make matters worse, the passenger's young son was still at the airstrip waiting for his father to return with another family friend and had to be fetched by the police as news of the tragedy became known. The new owner Chris Jones and I did consider cancelling the planned fly in event as a result but carried on as the accident had happened away from the strip and we had not personally known the people involved. Unfortunately, on the next day, just after the fly in was over, Chris received a very irate phone call from an elderly lady in the village who said we should not have had the event due to the accident the day before; even though she had visited the airstrip and enjoyed my hospitality and free food! How hypocritical can you be, complaining about an event which you yourself took advantage of? I happened to be with Chris when this telephone call was received and was just as annoyed that someone who had known me and my parents all my life should have taken that viewpoint.

The new owner, who for legal reasons, had taken over ownership of the farm on the Friday before my final fly in, a week earlier than I had wished, has kept the airstrip going, leant to fly helicopters and then became a fixed wing pilot as well. He still allows the DHFS to use the site and like myself, gets an annual visit to Shawbury for a helicopter fight and luncheon. He does not promote the airstrip as much as I did but visitors can fly in, and he still has the problem with that one annoying and persistent complainer. His own fly in days are few and far between, partly due to new insurance requirements these days but he has allowed a rocket club to use the airstrip for legal rocket launches during the Sunday take off restriction, and once, before he woke up, over 50 hot air balloons were launched on a competition from the field; what a sight that was!

To end this chapter, here are some views of my legacy, Milson airstrip, as it is today in 2010, the first one looking at the airstrip from the nearby public road, the second looking back towards the road from the northerly runway threshold, the third looking north up the overall 2 degree slope and the fourth looking back down the slope from the north. The relatively wide width of the mown grass gives the illusion that it is rather short and it is only **450 Metres** (plus a little extra at the northern end on the pronounced up slope) but it is adequate for most light aircraft with a STOL performance.

1. View from the main road. **2. Looking back at the approach.**

3. Looking north up the slope. 4. Looking south down the slope.

Unfortunately, the prevailing wind is a westerly so a crosswind is often the problem and together with the wet ground during the winter months, it is only useable for about $1/3^{rd}$ of the year. The famous windsock pole can be seen to the left in the fourth photograph. The airstrip at Milson is not therefore a commercially viable proposition yet the local authorities came and put a Rateable Value on it for business purposes after planning consent had been given. See **Appendix Eleven** for a detailed summary of the planning sequence, seen from my perspective.

Readers who have learnt to fly can fly into the airstrip with permission from the current owner but do get in touch first. Details are given in the relevant flight guides available, which can be purchased by pilots. The current owner is aware I am saying this in the book, and would be happy to hear from anyone wanting to pay

Milson a visit sometime in the future. Shown below is a map plan of most of the Little Down Farm and Milson Airstrip which might be useful to anyone hoping to fly in one day; with permission of course.

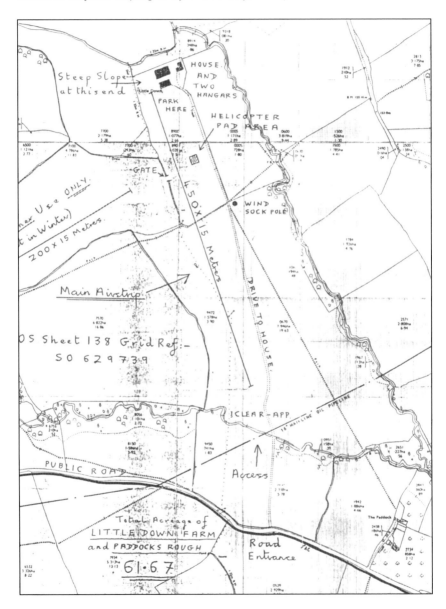

Chapter Eleven.
Other Matters.

Even though I do not now own Milson airstrip, I will always consider it "My" airstrip since I thought of it, constructed it over a number of years and by figure of speech, got it on the map! It is my legacy to aviation and I hope to will remain for years to come and not get ploughed up one day. When I was compelled to sell it in 2001, I was determined to see it purchased by a keen aviator and went to Chris Jones at his home in Coventry to see if his aviation interests were genuine before agreeing to the sale. They Were!

The time has come to devote a chapter to non flying matters which for the benefit of the reader will give a little more detail of my other lifetime interests and history. As I have already explained my sister and I were brought up living in the countryside on a hard working mixed dairy and arable farm. We had a varied lifestyle and enjoyed the freedom and variation of the farm, but both of us were sent to boarding school partly to allow our parents to get on with running a modern farm. Horse riding was a pastime for a while when we were young and again later on for me when I found myself living at home again in the 1980's and I used to help on the farm when needed. However, when my interest in flying became apparent, both my parents actively encouraged my interest to continue which for a farming family is unusual. Most farming families' hope their Son (or Daughter in some cases) will follow in the family tradition and keep the farm going but my Father never took that view, and let me develop my own interests for which I am eternally grateful; He still happily maintains his interest in my aviation activities today.

When I first left the college in Kidderminster, I worked as a farmhand but as I said in chapter two, whenever the weather was good for farming, it was also good for flying so I was not a reliable farm worker. When I had learnt to fly and after I became a flying instructor, I still lived at home but was away at Shobdon most of the time. I did not show much interest in girls at that stage as I was too "in love" with flying and found myself mixing with people a lot older than myself. I used to enjoy a drink at various pubs on the way home and once hit a tree in my mini van on the way home but got away with it. I lived away from home while at Cardiff and during my army experiences but was back at home during most of the 1980's after I was made redundant from Express Air Services and worked at Shobdon and Gloucester for Flight One Ltd. As the flying was intermittent with very long periods with no work, I used to help on the farm and ride my father's horses, as well as following the Ludlow Hunt. It was during that time that I formed a close friendship with an immediate neighbour which frightens me every time I think about it today. After that relationship ended, no harm done, I became very friendly with a nice girl from Shobdon whose name was Debbie Wright but although I liked her very much and we might have married, it was not to be. Her mother resented me for some reason and had a harsh exchange of words once about my relationship so I let it go. However, we did have some good times and she enjoyed flying with me to air shows and other events including the trip to Germany featured in **Appendix Five**. I did see Debbie a few times years later but then she appeared to disappear. The reason was that she had died very young. As mentioned earlier, I was not to know about this until seeing her name on her gravestone in the same cemetery where one of my grandfathers was laid to rest in 1984. That was a very great shock to me and I took a while to get over it.

While living at home, my father's legacy to the world was created when he had two fishing pools constructed on the farm in a rough land area in the centre of the farm. This was where they eventually had a holiday chalet constructed in 1992 after they had sold the rest of the farm. They had to buy a separate small property in Tenbury Wells as well as the planning consent was only for a holiday let building, but they ignored that condition and virtually stayed there for another 14 years, only vacating the property for the month of February when the weather is usually bad anyway. Those pools were stocked with Trout but were regularly poached until I devised a system to catch them. Basically, a type of pressure pad was designed and hidden underground in several places, we had a total of five sets which if triggered would send a signal to an alarm bleeper in the house. It worked very well with only one regular false alarm when a very large wild cat used to roam the area. It was eventually cornered and shot.

The photograph over the page was taken from a DHFS Griffin helicopter and shows the strip of land between the two pools where a Squirrel helicopter once made two landings! Since it was sold, the site has been redeveloped by the new owner but none of our family has been back to see it but from the air it appears that a lot of the trees have been removed. I made a vow never to return as I am happy to remember the pools as they were when my father owned and created them. Due to ill health, my parents completed an agreed sale a year earlier than originally intended and as a consequence, a very poor sale price was concluded due to the rush.

160

One very nice, calm summer's morning, ideal for poachers, the alarm went off. We all got up, I went up the roads towards the airstrip where I found their vehicle and disabled it by removing the distributor cap and spark plug leads. My mother Edna phoned the police, and my father Guy went down to the pool with his shotgun laded with doctored cartridges; they had corn rather than lead in them. 5 poachers were caught red handed and luckily saw the sense to give up. The police arrived and expressed alarm that they had been called just for a few fish but that was not the point; they were poaching private pools. There was a funny side as well when one of the lady policemen went down to the pools and discovered to her horror that there was a dead grass snake wrapped around the barbed wire she was trying to get over it. The loudest shriek I have ever heard was sounded disturbing the peace at about 5 am one quiet morning! Later in the day, one of the culprits came and asked for the distributor cap for his car. He was led on a wild goose chase, firstly to Cleobury Mortimer police station, followed by Bridgnorth, and then on to Kidderminster before eventually finding it back at the Cleobury station. We had no more trouble from them but the owners of the Paddocks, a small property which overlooked the pools area, had all their cars vandalised one night a few days later. We cannot be sure but it might have been the poacher's revenge, taken out on the wrong victims?

Another memorable event was when a boy camping on the farm went missing. He had been told to follow the brook on the farm downstream to get something from the wood but vanished. He was eventually found wondering on the main Clee Hill to Cleobury

Mortimer road by some extra police who were on their way to join the search party. He was one of a group of children being cared for in a children's home by Phillip Bozon, an ex RAF fitter who, after the war, had worked as a farm hand for my father until he retired from hard farm work due to ill health. He paid for some of my flights as well!

After I had been given part of the farm which included the airstrip, I made an application for outline planning permission for a farmhouse to be built on the now separate Little Down Farm. The planning committee rejected it on the grounds that the acreage was not viable as an independent business and "that I could still live next door with my parents". The local planning committee did not appear to realise that I was only wishing to replace what was already there, on a derelict site. They thought, wrongly, that the application was an entirely new site in open countryside.

I therefore asked one of the planning officers to come and view the site. He suggested that I make a full detailed application for a REPLACEMENT farmhouse with a design similar in appearance to the original house which was in a state of disrepair. I also asked that he put in down in writing, something that was to become crucial evidence in the subsequent application a year later. This I did in due course but in the meantime, I took the old house down brick by brick and used the hardcore as a base for the floor in the new agricultural hangar building which was built primarily to accommodate aircraft. Interestingly, the old house was built with bricks held together with cow dung and lime rather than cement and concrete and the tile floors were laid directly on to a soil base with no damp course. After my father had brought the farm in 1967, he was advised to abandon any plans to restore the existing farmhouse partly for those reasons.

The new replacement farm house was designed by an architect who had a young housemaid working for him. Her name was Dana Hayward, and after one false start when she said she did not want to see me again, we began a courtship, eventually deciding to get married when the house had been completed. My marriage was to last for 12 years but was blighted from the beginning by my obsession with the airstrip problems and the fact that I was to be made redundant by Brymon Airways within 3 months of getting married. I was then out of work for the next seven years. She was to meet one of my student pilots whom I was teaching to fly on his Kitfox aircraft, someone with a flare for women, lots of money, and who gradually enticed her away from me while I was working away at Oxford airport and later with BAC Express Airlines.

Although we were divorced I am happy to include a mention of Dana Haywood because we did have some good times together and once had such a laugh over something when eating out that we both had to leave the table to recover. It is always sad when family life breaks down but there can be many reasons for it; such as an Airstrip! I found it difficult to reconcile what had happened but I was at fault as well, so have to take a share of the blame for this sad outcome. I had to sell the farm as a result, not just because of the divorce but also because of my mounting debt to the bank which gradually grew while I was out of work. The main objector thought he had possibly seen the end of the airstrip for ever but luckily, the new owner was a keen aviator as well and it has remained in place.

After I submitted a full planning application with architect's drawings, the application was recommended for refusal for the same reason as before; the farm land was not a viable business acreage. A site meeting was recommended which helped to convince the planning committee that it was NOT after all a completely new site. When some members said there was no old farmhouse to replace (I had dismantled it for hardcore after I received the council letter stating that a replacement should be applied for) I produced both the photograph showing the old house and bore hole driller with a letter stating WHEN the job was done and the planning officer's letter. The decision to approve the house but with a legal tie to prevent the house being sold separate to the 60 acres of ground, was eventually granted the day I made my bad approach into Birmingham airport; when the balance of my mind was disturbed! The house was built and I was able to spend my first night there on the day of my marriage to Dana on June 30th 1990.

The persistent objector was a thorn in my parent's side as well. Not only did he not like the airstrip but complained about my father's horse riding and shooting. When riding one day, this unfriendly individual stopped him and asked if he had anything better to do. Guy replied that he could have gone fishing, hunting, shooting, or just riding out on one of his horses that afternoon and had chosen to ride! On another occasion, his actions were rather more serious, in that he called the police when we were all having a duck and pheasant shoot on the farm, in the area of the pools. We had to stop shooting because technically, the new Wildlife and Conservation Act in 1991 prevented you from shooting at released birds for 24 hours. My father had for years always caught about 20-30 home bred ducks the day before a shoot and then had them released 5 at a time from the top of a nearby hill. After each batch had been released, the gun stands would change to give all the shooters the best chance of a good shot as some, not all, of the released ducks flew back towards the pools. His idea was that the ducks would be given a better, more sporting, chance rather than being flushed straight off the pools themselves.

Father was prosecuted in the courts for this offence and pleaded guilty but because he was not aware of the recent change in the law and had no previous convictions of any kind, he was found not guilty and given a conditional discharge. He was also a well known and respected local farmer in the district and some of the invited guests were solicitors, estate agents and a former police superintendent. Although he was not convicted, he was advised not to repeat the practise again and gave up all shooting afterwards. He then concentrated on his fishing pleasures on the River Wye for many years afterwards.

That same individual who, as we know does not like the airstrip, also reported me to the social services after I had been made redundant from Brymon Airways for owning an airfield. The net result of that was that, although the airstrip activities was never intended to earn any income as such, (it was purely a pleasurable activity as far as I was concerned), I had to repay over £14000 for all the unemployment benefit, mortgage interest, and so on that I had received since losing my full time job. He also made sure that the hangar and airstrip were rated as a commercial business. Not a neighbour you would want in your back yard but we were all blighted by his presence; and Chris Jones now has to deal with him today.

My parents also gave up the chalet a year earlier than intended in 2006 and the pools area was sold in a very bad sale financially to the same person who had purchased the rest of the farm in 1992. The purchaser of both the farm and the chalet 14 years later negotiated a very hard sale which left my parents with much less than they deserved. The chalet and pools area had been valued by our own estate agent at well over £200,000 but in the end, my Mother who was suffering stress over the sale; let it go for just £125,000. There is a saying that you should never do business with your friends, the family of the purchaser of the farm at Milson had been friends of the family for over 30 years, so consequently they felt betrayed and very let down. Neither of my parents have been back to Milson since that bad sale was completed or seen their so called "friends" more than once or twice since the sale in early 2007.

In the course of my life, I have had a number of lucky escapes and a few laughs not connected with flying. One was when I was trying to move my saw bench on the farm in the airstrip hangar. Because the long bar used to prop up the heavy end would not lock into position, it was parked on some concrete blocks. As I tried to move it slightly so I could attach it to the tractor, it slipped off the blocks and fell to the floor. I went with it but the long vertical bar came up to meet me and stuck me just an inch away from my right eye. Another inch and I am sure I would have lost it for good. Another lucky escape for me, not witnessed by anyone else but a forgiving God, was when I was thistle cutting with the tractor and got off to remove a fallen branch off a tree. As I carried the branch away and put it in the hedgerow, the tractor started to move on its own. I turned round and stupidly shouted "Stop", but it continued down the hill gathering speed. It went through an open gateway, down between the two narrow walls of an old silage pit we used to use, and then crossed a field towards a deep pool on the small brook which crossed the land. Luckily for me, an old large tractor tyre which had lying in the same spot for many years was directly in the path of the runaway tractor and it got jammed under the two front wheels stopping it from falling into the deep pool at the bottom of the hill. I was able to recover the tractor and thistle cutter undamaged, and continued my days work as if nothing had happened! Accidents can happen all too easily on a farm and I have heard of many near disasters from others over the years.

I also caused a lot of unnecessary expense once when I had a large bonfire on the farm close to the newly constructed hangar. Unfortunately, the hot smoke and burning embers were blown over the roof area by the wind, and some landed on the PLASTIC skylights. A month or so later after a long dry spell, I was in the building when it started to rain. To my horror water began to drip on to the floor from most of the skylight windows. The realization of what had happened dawned on me when I got on to the roof to examine the damage. All the skylights had to be replaced but I was able to make a claim on the farm's insurance policy. I am now much more careful when having a bonfire. This was an innocent mistake from which I learnt a valuable lesson; only have a fire if the wind is blowing the smoke away from buildings and other valuable assets!

One of the funniest incidents on the Little Down was when the tenant farmer spent an entire morning sorting his sheep, with some to keep, and some to sell. Those to be sold were then put into a horsebox type trailer to be taken away and the rest released from their sorting pens. As his wife drove the tractor and trailer away while he and I were some distance away at the top of the one field opening a gate, the back door came down and one by one the sorted sheep ran out to rejoin the rest of the flock! Neither "Candid Camera" nor "You've been Framed" on TV could do better than that. Although it was not funny, the entire flock had to be sorted all over again, but I must say I had a very long laugh, at someone else's expense. I also had a good laugh as a child seeing my father getting stuck in the mud and trying to dig the tractor out. I found serious things like that funny and still do, as long as it is not happening to me.

After being given notice of redundancy in 1990, just three months after getting married to Dana and starting to live at the Little Down in our new house, I first of all went on a two month training course at the London Polytechnic to obtain my full Airline Transport Pilots Licence. In many ways, I had to completely re-study all the work I had done 10 years earlier plus a little extra. The extra subject material included climatology and inertial navigation systems which I missed in the classroom due to a spell of bad weather. In the appropriate exam, there were 7 questions on that very subject but once again, I passed all my exams at the first attempt. It was all to no avail however, as the 1991 Gulf War erupted and the general recession got worse so I ended up out of work for about 7 years.

Whilst unemployed, I made enquiries about becoming an instructor at the Joint Elementary Flying Training School (JEFTS) at RAF Barkston Heath in Lincolnshire and was invited along for an interview, which surprisingly for me, included a 45 minute training and assessment flight in a Slingsby Firefly (military version) G-BWXC which is shown in the small photograph over the page.

 A similar aircraft is shown in the larger photo with incidentally a Griffin and Squirrel helicopter from Shawbury in the background. Note the excellent all round visibility available with the bulbous canopy. The only poor feature in my view is the fixed undercarriage assembly.

I was given a thorough and detailed military style brief about how military pilots are taught to make a circuit and approach, something I was to practice later. They do not fly a square circuit as such with a crosswind and base leg but fly a running break from overhead with two 180 degree turns, one on to the downwind leg and the other directly on to finals. The angle a bank and rate of turn are adjusted to ensure you arrive on the runway centreline. Also, the final approach is flown differently to most civilian flying clubs in that you use a **"Point and Power"** concept to reach the threshold or touch down point. You simply aim the aircraft at the appropriate point and use the power to ensure you get there. The reason for this is that that is the way a jet is flown; and all students are assumed to be candidates for fast jets when they start their initial flying training. In civil flying, I always used to say "Stick (or control column) for Speed" determined by the aircrafts attitude, and "Throttle for Height" which is broadly correct unless you are making a glide approach or have no engine at all as in a glider.

As I walked out to the immaculate aircraft I was asked by the instructor, Captain Hewitt, which seat I was going to sit in as a trainee instructor. I replied that it would be on the right or starboard side as is the case in all civil aircraft during basis training but I was **WRONG**. In this special version of the Firefly, the student flies in the right seat with the instructor in the left. The reason is that the various controls are laid out in a similar manner to that found on the Shorts Tucano and Hawk training aircraft which a successful student may well fly later on in his career.

The flight itself was a useful experience for me which I enjoyed. It included me flying some aerobatic sequences under instruction above a complete cloud cover. I remember the small G force affecting my head and neck as I was not used to flying with a military style bone dome or helmet. One error I made as I did not know the area was to miss-identify an airfield during our descent. As we came out of cloud using eastern military radar I saw an airfield which I assumed to be Barkston Heath; it was in fact the RAF College airfield at Cranwell which is close by.

I had high hopes that I might get a job there as this was before I had the "as or with a co-pilot" restriction put on my medical but in the end I was not selected as there was a clear preference to employ ex–military pilots rather than pure civilians if at all possible. That was a pity, as I liked the environment, the aircraft were of a very high standard and I would have done my best there; but I did have a useful learning flight which was well worth the effort of making the initial enquiry.

I was not idle during that time and not only developed the airstrip but also did a lot of general farming work such as fencing the entire boundary and re-surfacing the long drive. I was able to keep flying a little, often due the generosity of some of the aircraft owners who had their aircraft based at Milson but I was very much out of practise from a commercial flying point of view. In the end I felt I had to get back into some kind of work and first took a job as a security agent at Birmingham airport. That job at least got me working to a routine which included getting up at 5 am some mornings when on the early shift but I hated it. It was poorly paid with over half my salary going in fuel costs getting to and from the airport, a 100 mile round trip. The best part of the job was the 4 days off after a gruelling 4 days on with two early and two late shifts between 5.30 am and 13.30 and 13.30 to 22.30 Hrs but I did once get the chance to do as security check on a Concorde aircraft which included a look over the flight deck.

I next tried a job as a ground instructor at the Oxford Air Training School where I had done my initial CPL/IR in 1979. That job was interesting and better paid but I found it very hard work. You never switch off as you always have to think and plan ahead for the next day, or weeks, teaching. Once again daily travel to Oxford took its toll as that was a 200 mile round trip and I had to be on the road each morning by 7am. I tried the idea of flying to/from Oxford once or twice but that is not a practical proposition due to the expense and the British weather which is not always co-operative. I did manage to get about an hours flying training on a small training helicopter which I enjoyed and just about managed to hover it. However, I did not like the job very much and had some difficulty in the class room due to my hearing problem. People kept asking me why I was teaching ground school there when I had a valid Airline Transport Pilots Licence which got me thinking about what I was doing there? I used to speak loudly and they always knew when I was in a classroom due to the loudness of my speech. I eventually left after nearly a year when I eventually found another full time flying job with BAC Express Airlines but had to wait for 6 months before starting it, so I went and did some worthwhile flying instructing at Gloucester for Archer Flight Training. During this time I mainly flew a Piper Tomahawk aircraft, usually G-BTJL and several Piper Cherokees.

Whilst I was a ground instructor at Oxford, I made arrangements with an old Cardiff flying club friend, Barry Mahoney, to have a flight as an observer in the cockpit of an A 320 Airbus. During my time at the flying club I had taught him some basic instrument flying and he eventually went one to fly with various airlines flying types such as the BAC 1-11, Boeing 737 and the Airbus. I was teaching the basics of "Glass Cockpit" presentations on modern aircraft in ground school and wanted to experience and see the systems operating in the air. He kindly arranged for me to fly on a trip to Tenerife in the Canary Islands and I duly presented myself at Cardiff on the arranged day. Security annoyed me as I had to board the aircraft as a passenger and then move into the cockpit; before that practise was discontinued. They also took an army style "compo rations" tin opener off my key ring as they considered it a potentially offensive weapon despite the fact that I had had it on my keys for the past 20 years or so with no trouble before hand. However, they did agree to return it and I got it back a few days later.

The flight itself was very informative and I was able to see all aspects of the flight from the jump seat situated between the two pilots. The operation of the Electronic Centralised Aircraft Monitor (ECAM) and Electronic Flight Instrument Systems (EFIS) were explained to me and I was impressed by the way the flight parameters were displayed to the pilots on an "all in one" presentation. However, there were a few conventional standby backup instruments just in case it all failed. Getting a technical update from ground control automatically during the flight also intrigued me. Barry did tell me that they were more of a systems manager rather than a pilot and wished he could fly a real "hands on" aircraft. He also said that occasionally the systems would sometimes jump 50 miles in an instant and told me how you had to think ahead and still **fly it in your mind** rather than sit back and let it fly you automatically. A good tip I learned from him was that a black hole on the approach charts where there was very little detail was almost certainly high ground. Unfortunately, a Dan Air Boeing 727 (G-BDAN) flew into the mountains in question in 1981 killing all on board. Controlled flight into Ground (CFIT) is pilot error!

I remember how warm it was on the ground in Tenerife despite a strong wind which made my eye catch an attractive Airtour's representative whose dress was being blown up to reveal a nice set of legs! I was also convinced that there was another aircraft flying alongside us during the cruise but I eventually concluded that it was a star low on the distant horizon. Although Barry was now earning much more money than I was ever likely to get, he said on several occasions how nice it was to fly a more conventional aircraft.

After the farm was sold, I first lived in a rented cottage at Aston Bank, near to Tenbury but after I met Wendy Turner, moved in to the "Brickyard", an isolated farm cottage in Milson about a mile from the airstrip. I could therefore keep an eye on what was going on there. However, when the landlord wanted Wendy to leave, we both decided to buy a property and eventually moved to "The Willows" at Wyson, near Ludlow where we still live with three dogs and a cat. My father gave his blessing to the purchase and indicated that the sale of the pools and chalet later would help to pay off the mortgage but due to the very bad sale he had, this was not to be.

A Picture of Wendy and I close to my Father's Pools, taken in 2003.

I still keep in touch with Chris at the airstrip and fly in occasionally when doing type rating training for LAA members or bi-annual flight checks for PPL and NPPL holders. Due to my hearing problem, the CAA have stopped me doing any ab-initio instruction, so I can only fly with someone who has already got a licence, unless it is in a microlight in which case I can be paid. Ironically, I can still instruct early students if I do not get paid for it, something I cannot really understand but it has something to do with an accepted standard.

The Little Down as it was when I sold it in 2001. There have been changes since.

It is worth comparing it to the photo taken just before my father brought the farm in 1967, shown on page 140. It bears no resemblance to the original at all as the site was completely re-developed. The Currie Wot G-ASBA which was then owned by Martin Kay, is shown parked on the lawn.

Finally, in this chapter a brief mention that when the airstrip and Little Down was "For Sale", the Daily Telegraph newspaper printed a very interesting article on the property with a good write up. It is produced as **Appendix Seven**. The comment about the occasional helicopter activity is very appropriate don't you think?

Chapter Twelve.
The Shorts SD360 Years.

During the years when I was unemployed in the early 1990's I tried to find a flying job and once contacted Keith Jones whom I had known at Shobdon. He was now the chief pilot of Celtic Airlines based at Bristol, but I had flown with him during the last few months of the Brymon job when, for a short while, I was flying the Shorts SD-330. I asked him if I could come and do a renewal of my Instrument and type rating in the hope of getting another job. He was keen to oblige but the cost would have been a minimum of £1750 but with no chance of an immediate job afterwards so I gave up the idea. However, by about 1997-8, jobs were starting to become more plentiful and Keith then asked me if I would like a job with BAC Express Airlines, to be based at Cardiff. I had an assessment flight with him in a "Shed", the common nickname for the Shorts SD-360 aircraft and was told he would recommend me to be recruited as a direct entry Captain. I remember the day I went for my interview at Horley, near Gatwick very well because I was caught by the police and subsequently given a fixed penalty for overtaking a very slow lorry on a double white lined road; despite the fact there was no other oncoming traffic. I was promised a job fairly quickly but it was more than 6 months before I actually started training.

During that time I flew as an instructor at Gloucester and once went to Shoreham Airport to fetch another aircraft. I was a passenger in the back going there, and was monitoring an instrument approach which was being made in bad weather when the DME line of sight UHF radio aid suddenly went off the air; as the aircraft was descending through cloud over the South Downs. Realising that the pilot had probably descended below the instrument approach vertical profile I urged him to abandon the descent and climb immediately. Had we not done so, it is very probable that the aircraft would have hit the hills. An awareness of what is going on in an aircraft even if you are not actually flying it yourself can possibly save your life. Keep that thought in your mind?

After a self study ground school using some notes I had purchased from Jersey European Airlines I started training in May but had an unfortunate landing accident when I inadvertently landed with the brakes on and burst both main wheels. I thought that had ruined my chance of a job for good and went home feeling very sad about myself but it was the training captain, Tony Harris, who really got the telling off for not checking the position of my feet. I did not deliberately have my feet on the top part of the rudder pedals but my toes were touching it. You do not have to have any pressure applied to have an effect. The wheels on the aircraft have an anti-skid system which prevents the brakes from locking on but it will only work once the wheel are actually turning but if there is any residual pressure in the brake lines at all it will lock a stationary wheel. I hasten to add that I did not claim for my travel and hotel expenses at Exeter on that occasion but did write to try and explain how it might have happened. One of the approach checks was brakes on/off, to check pressure in the system and that is why my toes might have been in contact with the upper part of the rudder. Keith Jones himself once landed with the brakes on at Manchester Airport which closed the airport for a few hours with a corresponding cost to the insurance company but in my case, we were flying from the companies maintenance base and had the aircraft removed from the runway within 20 minutes at no additional cost due to any diversions or holding aircraft. The most annoying thing about the whole incident was that only the day before the engineer had shown me two burst tyres at the back of the porta cabin office and said, "Never land with the Brakes On". I said I would never do something like that but did exactly that the very next day! After a few weeks to contemplate what had happened, the operations manager John Villis rang me and suggested we start again. The company were very good about the whole episode but I learnt later that it prevented me from being considered as a Captain for a very long time; an unfortunate black mark on my record.

The subsequent training went well and I was finally signed off at the end of June 1998 after which I then started to get paid. However, it was all to come to a sudden and abrupt end for a month following a road accident while I was positioning as a passenger from Exeter to Bournemouth. I will always remember it as a slow motion replay, as I can remember the oncoming car swerving from side to side as the elderly driver lost control until it hit us head on. You are completely helpless to do anything and just have to wait for the impact. After getting out myself and then pulling the Captain, Dennis King out, who was the driver out of the car, I remember waiting for what seemed an awfully long time for the police to arrive. We soon moved our position on the grass as we had sat on an ant's nest but I had great difficulty remembering any telephone numbers as shock was setting in, just like the flying accident I had in Germany and it was a long time before I was able to get in touch with the company and tell them the bad news.

After being taken to Dorchester Hospital where I was wrongly told that I just had severe bruising, I was advised to drive myself home and rest later the same day. It was just as well because although I was already in agony and could hardly lift my arms, I was much worse the next day. I had in fact broken three ribs, the upper sternum breastbone and bruised my kneecaps and toes as, despite wearing a seat belt, I had been thrown against the dash panel and window, breaking my glasses in the process. If I had not been wearing a seat belt I am sure I would have gone through the windscreen and might not have been here to write this book. I later calculated, using a formula about "G" forces taken out of some RAF medical notes, that the Captain and I had been subjected to a momentary "G" Force loading of 42 G's as we decelerated from 50-60 mph to zero in about two feet.

Flying for BAC Express was hard work, not physically as such but as almost all the flying at night, it was very tiring and by the end of the working week, or after you had flown the allowed hours, you were always exhausted. My main company base and route to start with was CWL-EMA-CWL but I also flew routes to Dublin, Belfast, Liverpool and as time went on, many other places around parts of Europe when we started flying routes for Air Contractors. Tiredness and fatigue were a constant problem and I well remember flying into Marseille in southern France early one morning as the sun came up after flying 4 continuous nights of work and being almost asleep at the controls. We had to wake up quickly as a white transit van drove across the runway just as we were about to land and a "Go-around" was flown but I remember it was a very messy affair as Medi Imani, the Captain and I, were so tired. It took a lot of getting used to, arriving at your hotel for breakfast and then going to bed but that is what night flying was all about. It was important to have good quality hotels with quiet rooms.

Once on my way home from Cardiff one morning, I was stopped by the police for wandering all over the road. They thought they had got a drink/drive case and got out their breathalyser but I told them not to bother as I had not been drinking but was just over tired. After explaining why I was on the road at that early hour, they suggested I stay at Cardiff in future and I said I would if the company would pay for the accommodation. One of the police officers was actually learning to fly at Shobdon, which helped. However, being based at CWL did not qualify me for free accommodation so I always drove to and from my home for all of my duties there. It was a nice change to be rostered to fly elsewhere other than your base as this qualified you for local accommodation and duty pay so I was always a volunteer if they wanted me to go anywhere other than my home base.

During my continuous employment with BAC Express, Air Contactors, and HD Air, it was effectively the same company operation but with different names as ownership changed. I was based at Cardiff, Bristol, Exeter, Southend, at home while with Air Contractors and flying all over Europe (which was the best arrangement for me financially), Exeter again, Coventry and finally Birmingham while we were flying in Scotland. As most of the work was long hours of duty at night, Air Contractors had a good rostering arrangement of two weeks on duty including a weekend away, one week on contactable days where you were given 12 hours notice of being required, and one week off plus an annual leave of 42 days. They also paid you well, with good duty pay, excellent hotels and car travel all the time you were away from home and I enjoyed it while it lasted. The job included time in Hamburg, Venice, Marseille, Naples and Paris as well all parts of the UK including Aberdeen and RAF Kinloss, near to the delightful town of Forres in Scotland.

I flew with various Captains and got on well with them all learning all the time from their collective experiences gained over the years. I cannot remember all my flights as I was with the company for nearly 12 years, but will now recall some of the events I can remember which I hope will give the reader some hints about what can, and does happen from day to day whilst flying the line under pressure; to be on schedule most of the time! However, these recollections may not be in strict chronological order but that does not matter in the context of this book.

When flying with Dennis King, he once asked me to look at the one main wheel before we flew which was almost down to the canvas due to some spot marks. If a wheel is slightly out of balance, it is possible for the wheel to make contact with the runway on exactly the same spot on the rubber each time you land. Also, on arrival at BFS, the loaders were once unable to open the rear baggage hold which could take up to 406 Kgs of freight but did not tell either of us at the time. They continued unloading the rest of the aircraft until it was so out of balance that, as we left the flight deck and walked to the rear of the plane, it tipped on to its tail damaging some air vent scoops near to the tail. You were supposed to put a metal bar on the tail, known as a "Pogo Stick", to prevent this from happening but they had been withdrawn after one aircraft had flown on a flight with it still attached to the rear fuselage. In our case, by walking gently back to the cockpit, the nose went down again after which some heavy ballast was put into the nose compartment until the door was opened. When loading an aircraft, it is not just the weight which matters, but more importantly, is the distribution layout of the load. A little weight on a long lever arm gives the same affect as a heavier amount on a shorter arm near to the Centre of Gravity. 20 Kgs X 200 inches is the same as 400 Kgs X 10 inches. At Liverpool I once came out of the canteen on the apron to see the tail of my "Shed" very low. I went and told the loaders to stop loading and got a mouthful saying they knew what they were doing. They didn't as there was nothing in the nose, just 50 Kgs there would have been sufficient to stop the 300 Kilos in the back tipping the aircraft on to its tail. Awareness of what is going on around you can be helpful in preventing an incident from happening.

Fairly early into the job as a junior first officer, I used to stay in the office at Cardiff and do the paperwork including the load sheet while the Captain went and did the walk round and other checks. On coming out to the aircraft and climbing on board, the Captain, who used to fly the Cessna 150's up to Shobdon for servicing from Staverton some 30 years earlier, shouts back to say that we were not going anywhere; the aircraft was unserviceable (U/S). I therefore relaxed my rush up to the flight deck where on arrival I found Ian Statham trying to ring the company engineer on his mobile phone.

Colour Photo of Twin Pioneer Cockpit, flying at 2000 feet, while in a slight descending turn to the right flying a 100 Knots.

The Best Twin Pioneer, G-BCWF at Prestwick airport for a Special Occasion in 1984.

Twin Pioneer approaching to Land.

Twin Otter G-BIHO at Birmingham Airport in 1989.

Seychelles Photos taken during Interview Visit in 1990.

Twin Otter Cockpit, taken at Birmingham.

Photograph of my Mother when she had a Flight in the Twin Otter to the isle of White and back.

Father in Twin Otter before Flight to Gatwick.

Debbie Wright at Schiphol Airport, Amsterdam.

Shorts SD360 G-EXPS in Flight.

G-CLAS in the last Company Colour Scheme.

The Isle of Lewis on the TCAS Display.

Shorts Cockpit Instruments, en route to Stornaway.

Typical Scottish Scene One Morning flying to Stornaway.

The Arrester Cable Held Up on a Military Runway
By small Rubber Disks.

"UP" cable

The Metal Sheeting Helicopter Pad.

Griffin "T" landing on Milson Airstrip.

RAF Gazelle Flight from RAF Shawbury in 1997.

The ARV Taking Off from Milson.

Acrosport Biplane G-BKCV.
I did a type conversion for a new owner once.

Europa G-DURO at Milson Airstrip.
One of my Favourites!

One of two Turbulents I flew.

A Mishap at the Airstrip.

The Aspire Centre, Where I wrote this book.

Final "Fly In" Line up, on the ground. Taken in 2001.

Final Fly In "Legacy" Photograph. I am proud of this recognition of my contribution to general aviation.

A Total of 50 Aircraft, Microlights, and Helicopters can be seen.

Wendy and I close by Father's Pools in 2003.

In Happier Days; before being made redundant yet again!

Wendy and Two Dogs with Jabiru G-CCAE behind.

Issy and Jenny in 2009.

He told me the electrics were not working correctly. I replied that it was hardly surprising since a number of circuit breakers (c/b's) were tripped or had been pulled out on **MY SIDE** of the aircraft. Keith Jones had been flying it earlier and had been simulating various electrical failures but had not left the aircraft in the correct configuration. The quote, "Never Assume Always Check" comes to mind again. Doing your cockpit checks are a must before ringing the engineers as in a lot of cases, the apparent fault can be rectified easily. One switch which often found itself in the wrong position was the "Start Master" which engineers often forgot to reset after doing an engine run or compressor wash. On just one of the company's fleet of aircraft, it was vital that you pulled out a certain c/b at the back of the aircraft as for some reason, the emergency exit lights below the two rear doors would remain illuminated and flatten the batteries while parked during the day if you forgot to do it.

At one time, BAC Express also did passenger work on an ad hoc basis for other companies such as Jersey European (Now Fly-Be) and British Airways out of Belfast during the day, as well as the main freight and mail work at night. Once I was told to drive from Cardiff to Birmingham airport and position to Dublin by commercial airline where I would meet the aircraft. On arrival, the Captain of the day told me we would now be going straight back to Cardiff to fetch the seats which had been left behind by another crew who had wrongly thought that the aircraft cabin seats were waiting in Dublin. That mistake cost the company two hours of unnecessary flying thus reducing any profit made by helping out other operators. Once again, asking a simple question like the wrong wheel case on the Twin Otter (mentioned in a previous chapter) would not have gone amiss.

Trying to be on time was always an issue with the post office and the night mail flights we used to do. As a result, incidents often occurred to due to the pressure of getting a move on! One night at Liverpool, we were the last aircraft to leave because the royal mail loaders had forgotten to give us the mail weight figures for the load sheet and Captain Dave Welch and I rushed our departure. As we taxied out an Emerald HS 748 aircraft was positioning to land and ATC asked if we could accept an immediate take off? Not wanting to be any later, we accepted and ended up taking off with the flaps UP. As we accelerated down the runway I realised the error as Dave tried to raise the nose using the landing speed which was still bugged on his Airspeed indicator (another error as it should have been set to a higher take off speed) and I automatically selected the emergency reserve take off power (RTOP) on both engines. We got away with it because on that night there was a 20-30 Knot headwind component on the runway, but it was a close shave. This incident is a good indication of how a near accident can come about due to the combination of a number of relatively minor mistakes which can be **linked in a chain** leading to a near disaster.

As part of our re-training programme, the same for all airlines, you are required to have refresher training in first aid, security matters, human factors, fire prevention, and so on; usually every two years. I once attended a one day refresher at the Salston Manor hotel near to Exeter and wrote on a piece of paper the words "Al Qaeda" and "Afghan Hijackers" to remind me of questions I wanted to ask later on about security matters. A few days later when I was in the control tower building at Exeter getting my weather and Notams for the flight to Stansted I put this piece of unwanted paper into the waste bin. Next day, a cleaning lady saw it, considered it suspicious and gave it to the ATC assistant, who promptly triggered as MAJOR Security alert which almost closed the airport. Unluckily for me, on the back of this piece of paper was the telephone number of an old friend of mine, Roger Lloyd, who used to keep an aircraft at Milson airstrip. He very quickly got a visit from a special branch policeman at his home in Herefordshire where eventually they were able to piece together the connection. An hour or so later I got woken up with a phone call from the company boss Mike Forsyth asking some odd questions about hijackers at Stansted and Al Qaeda. After initial denials that I had ever written anything like that down, the penny dropped. We had a laugh about it as I had not actually done anything wrong, but it goes to show how an innocent piece of paper or a careless remark can have very serious and unforeseen consequences. I did say that, at the very least, it was not a list of my many girlfriends or call girl contacts!

I have to say that today's increased security has had a very negative affect on flying as it is now virtually impossible for you to take a friend for a free flight. Security officials can show a complete lack of understanding about crew needs, the best example being a complete refusal to allow any aircrew members to take a drink of any kind with them when they go flying. Marcus Chandler and I were once refused permission to take any liquid refreshments with us and this led to both of us becoming seriously dehydrated. On this particular night, Marcus and I were due to fly from Exeter to Stansted, then on to Coventry and Dublin finally ending up back at Exeter as the sun came up. All was well until we were diverted to

East Midlands airport due to fog at CVT. It was decided to send the freight load to EMA by road so we had to wait on the apron for about two hours. When the load arrived on a lorry from CVT, the security gate at EMA would not initially allow it on come to the aircraft as the Coventry personnel had not got passes valid for EMA. The apron supervisor was also wanting us to move on as the stand was required by an inbound from elsewhere. The load happened to include the coffin of a deceased lady who was being returned to Ireland for burial. When I suggested to the supervisor that the security delay showed a complete lack of respect for the deceased he took it on his own head to authorise the load to be taken to the aircraft but Marcus, the apron supervisor, and I had to load the aircraft ourselves including the coffin which was surprisingly heavy. We eventually got the aircraft loaded and flew to Dublin about 4 hours later than planned where we then had to stay as we had exceeded our duty time hours. The whole nine hours were taken without a drink of any kind and we were both dehydrated on arrival, all because of the security officer's refusal to allow us to take any kind of drink with us. I wrote a Confidential Human Factors Incident Reporting Programme (CHIRP) report about this suggesting that in future one crew member be nominated as a baby and the other as a mother! That would then allow some drink or water to be allowed airside. Seriously though, the outcome was that, for a short time afterwards, bottled water appeared on the aircraft for crews to use, put there by engineers whose rules to get airside were slightly different, but the practise slowly ceased as time went on.

BAC Express was lucky to be awarded a contract to fly some of the feeder routes into Paris Charles De Gaulle airport for Federal Express (Fedex). This made our operation an attractive proposition to buy and in 2003 Air Contractors, an Irish based freight company purchased the company. This was to have a profound impact on both my working hours and my income as I now found myself away from home for up to 2 weeks at a time. As I was now paid duty pay **all** the time I was away from home plus accommodation and travel, the difference in income for a typical 5 day week at Exeter was about £500 a week. It wasn't £500 in cash terms but I no longer had to pay for my own accommodation or travel to/from Exeter, and was paid duty pay all the time I was there, not just when flying. However, the biggest change was that we all had to have our licences modified to European Joint Airworthiness Regulations (JAR) standards, as all the aircraft were transferred to the Irish register; and the way training on the aircraft was carried out was to change dramatically.

The Irish Aviation Authority had a rule that if there was a ground training simulator for a particular type of aircraft anywhere in the world, it **MUST** be used for recurrent training. This ruling came about following a training accident in which an IAA inspector was killed as he monitored a training flight which went badly wrong. As there was a simulator for the Shorts SD330/360 in America, we all had to fly to New York every 6 months for our bi-annual base checks and I/R renewal. I managed to have two visits to New York and on the second agreed with the company to stay on for a week's holiday with my new partner Wendy Turner who I had met after I had sold the farm and started to live nearby in a rented cottage at Aston Bank. I obviously paid for Wendy to fly over but my own flight to the United States was taken care of.

The simulator was obviously not the real aircraft but was very useful for simulating systems failure such as electrical and hydraulic problems that you would not want to try in the air. You could also repeat the same procedure time and time again. While doing a series of engine failures just after taking off, it made me feel very ill. Repeatedly pushing a button and finding yourself in an instant, back on the end of a runway ready to try again, felt very weird. On my first trip there, we treated it a bit like a game and tried some variations on the companies Standard Operating Procedures (SOP's). As a result of that, during the one session, we found the aircraft getting airborne with no one holding the control column! It was also a very tiring time, as, to save unnecessary costs to the company, we were flying out to New York and going straight into the simulator when our body clocks were saying we should have been in bed asleep! By going to New York you were putting yourself 5 hours ahead of their time zone; a long day.

On the second occasion, the whole visit was more seriously handled but we found ourselves trying to fly without headsets for some reason and I had difficulty hearing what was going on. Our training Captain, David Smith hinted that if my hearing was that bad I should not be flying and that worried me but I should point out that we were all suffering from jet lag and a very long travelling day which can make my hearing more difficult. I was to make one of my worse errors during this training session when I tried to be clever and deliberately put my hand on the incorrect fuel level during an engine shutdown practise. The other crew member always has to confirm that the correct lever has been selected BEFORE it is moved and Captain Steve Thursfield who was doing his test correctly recognised that. The problem was that the training captain and examiner, Dave

Smith apparently did not notice my deliberate mistake and when, during the de-briefing session, I told him what I had done, he went ballistic. He was really angry with rage saying I should never ever do anything like that again. I would not have done so in the real aircraft but he was certainly not happy about my conduct. The idea came to mind because during training in the real aircraft four years earlier at Cardiff, Tony Harris DID put his hand on the wrong fuel lever and I wanted to see if Steve noticed it, which he did. I managed to calm things down when I asked him to at least give me some credit for being honest; had I kept quiet, he would never have known about it! That incident I am sure put a black mark on my training record and delayed my promotion to Captain but I did achieve it for the last year of my flying on the "Shed" a few years later.

The holiday part of that visit to the States was more enjoyable and Wendy and I drove to Washington DC, visited a number of important places such as the Smithsonian National Air and Space museum, the Lincoln Memorial, John F Kennedy's grave in Arlington National Cemetery, saw The White House and went to many other places of interest. I particularly enjoyed the driving experience on the Freeways but was shocked by the road standards in some areas.

When back in New York, we visited the site of the World Trade Centre and the 911 terrorist atrocity in 2001, sailed around Manhattan Island, saw one of the Concorde's at the Intrepid Aircraft Carrier museum and I had my second visit up to the top of the Empire State Building but Wendy was too ill for that, exhausted by the amount of activity we had tried to pack into just one week. In retrospect, we had both tried to do too much in one week.

Although I had been to Scotland and flown there with Loganair, I thoroughly enjoyed my first one off trip to Scotland when I was told at short notice during a standby duty at home to travel to Exeter, fly as a passenger to Belfast, before flying on to Glasgow and THEN fly the next days mail flight to Benbecula and Stornaway on the Outer Hebrides with Steve Thursfield. I was exhausted after having been up for almost a day and a half but luckily the weather was absolutely perfect with almost unlimited visibility and clear sky. The actual flight was therefore a pleasure and I was able to enjoy the beautiful scenery in the Western Isles. Little did I know then, that the last eighteen months of my time with BAC/HD Air, flying as a Captain, would be spent mainly in Scotland flying to the same places from Inverness. The reason why I was asked to fly that flight was that another crew member had fallen ill in Glasgow and had to be replaced at very short notice. To cover the rules, it was put down on paper that I had travelled to Glasgow the day previously and had been in the hotel overnight. I was also to fly the route again with Aero Condor, a Portuguese airline when Air Contractors lent me to them for a short time. Their own SOP's were a little different from BAC/Air Contactors but it was not all bad and they did have a final call as you started the take of run of "Black Panel", i.e., was the Central Warning Panel (CWP) clear of any warning lights? The only important missing item not covered on the CWP was the Flaps so beware but it was a useful final check nevertheless!

Airframe icing on any aircraft can be a serious risk especially if it has no de-icing or anti-icing equipment fitted. Light aircraft are particularly prone to icing which can occur anytime if an aircraft is flying in cloud when the temperature is below freezing. Cloud, or fog on the ground, is in fact minute particles of condensed water vapour and/or ice crystals which due to their minute size often remain in liquid form even when the temperature is below the 0 Degree Isotherm or "Freezing level". This is known as supercooled water droplets which, if they come into contact with an object such as an aircraft's wing, WILL begin to freeze. Those droplets just below freezing are the worse as the colder they get the greater is the concentration of ice particles to water, which is why in very cold temperatures serious airframe icing is much less likely. In very cold cloud, the ice particles simply bounce off the airframe or wing, but supercooled water at between 0 to -15 degrees is a different matter.

I was once asked to fly an aircraft from Venice to Lyon in France which even in still air conditions was at the extreme of the Shed's range. However, the Captain and I decided to give it a go as on part of the route, you could not fly direct due to the Alps, a tailwind was forecast. However, just after getting airborne from Venice, we encountered very heavy icing in heavy rain preceding an advancing warm front. This is where warm liquid rain can fall through cold air which is below freezing casing the rain to become supercooled. This rain will the flow back over the aircraft's airframe and wings causing what is known as Clear Ice, the heaviest type of ice accretion. The effect of this encounter was to see us back on the ground very quickly. The ice build up was so quick that we felt a control reversal was taking place where the elevator controls had started to have the opposite effect due to a change of shape over the tail plane and elevators. Medi and I landed back at Venice less than 20 minutes after taking off and half an hour later, the aircraft was still covered in ice with large build ups on the struts, nose cone, wheel arches and so on. We were lucky. I myself suffered heavy icing over Yorkshire on one occasion as Captain but was able to safely descend into warmer air but this is not always the case. Ironically, if you have plenty of excess power and can climb, you stand a better chance of getting out of a heavy icing encounter by **CLIMBING INTO COLDER AIR**. One variation to UK rules was that in Italy any de-icing of an aircraft on the ground has to be done in specific areas. If you required de-icing, then you had to taxy from your stand to this area and in our case shut down the turbo-prop engines while the spraying was completed.

I spent a lot of time flying out of Venice, flying 4 nights a week to Milan and back. We use to do a two week tour with a weekend away so I got to know Venice very well. It is an incredible city that is almost floating on water. There are no roads as such as they are all canals and it is full of historical buildings, churches etc. I once brought Wendy a small plastic Gondola from there which she did not like very much but we still have it on a shelf. One weekend, I hired a car and travelled up the Alpi Pioneer aircraft factory at Comina in Northern Italy where I had a flight in one of their new aircraft. I wrote a report on it for both the Light Aircraft Association and the Flying Farmers Association.

When I found myself based at Bristol, I used to fly a regular two day trip to Norwich and back via Stansted during which we used to do a day stop at Norwich. This used to suite me well as I always had a good carvery meal using some of my duty pay which was about £25 per round trip. When coming in to land once at BRS, ATC asked us to expedite as there was another aircraft approaching from the northwest. Despite my protestations that we were too high and fast the Captain, John Mountain, persisted in making a tight approach and we had to do one of only two "Go-arounds" (previously known as Overshoots) I have ever had to make in anger rather than during training. In a similar case to the LPL take off without flaps mentioned earlier, rushing does NOT pay; it is sometimes much better not to be tempted by an ATC request to speed things up.

Norman Newbiggin, who was one of the companies Captains for a short time, once flew into Bristol with me and landed well below the cloud base and Runway Visual Range (RVR) limits of 220 Feet and 550 metres. Although the meteorological observation given was well below the limits allowed for a landing, we could still clearly see the runway AND a wall of fog advancing towards us from the other end of the airfield. ATC had advised us of the approaching fog and we just made it in time but after landing we needed a "follow me" vehicle in order to find our way off the runway. I sometimes used to do my paperwork in the Bristol Flight Centre prior to a flight from there and once got locked in when the cleaning lady left without realising I was inside. I rang the company who in turn rang the airport and their security people came and let me out. Norman once asked me in confidence if I would fly with him without a valid medical. He had a renewal booked but we had been diverted due to bad weather and ended up being away for an extra day. It was a technical oversight and was not a deliberate act. Conversely, I once had to confide in him that I had suddenly had a serious medical problem develop. I had had surgery a week or so earlier and although I had already flown one night with no problem, I suddenly started to bleed and had to go to Exeter hospital to have the wound re-stitched. That mail flight was regrettably lost but there was nothing that could be done at such short notice.

During my time at Cardiff, Bristol, and Exeter I flew on at least three trips to Maastrict in Holland but in each case the flight was a rushed ad hoc sudden charter usually after we had completed the normal mail flight. On the one occasion, we had to position the aircraft from Norwich to Southend after the normal mail flight from Bristol but we had not enough strapping to tie down the bulky heavy load. We managed to improvise and got away with it but we did make a mistake which was not apparent at the time, but was picked up during an audit of the paperwork later. The cabin of the "Shed" has three loading bays, A, B, and C. Bays A and C had a 1000 Lbs weight limit, and Bay B, the middle one, a 1500 Lbs limit. We had inadvertently loaded the small bulky load weighing over 2000 Lbs in just Bay B only. Had we realised, it would have been necessary to use spreader beams to distribute the heavy localised weight more evenly. Before flying from Cardiff to Maastrict once, shortly after starting my job with BAC, I went to get the necessary European charts out of the folder kept in the office before we went intending to get just Maastrict and several other alternates such as Brussels and Ostend. The Captain of the day, Simon Thesinger, told me to take them all which turned out to be a good thing. We thought we were just going to MST and after a duty rest, positioning back to CWL. In the event, we were asked to fly direct to Paris Charles De Gaulle, then on to Stansted and Dublin but due to strong headwinds and heavy icing ended up at Liverpool. Always be prepared for any eventuality. This trip was actually a forerunner of the Fedex Contract which BAC was awarded before being purchased by Air Contractors. They had a good system for chart updates and all aircraft had individual "Nav Bag's" with the whole of Europe included which were changed and updated weekly by a specialist company. On another occasion when I flew to Glasgow with another Captain by airline to retrieve an aircraft which had been on loan to Loganair we arrived to find there were NO navigational charts on the aircraft at all but luckily I had copies of my own charts for the two or three regularly used airfields we were intending to fly to, so we elected to continue.

Just before we got our last major contract in Scotland flying the mail to the Outer Hebrides 6 days a week, I found myself having to fly a flight from EXT to STN and return with only ONE Headset. Just before departure, the one headset fell apart and there was no spare in the aircraft (which there should have been). As it was a CAVOK night with perfect weather conditions, Captain Mike Byrnes and I decided to go with me doing the radio and him doing the flying. We managed reasonably well until, in the vicinity of Stansted, ATC started giving radar vectors and heading changes for sequencing in traffic. It was not easy to communicate the information and it was not an enjoyable experience. I would never want to do that again and certainly would not have even contemplated it if the weather had been bad with low cloud and/or poor visibility. On another flight with Mike, we had to position to Bournemouth from Exeter and take enough fuel for our flight to Edinburgh, as fuel was not available there. All went well until we had to hold on the ground for 20 minutes waiting for another aircraft to leave the freight stand. That used up our precious reserve so the flight to EDI was flown with barely enough fuel flying across a fog covered UK. I kept on using the GPS in the aircraft to "Go To" EDI, to get the latest "Time to Go", and using the known 18 Lbs a minute fuel burn rate, kept on working out how much fuel would be left on arrival many times over. Normally, it would not have been a problem as you can always land for a Tech Stop to re-fuel but on this flight there were very few airfields available due to a widespread fog blanket. With hindsight we took a calculated risk but our nerves were on edge for most of the flight.

On one of the contracts we flew, it involved flying into RAF Kinloss in Scotland and staying locally in various hotels in and around the delightful little Scottish town of Forres. This was interesting as their military operating procedures were slightly different and you were often asked "what are your intentions" and "confirm three greens". Dave Welch once answered the first by saying "To Land of course" which was rather funny but in reality what the military controller wanted to know was what type of approach did you want to carry out. There was a standard ILS on R/W 26 but coming the other way it was either radar to visual or a full PAR approach where the radar controller talks you down with left/right and up/down commands. There was also an arrestor wire laid across the runway which could be up or down. Ian Statham was so unsure about the significance of that that he once arranged to touch down after the wire but in actual fact, the wire up meant it was supported by small rubber disks just two inches off the runway surface and our large wheels would pass over it with no problems. The only information I could find about this wire was in a CAA safety sense leaflet, currently number 26. A photograph of the wire in the "Up" position is shown in the one coloured section. It was while staying in a very nice hotel at Forres on a night off while flying for Aero Condor, that Steve Thursfield suggested a name for this book. I enjoyed my stays there and enjoyed walking around the local forests in the area.

One of my most frightening approaches was into RAF Kinloss one night when we declared we would go visual; you could often see the airfield from about 40 miles out. However, as it was on the coast, it was possible for showers off shore to suddenly pass over the airfield and we got caught in one when we were a little below and to the left of the glidepath angle, Not only that but the wind went from being reported as calm to a 20-30 knot crosswind. Never declare or go visual at night unless you are convinced all will be well, always accept ATC help to position for a visual final approach. There was also high ground to the south and if you descended too early it was possible to get a GPWS warning off one prominent peak even if you were complying with the radar controller's step down altitudes. It was a company rule to always react to a warning in case you were not where you thought you were in which case you made a rapid max rate climb back to the safety altitude and then re-positioned using radar or the correct procedural approach from the local NDB beacon.

One day in 2004, while resting in the hotel in Forres, I got a telephone call from the CAA. It was the Chief Medical Officer, Dr

Robert Hunter, who said that the CAA medical branch had been reviewing my records and **they did not think I should be flying any more**. I was shocked to hear this and asked whether I should cancel that evening's flight. They said go ahead and fly but that I should come down to Gatwick to see them soon. I told the company fleet Captain, David Smith thinking I would get support from him but he sided with the CAA and suggested I should give up flying. I do not think he liked me very much and thought I was a danger to aviation but he was overruled by my friend Keith Jones and some of the other Captains I had flown with who considered I had lots of experience to help overcome the hearing difficulties I might have.

Before I went to see the CAA, I obviously made some urgent enquiries and found to my pleasure that the harmonisation of European regulations had reduced the medical standards slightly and that it was now possible for a pilot to fly using a hearing aid if necessary. However, a restriction would be placed on the medical requiring you to fly "as or with a co-pilot", which I now have today. I did go and have some hearing tests about getting hearing aids and was put on a computer programme where over a period of about an hour, my hearing was restored to normal, something I have never had. I found myself hearing sounds which I have NEVER heard such as the dripping of a tap and wind rushing through a door. I now know it is possible to give me a full hearing capability but it would be at a cost; about £4500 for each side I was told. In fact, because I have never heard some kinds of sound, I found the real world alarming and very very noisy.

Luckily for me, the CAA relented and I was able to continue flying. Initially they required me to have a set of NHS hearing aids but I found them annoying as I found I could hear the aircraft engines and the rush of air more than the required intercom and radio communications. After a year with them, a CAA medical examiner recognised the problem and allowed me to fly without hearing aids but I have since been subject to a yearly cockpit hearing check with a CAA appointed examiner. I am glad to say that I am fine with a good quality headset and have no problems if I turn up the volume. There was always a joke going round in BAC/HD Air that they knew when I had been flying as all the volumes were always turned up when someone else got on board. Once again, my experience as a pilot over 40 years has helped to save the day. After all it was the CAA, not me, who decided in 1978/9 to grant me a commercial medical based on my flying experience but I have offered to stop flying many times if they gave me a top job in the CAA for £40,000 a year; and they just laugh jokingly at the suggestion. However, that said my lucky flying career in commercial aviation will, or may, have already ended due to the unfortunate redundancy I suffered in 2009.

One of the routes we flew for a long time was from Luton to Kassel in Germany very close to where I had been stationed during my time with the army in 1977. This small airfield had a narrow runway with a convex curve on it which meant you could not see the far end as you touched down and the approach was a Localiser (centreline guidance) only letdown with altitude checks relevant to a DME which was NOT on the airfield or aligned with the touchdown point. The distances as you descended wound down, then up again, after you passed the NDB beacon. In addition to all that, you could only land one way due to high ground in close proximity to the runway. That airfield could therefore be a challenge especially when there was a strong crosswind and/or low cloud. To be truthful I did not like that route as the flight time back could be almost 2.5 hours against a headwind, but I did fly a few trips as Captain later on.

Another destination in Germany, this time from Coventry, was to Niederheim which was on the Dutch border. This airfield had once been RAF Bruggen before the air force moved out and was now being developed as a new passenger and freight airport on the German border with Holland. That route was also interesting as you always flew over the top of Amsterdam and the vast Schiphol Airport. On one flight with Marcus Chandler, when the various Volmet reports for European airfields were indicating a rather stiff north easterly surface wind, we were vectored for an ILS approach to R/W 27 where the surface wind was reported as being calm. I had my suspicions that the wind on our approach would be a tailwind and suggested we approach with an NDB letdown the other way but he decided to proceed. Due to the real tailwind, we had great difficultly maintaining the glidepath, had a very high rate of descent to maintain it which caused the GPWS and TAWS system to sound an alarm, and we ended up landing more than half way down the 10,000 foot runway. Once again that contract was not to last partly because one of our aircraft got damaged when it blew away in strong winds just after the chocks had been removed prior to starting up, hitting the Ground Power Unit (GPU). On landing at Edinburgh once in very strong winds we were told to park "nose in" on to stand which was normal procedure but we had a 40 knot wind on the tail. As we shutdown and before any chocks were put in place, the aircraft did a complete out of control 180 degree turn almost hitting a service vehicle which had just parked alongside the aircraft. It is vital that you are always conscious of the effects of the WIND, especially if it is strong and gusty. You do not have to accept ATC instructions if you think the safety of the aircraft is at risk and can always ask to be parked into wind. Immediately after this incident, other arriving aircraft were allowed to park into wind if they wished.

Several quick stories now before I end this chapter. First, I once had a bird strike at 6000 Feet at **night** flying into Stansted. We had hit a migrating Goose which hit the windscreen right in front of my face. I could not see anything and the Captain had to continue the approach and landing. When collecting an aircraft from Southend the handling agent lost the GPU off his vehicle as it approached the aircraft and all I could do was watch it slam into the side of the aircraft waiting for the impact. That incident cost the company a lot of money as the aircraft was off line for 6 weeks. Also at Southend, I went to collect an aircraft from a hangar where it was parked on a slope. While I was doing checks in the aircraft, the nose wheel chock was removed by the Captain allowing the aircraft to roll backwards down the hill across a live taxiway and on to the grass. I was helpless because without the engines running there was no pressure in the brake system. It was funny seeing the Captain running after the aircraft and once again, we got away with it but it is a good example of how careful you must be in the vicinity of aircraft on a live and active airfield.

Finally, on its last visit to Belfast before being withdrawn from service in 2003, I was able to have a close look around a Concorde G-BOAE and was alarmed to see how poor the nose wheel tyre was. Days later it was flown into permanent retirement in Barbados. Due to the significance of the occasion, our positioning flight in the "Shed" was delayed by ATC so we were able to see the Concorde close up. It was very noisy! Being airside, I was able to give it a very close inspection before being asked to move on. G-BAOE ended up retiring to a warm home in Barbados where it is now under cover.

Chapter Thirteen.
Captain at last; and Scottish Memories.

For a short time I flew with a temporary Captain who tried to change the way we flew the take off sequence. He suggested that the F/O held the control column during the first part of the take off run which we had not done previously when the Captain was handling the aircraft. For a short time, I felt confused until the matter was permanently resolved by the Chief Pilot who was persuaded to agree to the modification of the SOP's. He wasn't perfect however and we once took off from Benbecula without a take off clearance. We had been cleared to line up only; a bit like my error during PPL training 40 years earlier at Bristol airport. However, ATC were very lenient at BEB as there was so little traffic and we were forgiven!

Before becoming a Captain I witnessed quite a few other unfortunate incidents and accidents from the cockpit. Once a post office van tried to cut the corner and drove into an Emerald 748's wing. On another occasion, I saw an exuberant pilot taxy in far too fast in another Emerald 748, so fast in fact that he wasn't able to turn quickly enough, almost hitting one of the apron floodlights. He stopped just short of it and had to be marshalled backwards to be able to move later on. On the flying side just after I joined the company, we were given once clearance to line up and take off but had not received our IFR departure instructions. I rightly queried this as the weather was bad and ATC cancelled the take off but it led to an annoyed airline Airbus pilot having to do an expensive "Go-around". One Captain I was flying with received a mobile phone call telling him to fly with me to Edinburgh but he refused and cancelled the call. When the company boss rang back a few minutes later to find out why, he said it would have been nice to be asked, "Do you mind going to Edinburgh (EDI)?" We went but there was a sequel to this event one month later when he got a letter from the company asking why there was an unpaid bar bill back at Belfast where we were originally supposed to have gone back to! With a newly promoted Captain we once diverted to Cardiff instead of landing at Bristol due to low cloud and a poor RVR as he was not prepared to risk ending up short of fuel. The company always insisted going with just the legal minimum of fuel and we always had to fuel up BEFORE we knew the actual loading weight for the trip, so sometimes you ended up with a substantial underload which might have been very usefully used as extra fuel; especially if the forecast was bad. In Scotland, after I had become Captain I did indeed arrange for the fuel to come to the aircraft at Inverness every morning immediately after the load figure had been given to us. This allowed the company to sometimes SAVE about £80 a day in fuel costs as any fuel uplifted in Stornaway was about 20 pence per litre more expensive. Sometimes the weather could catch everyone out, especially when fog occurred which was NOT forecast. Once, I left Cardiff for East Midlands, was told as we approached Birmingham that it had "fogged out", and decided to divert to our alternate at Liverpool only to discover that the apron there was now full of other diverting aircraft. Although Manchester was a possible alternate, we did a 180 Degree turn toward the Brecon VOR and ending up back at Cardiff after 1.5 hours having gone nowhere.

After a long wait of nearly eleven years, I was at last invited to become a Captain while staying in the Holiday Inn Express at Inverness in return for accepting a base at Coventry flying a new route every evening to Paris Le Bourget. I had waited long enough and despite some concern about my hearing Keith Jones was confident that I had more than enough practical experience to cope. Unfortunately, that contract did not last for long and I ended up flying the Scottish routes for nearly a year which I enjoyed very much.

My training started at Coventry with one very bad flight in the left seat for the first time. I had just purchased a brand new noise cancelling headset to improve my reception but it not only cut out the background cockpit noise but also the intercom conversations as well. Also, I was a bag of nerves. However, after a rest, the second flight with one of the normal headsets went much better and I soon mastered the aircraft from the left side which now included having to taxy it on the ground and **respond to rather than doing** the cockpit checks as we moved. The areas and degree of responsibility changes dramatically when you become a Captain. That includes all the paperwork and documentation, as well as the decision to go, or not to go? You must also adhere to the companies agreed Standard Operating Procedure's (SOP's) even if you might personally disagree with the way a certain activity or procedure is dealt with. Continuity and standardisation are vital in a two crew environment especially in a large company like British Airways where you might find yourself flying with someone you have never previously met.

The photograph on the next page shows G-CLAS, painted in the final BAC Express Colour Scheme. Unfortunately, the aircraft was sold shortly afterwards as it was a leased aircraft so the cost of having it painted was largely wasted. This expense clearly showed a lack of planning for the future which was a pity.

I settled down flying as Captain very quickly, got on well with my fellow crew members and managed to fly nearly 300 hours in the left seat before the company messed it all up and the contract, and my job, ended. Scotland can give you all kinds of weather in just one day from unlimited visibility in the early morning to severe gale force winds gusting to over 50 -60 Knots on the ground by evening time. You certainly get plenty of variety and handling practise and I was grateful to get the experience. Shortly after I had become a Captain, Highland Airways approached me about coming over to them to fly a Jetstream 31, something I was keen to do as I liked Scotland and had started to think about moving there to live. Wendy and I had had a week's holiday in the area to get a feel for Scotland but I decided to stay with HD Air to get more experience in the left seat first, during a winter. Little did I know then that the job was to end suddenly and I later wished that I had gone to Highland Airways after all? As I learned later, they did not last for long either, so even if I had moved, I would now have been out of a job in any case. The loss of the contract was a monumental cock-up which I will return to later.

During my line training I flew the aircraft to Jersey for some maintenance before continuing to Paris to pick up the freight load and remember it as it was a beautiful day over all of France. The new contract, from Coventry (CVT) to Le Bourget was empty outbound and unusually appeared to have two call signs, one in UK airspace and a different one once you started talking to the French. Despite valiant efforts to get them to accept the correct call sign we eventually used what they wanted. The take off time from CVT was about 1600 hrs local time and you were usually back home in CVT by about 11 pm. I made one mistake during the line training when I inadvertently left the battery master switch on after re-fuelling but remembered in time and did not tell Keith Jones for fear of getting a telling off. In Scotland, I took the Flight Manual off the aircraft to

192

study it during our rest in Benbecula but forgot to put it back, finding it in my flight bag later the next day. Luckily the company had used a different aircraft that day and I was able to put it back without making a possible flight illegal. When I told Keith about that error he was not amused and ordered me to take it back to the aircraft immediately.

The Paris contract would have suited me very well and I was in the process of finding long term local accommodation in the Coventry area when for some reason, the company pulled out, so my two years ended up being just one month; a bit like the Cardiff contract with the Twin Otter. The only negative aspect of that job, if it had lasted, was that we had to help load the freight from a lorry on to the aircraft. The main problem was that the weights of the various items varied significantly and it was difficult to get a BALANCED load in the cabin area. However flying into France and back during which you flew over the South Coast, the Channel and Paris in daylight during the summer months made the route an enjoyable one.

While I was a Captain, I was asked to fly the Luton to Kassel route a few times and spent some time in the airport hotel at Luton. However, because I was not based there, it was always a problem getting through security even with your flying licence, passport, yellow jacket and an ID for some other place. I often had to wait until the based First Officer arrived until I could get access to the aircraft which was just yards away from the security gate; even when the re-fuelling tanker was waiting for me. I used to find that the airport security people were not very flexible in any way and never believed anything you told them; either at Luton or anywhere else. It is my own personal view that your airport security clearance to go "airside" should form part of your pilot's licence, to be reviewed or renewed every time you have a base check or instrument rating renewal.

Part of the Captains responsibility was to check the paperwork of the aircraft especially when flying a particular aircraft for the first time during a series of flights. At Luton, I once discovered that the "daily" inspection which I seem to remember was valid for 36 hours had NOT been carried out. Although it was valid up to midnight on the day in question and I could have flown to Germany legally, I would not have been able to fly back. I therefore rang the company engineer who lived near to Birmingham and told him to come and sign off the paperwork. He had in fact been at Luton earlier that day and changed a main wheel tyre but had forgotten to do the daily inspection. Needless to say, he was not amused having to drive at high speed down the M1 motorway just to sign a technical log sheet, but there was no alternative. A hint that I should overlook the matter was rejected as I could have been in a lot of trouble if something else had happened. Missing something unintentionally is one thing but deliberately ignoring the rules is another. Insurance companies like to find a reason for NOT paying a claim, even if it has nothing to do with the case. I am always mindful of a tale told to me and others at an instructor's seminar when a company did not pay an insurance claim following a wheel's up landing because the paperwork was not in order. The aircraft involved, a Piper PA-34 Seneca had had a radio modification done some years previously but there was no record of the work having being done. The aircraft's certificate of airworthiness was therefore technically "invalid" and the insurance company refused to pay for the repairs; even after the owner had taken the matter to court! This was why I would not deliberately overlook the fact that the daily inspection had not been correctly carried out. It was agreed that I would get the aircraft loaded ready to go and that he would meet me at the security gate with the tech log. He actually made it in time and we got away virtually on schedule that evening.

After that contract ended, I found myself flying mainly in Scotland and thoroughly enjoyed it. The mail contracts we had were Aberdeen to East Midlands which came to an end when Loganair took over the route and the out and back run to Stornaway and Benbecula in the Outer Hebrides flown from Inverness, which was expected to last for some time. On one of the flights to EMA, the forecast was very bad with an almost certainty of Fog. I rang the post office supervisor and suggested I fly directly to Stansted where the forecast of fog was a little better but he was adamant I went to East Midlands (EMA) first. This almost caused us not only to NOT land at EMA as I had thought would be the case and we only just got into Stansted before it too closed due to the RVR falling below 550 metres. I hasten to add that Southend was the so called "bolt hole" that night which was forecast to stay open otherwise I would not have gone at all that night. That flight caused me a few nasty thoughts as we were burning the fuel away. As Captain you have to look at the overall picture and ALWAYS think of **flight safety** as being the overriding concern rather than a commercial pressure to go. Syed Ali, my First Officer and I had an expensive nights stay in a hotel at Stansted before we had an enjoyable daylight flight back to Aberdeen (ABZ) the following afternoon routing up the East coast.

The other contract out to the Scottish isles was more varied and interesting. The only snag was the need to get up at 04.30 every morning when you were flying and then having to spend 7 hours on Benbecula every day where we had a rest house. We did however always get a good breakfast as we were able to go to the local Hospital canteen for a hearty meal if you wanted it. The picture at the bottom of this page shows the aircraft approaching Ullapool at about 6500 feet one clear morning.

If the weather was good I used to enjoy the long walks on an almost deserted beaches and I did for a while consider writing this book while there but never got started on it. The flying conditions could change dramatically and I once made an approach and landing at Stornaway where the wind was gusting in excess of 55 Knots. The taxying limit for the aircraft was 55 knots and the door limit was 50 Kts, so we were right on the limits that particular day.

One of the new First Officers at Inverness, Andrew Laing, was an ex RAF flight engineer who used to fly the Nimrod maritime reconnaissance aircraft out of Kinloss. His engineering knowledge and good common sense was very useful in times of difficulty but even he was not perfect as one day, when I was not flying, he flew to Benbecula (BEB) and then discovered that the base check and I/R on his licence had lapsed. That was as much the companies fault as it was his own. The company had to fly another pilot out to the island to legally complete the mail flight that afternoon. He and I flew together many times and during a particularly bad spell of weather over the Christmas period in 2008, we had to contend with thick fog at Inverness on more than one occasion. We once managed to get in with a "window of opportunity" as we were passing on our way to Aberdeen from Stornaway, but on another flight when we hoped to get back to INV, we had to abandon it and return to Aberdeen.

One day at Benbecula, I had a feeling something was not right and just before starting engines decided to re-check if the Pitot covers were off. The one side was not. Had we left it on, we would either have burnt it off or had only one ASI reading during the start of the take of run before reaching V1. "Stop Stop" would have had to be called had I not checked again. I had a word with the ground party about this saying

that they too should look for anything obviously wrong as they monitor a start up. On a daylight visual flight into ABZ, Andrew was flying and we were given permission to position visually for a landing on R/W 16. I was doing the checks and radio and could clearly see the airfield some distance away. What I had NOT realized, was that he had not correctly identified the airfield and runway and was in fact flying towards another feature which he thought looked like an airfield. This was an important learning curve for me as Captain as you must constantly monitor an in-experienced First Officer, just in case. Never assume he is thinking what you are thinking.

I had seriously considered moving up to Scotland as I liked the Inverness area very much but could not get a cast iron guarantee that the job would last. That proved to be the case as trouble was brewing with the one company owned aircraft which remained, G-TMRB. It was due for some major maintenance inputs such as a wing spar check and several extensions had been granted by the CAA to keep it airborne as long as possible but this could not go on forever. The company decided to use a Benair Shorts SD360/300 aircraft and in the week before our own aircraft was to be grounded, several of the companies pilots including myself did the necessary ground school on their SOP's and paperwork. It was planned that I would return to INV after a weekend at home and carry out the required base and line check training on their aircraft. What turned out to be my very last flight in Scotland, was on a Thursday 26th February 2009 with another F/O, Jay Suchowa but it started very ominously when, as I picked him up from the crew house in Inverness, I had a very severe nose bleed and went to the nearby hospital to be sure it was nothing more serious. However, that was not before I had visited the downstairs toilet and sneezed blood all over the walls and carpet leaving it as if there had been a murder committed! As time was tight, I had to leave it and in fact, have never been back there since, after the day's flying had been completed; I immediately got a commercial flight back to Birmingham; and as it turned out, never returned. In my log book, I made a note about it which makes it appear that I lost my job because of a very severe nose bleed, which was not the case!

It was planned that I would position back to INV the following Wednesday to do the Benair conversion training and I duly caught a FlyBe flight from BHX to EDI. I was then to pick up a hire car and drive up the A90 to Inverness but when I rang the company from EDI, James Pennington in the office said it was all over and that the company had lost the contract! Apparently, Benair had decided to put up the hire price for the aircraft and as the post office was not prepared to pay the increase, the deal was off. I remember being very shocked and my arms started shaking. He offered me a flight straight back to Birmingham but as I had already got the hire car, it was agreed I would have a leisurely drive back home during which I called on Terry Dixon, the chief pilot who lived near to Hexham in Northumberland. He was as shocked as I was to learn of the most recent developments.

I was glad to have volunteered to fly over the Christmas and New Year period for 2008/9 because it gave me a little more flying just before the job came to an end. During the period leading up to Christmas there were extra mail flights and one of those was a Fairchild Metro-liner which took off about 10 minutes behind me and climbed above my Flight Level. As he was faster he used to pass me at about the half way point at Ullapool on the Scottish coast and arrive at Stornaway about 15 minutes ahead of me. However, due to IFR rules and having no radar at Stornaway, he always had to wait for me to make my approach before he could descend. On one morning when the weather was perfectly clear with unlimited visibility I invited ATC to let him descend ahead of me but rules are rules and they would not allow it; despite the fact that we both had TCAS fitted in out aircraft and could "see" each other electronically. Personally I thought it stupid to keep him above me for about 20 extra minutes when, due to his faster speed he could have landed well ahead of me. He thanked me for trying to help but the rules said he had to wait.

I would like to make a brief mention about two modern aids, TAWS and TCAS. Changing ICAO regulations required all our Shorts SD 360 aircraft to be fitted, at a cost of around £40,000 each, with an updated Ground Proximity Warning system (GPWS) which can see the terrain ahead based on GPS and an internal computerised database. That was known as a Terrain Awareness Warning System (TAWS). The photo above shows the outline of the Isle of Harris on our way to Stornaway one early morning.

Also a Terminal Collision Avoidance System (TCAS) was needed which interrogates other aircrafts radar transponders and gives a warning of a possible mid air collision risk. You could see other proximate traffic on your vertical speed indicator and would receive either a Traffic Advisory (TA) or a more important Resolution Advisory (RA) if a possible risk of collision was determined. Both systems do enhance flight safety but in my view they take away the pilots needs to be vigilant and aware of his surroundings. I had one false warning when I was about to land saying "climb climb" as there was an aircraft at the runway hold and one real "Resolution Advisory" while climbing out of Coventry toward Paris in uncontrolled airspace. Below a certain height, some warnings are supposed to be inhibited to prevent false RA's but sometimes you can still get one.

Consulting my log books I see I made a total of 118 round trips to Stornaway and Benbecula during the course of that particular contract, 86 as a First Officer and 32 as Captain. I also flew many times out of ABZ to EMA. I only hope that one day I will get the chance to fly around the Scottish Islands again but I must be grateful for the time I did have in Scotland. Highland Airways whom I admired, were very good to the BAC/HD Air crews and we had the use of a company car with which I was able to tour the Western Isles of Scotland including the beautiful Isle of Skye. I fell in love with Scotland while I was there and would gladly go to live there if a suitable flying job came about. The weather is very changeable and you can have all four seasons in one day from gales and low cloud to hot clear skies with no wind, all during one flying duty period.

Incidentally, I did express interest in a BN2a Islander job which Highland Airways was starting up based at Oban on the west coast but it was to be a single crew operation and the CAA would **not** remove my "As or with a Co-Pilot" restriction which would have allowed me to be considered. My hearing problem had, it seems, finally caught up with me and denied me a job which I would have been more than happy with; to finish my flying career.

Due to the companies failure to get a satisfactory alternative arrangement when their one aircraft had to be withdrawn from service, my career flying the Shorts SD 360 ended after a period lasting for nearly twelve years. Apart from one other three hour flight in April 2009, when I flew G-TMRB to Karup in Denmark for the required essential maintenance work and storage, I have not flown commercially since. The way in which my flying career with BAC/HD Air ended is a good example of how an airline operation can sometimes **not** keep their eye on the ball. The aircrew had been warning for months that the aircraft required some major maintenance issues to be resolved and yet nobody seemed to recognise the urgency of the need to find a replacement aircraft in time. As I understand it, Benair insisted on getting more money for their Shorts aircraft as they were more expensive to operate before we had even started flying and the company regrettably lost the mail contract as a result. In my view it would have been a safer option to have started the work, and then tried to increase the revenue once the new arrangements had settled down.

One of my deepest regrets was that I agreed to return to Birmingham immediately. I should have insisted on carrying on up to Inverness to say my goodbyes to friends and colleagues at Highland Airways. I might even have been able to get a job with them but as things turned out that would not have lasted long as they themselves went out of business about a year later. However, I might have got another aircraft type on my license. Personally, I also lost an expensive solid state SW/AW/FM Sony radio which I had left in the crew house and was never returned to me. In the hangar at INV there was a saying on the wall which has always remained firmly in my mind, **"Those who fail to plan, plan to fail"**. This was sadly true, not only of HD Air but also of Highland Airways themselves just over a year later. A local Scottish company, Loganair, who I had worked for briefly in 1987, quickly picked up most of the resulting work. This was later sub let to a foreign operator for a short time.

The previous photograph is of HD Air's wholly owned Shorts SD 360 which, as I write this book, is currently in storage at Karup in Demark while the company seeks to find a new worthwhile contract. This aircraft is configured as an E class freighter which is allowed by the United Kingdom's Civil Aviation Authority. The other company operating Shorts SD-360's in Europe is Benair (who now owns HD Air) but Danish rules do not allow their own aircraft to operate as pure freighters and the galley area, together with the three rear seats and the luggage racks have to remain fitted to the aircraft.

HD Air has not gone out of business as such and the company Air Operators Certificate (AOC) remains in force to this day (August 2010). They have left Coventry and now have an office in the old terminal building at Birmingham Airport. I live in hope that one day Rob Davies, the company's current operation's manager who I regularly talk to, will ring me and say, "What time can you report for Duty"? At my last CAA medical, I again saw Dr Robert Hunter who told me regrettably to more or less call it a day. He allowed a renewal of my Class One medical but only expects me to only accept a job on a two crew turbo-prop type aircraft similar to the Shorts SD 360. At nearly 58 years of age, I was happy with that condition as no jet airline is ever going to train me to fly an Airbus or Boeing jet. I am however still flying light aircraft and this aspect of my life, and stories relating to it, are the subject of my next chapter.

These are two good pictures of a "Shed" Captain's instrument panel taken while en route to Stornaway in the Outer Hebrides, and while parked on a windy Benbecula during our regular day stop!

Chapter Fourteen.
Other Flying.

I have been a qualified flying instructor since 1972 and have kept the rating current for most of my flying career apart from a period when I was flying commercially for Brymon airways. I hold a full instructors rating with endorsements allowing me to teach night and instrument flying on single engine landplanes only. This allows me to teach on the multitude of light aircraft owned and operated by members of the Light Aircraft Association; formally known as the Popular Flying Association. I was formally invited to become one of their first Coaching Pilots when the scheme was set up in 1998 and had an assessment flight with John Brownlow at Cambridge where I was able to fly both an ARV and Europa aircraft solo for the first time. I found the grass runways at Cambridge to be one of the roughest licensed grass airfields I have ever flown from whilst some of the smoothest I have known have been at Hanley William and a strip at Lydney on the shorelines of the Severn Estuary. My legacy, Milson is getting smoother all the time as the bump at the midpoint is gradually worn away. I slowly levelled it with massive amounts of unwanted sand which I got free from an industrial site and sprinkled on the ground whenever a puddle appeared. I was also to get the opportunity to fly the new Jabiru Aircraft from a grass strip at Southerby shortly afterwards and wrote a good report on the aircraft, in which I offered to take the plane and leave my car behind!

Having Milson airstrip with resident owners based there often gave me the chance to fly different types of aircraft. Over the years, the various types included a Rans Coyote G-BSTT in which I had three cases of running out of fuel which hints at a design problem but more about that later, a Druine Turbulent G-BLTC, one of the classic Piper Cubs G-BGXA, an ARV Super Two G-BMDO, a Taylorcraft aircraft G-BREY and Kitfox G-HOBO, amongst many others. Flying all these different types gives you a good appreciation of flying and you are learning all the time one way or the other. This chapter should be interesting to the reader as I recall some of the experiences I gained while flying these aircraft and working as an instructor and coach pilot, mainly from Shobdon. Once again, these recollections may not be in chronological order but it should make some good reading nevertheless.

The Turbulent had been built by Graham Smith and although I did not do the initial flights primarily because I had not flown the type enough, I was to fly it frequently during my seven years of unemployment in the 1990's. You had to swing it to start and sometimes it could take a while but on other occasions it would fire up on the first swing; you never knew whether you were going to be lucky of not. You often read of pilots who after hand swinging an aircraft find themselves in trouble as the aircraft goes to full throttle, jumps the chocks, and then carers across the airfield to eventually hit something or get airborne on its own. As a safeguard against such a mishap, it was common practise to actually start the Turbulent with the Fuel OFF and then select it back on within a minute of starting up, if you remembered in time. One observation if running the engine with the top cowl off was how ICE formed on the Carburettor choke giving you a good indication of why you sometimes get "carb icing" even on a warm day. It was enjoyable to fly with the wind whistling by and your head exposed to the elements and I was thankful to Graham for letting me fly it. He had a red coloured pitot tube cover which was always put in to a small compartment behind the pilots head but it disappeared on one flight when it came out. I was to pick it up walking around my father's pools one day about a week or so later; talk about finding a "Needle in a Haystack"! Apart from the Turbulent, I was also to get the opportunity to fly other open cockpit aircraft such as a Currie Wot Biplane, G-ASBA, which I flew a few times and was something like a miniature Tiger Moth.

I later flew an Acrosport Two biplane G-BKCV, when I did a tailwheel conversion for the owner, but that was from Baxterley airstrip and Sywell in Northamptonshire. I did also once fly in a Tiger Moth but did not enjoy it, but that was in my earlier days when I had not got as much experience.

The Taylorcraft aircraft, G-BREY, which was based at Milson for a short while caught me out badly when I first went to fetch it and could not start it. As it had no fuel priming system and it was hand swung to start, you had to suck fuel in to the induction manifold of the carburettor with the throttle FULLY CLOSED to give enough of a suction and venturi effect over the fuel jet. I had repeatedly tried to start it with the throttle slightly open as we used to do on the Auster and many other types and eventually I had to give up and drove home. A few months later after the aircraft was sold on, I saw the aircraft again in Leicester. I asked the owner if he had had trouble starting it, which he had and told him the tip which he was pleased to learn about. You are constantly learning new things about flying almost every time you fly a light aircraft or microlight.

One aircraft type with which I have had a long association is the monowheel version of the Shaw Europa. With one large main wheel under the centre of the aircraft and two small outrigger wheels to stop the wingtips from touching the ground, it is one of the more difficult aircraft to take off and land well, although it flies like a fighter plane in the air and is surprisingly difficult to slow down due to its very low drag profile.

In some ways it resembles a glider with an engine similar to the Motor Falke and being a tailwheel aircraft is hard to keep straight on the ground. However, although having any previous tailwheel experience is useful; I have always said that having no previous experience is NOT a problem as the Europa is unique to itself. Careful training when the time and weather are right is what is needed when doing a type conversion. Ironically NO wind conditions can be the most difficult to handle as the pilot often becomes complacent and relaxes too much just when he or she should be concentrating the most.

After my initial check out on type as part of my LAA Coaching check, I was first introduced to the aircraft in a big way when Dari Sagar purchased a Europa G-DURO, and asked me to carry out his type conversion training. The very first time I was ever introduced to him by another friend, I made an embarrassing slip of the tongue and said, "Oh, Hello Dari, the pilot who is always getting lost"! This was in fact true as his sense of direction was very poor and he was known to always follow someone else when flying to air shows or going to "Fly-Ins" but I should not have said it at the time. He forgave me for it however, and we got along fine. He was a nervous pilot in some ways but did a lot of flying on the aircraft until increasing costs made him sell the aircraft. He knows I am writing this book and has already reserved a copy so I hope he agrees with my comments.

I carried a number of other type conversions on several more Europa aircraft among them G-BVRA, G-BWJX, G-BHUG, G-DAYS and G-CBOF which, for a reason yet to be determined, wants to roll slightly to the left all the time. I suggested to the owner that he takes it to the Europa factory for investigation but I suspect that the one wing is slightly deformed although it is not noticeable. I also air tested and type rated the owners of G-BZAM and G-ROOV but the one pilot type conversion course was to result in an accident and the owner, even after converting it to the safer nose wheel version, suffered yet another unrelated accident and decided to sell it. When the Europa first appeared it was hailed as a revolution in aircraft design but since then, many other types, which are much easier to fly, have appeared on the market. If the reader is thinking of buying an aircraft, he or she should first decide what you want the aircraft for, either for long cross countries with plenty of baggage space, or do you want to fly in and out of short grass strips. The choice of aircraft is mind boggling these days, so take your time before deciding on the type you wish to buy. My recollections of flying the Europa are best summed up by re-producing an article (**Appendix Eight**) which I wrote about the aircraft and was published in the Europa Club magazine rather than repeating all the information here.

When doing a type conversion on to another Europa, G-BVLV, flying from Bidford on Avon, I decided to go and do some circuit work at Long Marston airfield, near to Stratford upon Avon, which had one fairly long hard runway 04/22. I arrived overhead, circled several times over what appeared to be a market day and ended up landing in the middle of a drag race which was using the main runway I landed on. This caused a lot of angry faces, threats of legal

204

action, and a possible report to the CAA but there was no NOTAM action for the event and no one on the ground replied to my calls on the accepted microlight frequency 129.825 MHz. There were also no visual signals on the ground, such as a white cross on the runway, to say the airfield was closed. This was an embarrassing incident which could have been nasty and was caused by not being sure about the operating status of the airfield. I have never been entirely happy flying from this airfield as it is apparently owned by three brothers, each of which has a different interest and plans for the airfield. You can never be really sure what is going on there, or who is in charge. I have been there when people have been using the runway to learn to drive on, or flying model aircraft from the site and I have had other microlights using a completely different grass runway, taking off in the opposite direction! Beware at Long Marston airfield; I certainly learnt to be on my guard there.

Another aircraft I was to have a lot to do with was the homebuilt Kitfox which was a robust two seater tailwheel aircraft similar in shape to an Auster. Most Kitfox aircraft are powered by a Rotax 582 two stroke engine originally designed for a snowmobile vehicle and modified with a reduction gearbox for a propeller. As the photo shows, they are a useful aircraft for a farm strip as they have STOL performance but also can be safely stored in a lorry trailer sized container.

I also owned one for about two years after I sold the airstrip and had a bit of cash to hand but that came to a sad end when I suffered an engine failure. That story has already been accounted for in the first part of this book. Apart from the one I owned, G-BTNR, I have also flown G-BSRT, G-CJUD, G-HOBO, G-TFOX which was a mouthful to speak over the radio so I used to say "Kitfox" instead and recently G-LEED but there are others as well.

One of my resident pilots at Milson was Adrian Lloyd who had a flex wing microlight until he decided to convert to a fixed wing aircraft for more comfort and a greater opportunity to fly. He purchased his Kitfox G-BSRT with the help of his father and asked me to carry out his type conversion training which we started at Shobdon. His general flying was very good partly because he had been a gliding instructor some years before and understood the need to use the "Stick and Rudder" in close co-ordination. However, when we came to start doing circuits, his take off efforts were interesting to begin with; he was swinging all over the place and barely staying on the runway. That was caused by his failure to look down the side of the engine cowling rather than straight over the nose. His landings however, weren't so much of a problem, especially on the grass.

I flew one cross country with him and left our timing a little tight as darkness appeared and we landed back at Milson in almost night time conditions. As we were late that day, he did not, as was usual, refuel the aircraft. The next time we flew, we were on our approach into Shobdon when his low fuel warning light started to flicker. "Some bastard has nicked my fuel" he kept repeating until after landing it dawned on both of us that he had not re-fuelled it. Luckily this Kitfox had a reserve tank which holds about 5 litres of fuel; enough for about 20 minutes of flying after the warning light has come on. Yet again, never assume always check, comes to mind. I was to make a bad mistake myself when in very low cloud, rain and poor visibility conditions we attempted to fly back to Milson. Knowing the road and countryside, I had said we would follow the main road at low level; the problem was that at Mortimer's Cross roads just north east of Shobdon, I started flying up the WRONG road which put us in the dangerous situation of flying up a steep sided valley where the ground height slowly increased into the cloud covered hills. I suddenly realised what was happening and taking control, increased the engine to full power and made a tight 180 degree turn. That was a close shave and a good example of the "Get Home" syndrome where against your better judgement you take a chance; it is simply not worth it as you may never arrive at your intended bed for the night. "Get home itis" (a saying) can be a fatal flaw in our thinking so beware!

Another very nice Kitfox I flew was G-HOBO which handled nicely right down to the stall and was easy to land without being heavy on the nose like my own aircraft which had a forward C of G. However, I went to fly it one day and felt a little uncomfortable about the engine sound and I had a

206

slightly reduced max RPM during the engine run up. As it was also a little on the windy side, I decided to call it a day and put it back in the Hangar.

Unluckily for Adrian who flew it next, the engine seized solid just after take off and he had to make an emergency downwind landing on one of my fathers old farm fields during which he broke the propeller, damaged a wing tip and strained the undercarriage up to the safety wires. This was why I had asked him to check my own aircraft a day or so before I had my own failure. It appears someone was looking after me yet again. You have to have a feel for an aircraft and if you think something is not right, that is probably the case.

One of the aircraft I flew was G-CJUD, which one elderly gentleman decided to buy without even seeing it. I was asked to do his type conversion but when we took off on our first flight together, he could hardly control it due to the very sensitive aileron and rudder control caused by "Adverse Yaw" which occurs when the increased drag of the down going aileron causes the nose of the aircraft to swing or yaw in the OPPOSITE direction to the intended direction of turn. This problem is now largely eliminated in most modern aircraft and can come as a sudden shock to an untrained or inexperienced pilot. Neil Martin kept saying "What have I done" (buying this machine) but I must say he persevered and eventually was able to fly the aircraft quite well. He was reluctant to turn by banking the aircraft sufficiently, tending instead to slip it round the turn with the rudder and he kept remembering my comment after the training was completed that "If you are going to turn, Turn!"

One day I was asked by the chief engineer of the Light Aircraft Association to go and evaluate a newly built but different model of a Kitfox to determine the absolute safe forward and aft limits on the Centre of Gravity envelope. At the suggested forward limit for G-CDXY, I could hardly get the tail down during the landing while at the aft limit the take of run was extended considerably as it was hard to raise the tail. However, my big mistake was that when I first arrived the owner had already prepared the aircraft ready for flight and had, so he said, done a detailed external check. I believed him and after a cursory check, got in and off I went. After landing back and getting out I then noticed that the locking pin on the port main wing pin was NOT in place. He had been interrupted by my arrival and had had his mind taken off the task.

Something similar happened to me a few years earlier when I flew a Cessna 150 to an air show at Badminton. While preparing for departure, I was interrupted by an old friend I had not seen for a while and subsequently left both my fuel filler caps off after I had just re-fuelled. Luckily someone noticed as I started up and waved me to shutdown. If I may now just recall another event; the prototype Britten Norman Tri-Lander aircraft was photographed during an air test from another aircraft. The photo was shown on the front page of the "Flight International" magazine, unfortunately and embarrassingly for the company sales team, with one of the fuel filler caps hanging on a piece of chain. It can happen to anyone, so check, and check again! I went out to the "Shed" at Inverness one morning and found the pressure re-fuelling cap hanging below the starboard wheel arch, so it is a recurring problem, usually brought about when the **routine is interrupted** for some reason.

Re-fuelling any aircraft can be a problem requiring your utmost concentration, as so many different units of measurement can be used. In commercial flying, the gauges sometimes give fuel in pounds weight, the load sheet weight is in kilograms and the fuel is uplifted in litres! You can easily get the conversion figures mixed up which is exactly what Air Canada did when they first introduced the Boeing 767 into service causing one of their new aircraft to run out of fuel during a flight. Luckily, they managed to glide and land successfully at a disused airstrip once used by the First Officer when he was a school cadet some years earlier.

The ARV Super Two aircraft was an interesting little light aircraft which had an unusual Newland engine with some kind of electronic ignition. The aircraft I was to fly was G-BMDO which I first saw in the Flight One hangar at Gloucester when I used to fly the Twin Pioneer. Roger Lloyd had it based at Milson but it was not really suitable for a small grass strip of just 450-500 metres and he had to normally fly it out on his own with just a little fuel on board. At that time it had very small wheels on it which were not conducive for use on grass strips, especially if wet or damp. After he sold it to John Eden and his son Louis, I was asked to teach them both to fly it. I managed to get Louis solo no problem but as hard as I tried, his father never mastered it enough for me to be confident to let him go on his own. Sadly, this flying all came to

208

an end when the aircraft was blown over during gale force winds at Tatenhill Airfield, close to where they lived. This was a pity because the performance of the aircraft was transformed when they decided to put much bigger and thicker wheels on it. It simply jumped into the air with ease. The aircraft was kept at Milson and I used to position it to either Shobdon or Tatenhill for the training details. One drawback was that it did not have a reliable fuel; gauge so it was always dipped with a stick before flight. Whilst positioning to Tatenhill one day, I ran into bad weather and low cloud over the Cannock Chase area, and became so concerned about my possible fuel state, that I decided I MUST make a precautionary landing.

I looked at one long field which had cattle in it but decided to land at a disused airfield near Stafford called Wheaton Aston. Wisely as it turned out, I decided to land on the old hard runway, landing between two rows of rounded Straw bales which had been stacked on either side of the runway with a track line between them. The wingtip had about a foot or so to spare on either side but it all worked out. Had I chosen to land on the flat stubble fields on the site, I would have probably turned it over as the ground was waterlogged and very soft. I did not panic but I must say the heart was beating and your thought processes seem to go out of the window under stress. Doing all the necessary checks and procedures during simulated training is one thing but when you are confronted with an **actual** precautionary or forced landing, the feeling is totally different, and scary. As it turned out I actually had 15 litres of fuel left, enough to divert to Halfpenny Green airfield but I was not sure of that at the time. The farmer was amused as he had only ever had gliders land there previously but he did go and get me 10 litres of fuel before I departed when the weather had cleared up. Do not rush a decision, evaluate your options and be careful to do all your checks when under pressure.

Now let's explain the stories behind the Rans S-6 G-BSTT. It was built at Milson by Mike Holmes and successfully test flown from Milson by myself but not without some incidents. First of all, the tailplane incidence was wrong giving a permanent and strong nose down force when first flown. This was corrected by making several sets of brackets until the incidence was finally corrected and acceptable during all phases of flight, from take off to landing; but the original builder's plans clearly had a mistake on them. The fuel system was also less than ideal and caused me to run out of fuel at least three times, although on of those I was supposed to have been the passenger, not the pilot flying it. During flight the design of the vent allowed fuel to escape freely due to suction and the fact that fuel in the climbing attitude flowed towards the vent pipe. The net effect of this was that about a third of the volume of fuel was lost during the early part of every flight. While I was doing the intended two hour endurance flight as part of the fight test programme, I ran out of fuel just after getting airborne from the airstrip in a high nose up attitude. In the corner of my eye I could still see part of the airstrip below me so, without a moments hesitation, I lowered the nose, ensured I had a high airspeed and did a rapid 180 degree turn. I then landed back on the airstrip about half way up the strip just as the engine started again. They all say you should <u>never attempt to turn back to the field if you suffer an engine failure after taking off</u> and that is broadly true but there are occasionally exceptions. I had nowhere else to go at Milson as there are woods ahead as I and Adrian Lloyd had found out in the Kitfox incident already mentioned. I distinctly remember seeing the air bubbles going down the fuel pipe as the engine was failing but I kept a cool head and reacted very quickly to the situation.

The second case was much later on when Mike was flying it with me as an innocent passenger and we had flown to Caernarfon in North Wales. On the way back while passing over the Brown Clee Hills at 3000 Feet amsl, but only 1200 feet above ground at that point, we ran out of fuel. Mike's reaction could have been better as he immediately pushed the nose down, increasing speed rapidly and losing height more quickly than we need have done. He then shouted to me, **"You have control"**. I did not really want control with nowhere to go on the side of the hill with numerous very small fields with hedges or stone walls around. The result was that we very quickly passed between two trees taking off the one wing, landed and spun round; all in about 45 seconds from when the engine had stopped. As luck would have it, the fuselage was intact with NO damage to the front end or the propeller but had we been just a few metres to the left would have passed through a wider gap in the trees without causing any damage. Both of us were shocked and Mike has sprained his back but I was fine. Later, when doing the paperwork and the report for the AAIB, I had to accept responsibility and be recorded as being the pilot in command as Mike's medical certificate had expired a few days earlier. Mike later had yet another engine failure when the engine seized up completely and on that occasion he did not reach his chosen field and stalled it just before landing but got away with it a second time.

The third time I ran out of fuel was after flying it to the LAA rally at Cranfield and having to hold for a period of time. The engine failed during the last stage of the long approach but I had enough momentum and height to land it normally, pull off the runway and park it where they wanted us to go; just as the engine started up again. I was lucky again, but in reality the fuel system and stated endurance of the aircraft was inadequate and needed a complete re-design. The system was indeed improved as time went on.

One other aircraft I have enjoyed flying is the Australian designed Jabiru which can be built and flown as either an aircraft or microlight version depending on the model. It is easy to fly but has two faults from a piloting point of view. Firstly, the lookout in it particularly during turns is VERY POOR, especially if you are a tall person and secondly, the aileron and roll control is very poor and sloppy (or unresponsive) during an approach to land in crosswinds. You MUST use the rudder to maintain the centre line of the approach path and try and keep the wings as level as possible. My own view is that all the flying control surfaces, aileron, elevator and rudder are too small and need to be larger. However, it does have some good features in that it has a nice little aero engine on it and it is very economical to run. I have flown several of these aircraft and taught a flex wing microlight pilot to fly one with no great difficulty a few years ago. That lady, Rachel Wells, would have made a good professional pilot but she has left it to late too realise her dream of flying full time and actually runs a small provincial bank for Lloyds in a small county town in Worcestershire probably earning more than I ever did?

During the 1990's while I was out of a full time job I not only did some LAA Coaching and type conversions but also flew as a part time instructor at Shobdon. One day an aircraft landed and the young pilot got out and surprisingly asked "Where am I?" Before I told him he was at Shobdon, I asked him where he had come from and been hoping to go. It turned out that he was supposed to have been flying from Gloucester to Oxford but had set off in the completely opposite direction. The reason, his Directional Indicator (DI) in his aircraft had been set 180 out of position and he had not realised that the sun is always to the south. After a suitable brief and discussion with his instructor at Gloucester, he was allowed to fly back home. It is important whenever you set off on any cross county flight to make an early GROSS ERROR check such as looking for a prominent landmark to ensure you are at least gong the way you want to go. It is also vitally important to regularly check that your DI is set correctly to the compass reading; normally done as part of your regular **FREDA** checks every 10-15 minutes or so. That mnemonic stands for **F**uel On correct tank and sufficient, **R**adio correct frequency and volume turned up, **E**ngine temperatures and pressures including a check for carburettor icing, **D**irectional Indicator (DI) correctly set to the magnetic compass with the **A**ltimeter set to correct atmospheric pressure setting, be it the QNH (altitude), QFE (Height above an airfield), or set to 1013 to give a flight level reading like when flying on airways.

When an instructor at Shobdon in the earlier years, I was asked by "Woodie" the CFI if I would sit in an aircraft and let a student do a "solo" cross country without saying anything at all unless flight safety was at risk. He was supposed to fly a short triangular flight from Shobdon to Hereford and Bromyard but ended up turning over Tenbury Wells which he thought was Bromyard. The reason was that his DI and compass had a <u>consistent 15 degree error</u> on the entire flight. The weather was a little windy (which is why I went with him) but with good visibility so he could virtually see his turning points as he set course but saw Tenbury instead of Bromyard on his second leg. When flying with a student on a cross country once, he called up Turweston airfield, proceeded to join overhead as instructed and completed a full circuit to then land at Finmere aerodrome about five miles to the south. It was no wonder that the controller at Turweston could not see him! I found it difficult not to open my mouth and reveal the error myself. The difference between the two airfields is that Finmere has less evidence of aviation use and has a dual carriageway running directly alongside the runway while Turweston is in open countryside. Check and check again. A USAF F-111 swing wing bomber pilot once did a wonderful display at Bruntingthorpe airfield rather than at Coventry, so it can happen to anyone!

During one flight with a student, he appeared to be tense and finding his flying hard going. I told him to take his hands off the control column which caused the aircraft to pitch either up or down, I cannot remember which way, as he was flying it completely out of trim. Apparently he had been flying like that with other instructors and on his own for some time without realising the significance of the trimmer for the elevator control. Sometimes an aspect of your flying training can be overlooked quite by accident, so always look for something which does not appear to be right.

A BBC television programme called "999" once featured a story where two pilots had got trapped above cloud at night with insufficient radio aids and experience to get down safely. This flight had originated from Shobdon on a night when I went flying in the circuit and discovered very low cloud in the vicinity of the airfield. I landed and advised the Chief instructor, Dennis Davies that flying should cease and met these two pilots as they were leaving the clubhouse to fly. I told them the weather was no good but they still got airborne. They were escorted down through cloud by an RAF Sea King helicopter from Chivenor in Devon and landed at Birmingham airport virtually out of fuel.

I was occasionally asked to do extra flights, flown on behalf of other people or the club. One was a flight to East Anglia in a Grumman Tiger G-ERRY, where I had planned to land, with permission, at a private grass airstrip which had been used by Piper Pawnee crop spraying aircraft in the past. The grass airstrip was about 900 metres in length and perfectly acceptable for this type of aircraft. On arrival, I descended through cloud flying towards the BBC world service transmitters on the coast, using the ADF set to 648 KHz and being absolutely spot on course, quickly found the airstrip. However, I noticed some very large trees at one end of the runway and felt a little uneasy about landing there; It is usually easy to land but you have to be sure you can take off again later. I therefore decided to divert to Ipswich airport which no longer exists, having now been covered in houses. When I went and had a look at the airstrip the next day, I found it was OK but with a few mole tumps on it BUT more seriously, about a third of the way down it, someone had hammered in a short stake with a "Number 7" on it. Had I actually landed I would have almost certainly hit it resulting in possible serious damage to the one wing. Someone looking after me again, I wonder? When I rang the lady of the house before the flight, she had said everything was fine, so be careful; whenever you plan to fly to an unlicensed grass or hard strip, be on the lookout for the unexpected. I do remember that the Directional Indicator (DI) on this particular aircraft was almost useless as it would not hold a steady heading when reset to the compass.

Another flight I did was to fly a Cessna 150 G-BEIG to Andrewsfield near Stansted to have a propeller changed. Unfortunately the proposed new propeller would not fit as the holes were a different diameter so the three hour flight there and back was a waste of time but a good day out for me. This aircraft had a very poor rate of climb at full throttle and the club was trying to improve its performance. The reason turned out to be nothing to do with the propeller pitch or engine power. What was wrong was the propeller incidence was slightly out of position following a possible heavy landing on the nose wheel and at full throttle the Thrust line was actually trying to pull the aircraft down slightly when it was trying to climb. The bend in the engine alignment was so slight it was not noticeable to the naked eye. The significance of this example is that if you ever have a heavy landing or suspect you might have damaged an aircraft in any way, report it, even if you gets you into a spot of bother. One of the companies Shorts SD-360 aircraft I used to fly was once found to have seriously bent undercarriage legs when it went for a routine check; someone had landed it heavily and said nothing thinking he or she had got away with it.

Finally in these reflections, (and there are many more I could tell you), was the occasion when I was staying at Shobdon on my own in the evening and had a telephone call from the London Air Traffic Control Centre (LATCC). "A Beagle Pup aircraft had been stolen and should it land at Shobdon, could I apprehend the pilot and call the Police", was the message. Just as I put the phone down a Beagle Pup did indeed land and my heart started to pound, but luckily it was a different registration to the one I had been given. The stolen aircraft was to crash in the English Channel killing the pilot in an apparent suicide. Something similar also happened to a USAF Hercules some years later which was taken from RAF Mildenhall.

Also, watch out for crooks in aviation. Phillip Cadman, the owner of the Auster mentioned earlier in the book was persuaded to purchase a Miles Messenger aircraft, G-AKKB, and it was duly flown to its new home at Milson where it was parked in the corner of the field. Unknown to him, it had been condemned by the CAA due to glue failure in the wings and eventually fell apart on the farm as the wooden wing spar rotted away. He thought he had got a bargain for £600, but in reality, he had been robbed. The engine however was saved and used again on another aircraft.

I am often accused of having too much to say but as an instructor that was a good fault as I used to keep on about something so much that whenever a student was flying on their own, they could still hear my voice! I enjoy teaching but as I have said many times over the years, an instructor cannot actually teach you to fly; **you have to do it yourself**. A flying instructor can only demonstrate, evaluate and help to correct student errors. As I have always enjoyed instrument flying, I have written some basic notes on that subject during which I point out that you are still flying the aircraft in the same way as you do visually but you have to trust the instruments and suppress your own feelings sometimes. Those detailed notes are given to you in **Appendix Nine** of the book.

214

Chapter Fifteen.
A Non Flying future?

It is sad that I am writing this concluding chapter at the age of 58 rather than 68 but redundancy, the state of the airline industry in 2010 and the CAA's doubt about my hearing may well have ended my commercial flying dreams but I hope that I will continue to fly privately for many years to come? However by writing this book now, my parents who are still both well and reasonable active have been able to enjoy reading the text as I have been writing it. I got the inspiration to get on and write it after reading Air Vice-Marshal, Sir John Severne's book "Silvered Wings". Although it is about a military pilot's career, it was written in a similar way to this account of my life and shows determined enthusiasm and oozes the sheer joy of flying. Another book, this time written by a civilian pilot who also achieved success against the odds was "Defining Moments" by Robin A Rackham. Had I not had a medical problem to overcome, I am sure I would have strived to get up the ladder more quickly and could have ended up flying Concorde, but I am not complaining. Over the years I tended to be loyal to my current employer at the time and only left one flying job of my own choosing. Another good read which has helped me to write this book has an unlikely title, "Fall Out Roman Catholics and Jews", written by Anthony Haig-Thomas.

The 911 terrorist atrocities in 2001, the volcanic ash cloud in 2010 and a glut of surplus pilots worldwide looking for work has taken the shine off aviation as I used to know it. Instead of being invited to join a company and having the type rating paid for, the industry now finds that rich parents are asking airlines to employ their sons or daughters as pilots, and are wiling to pay for the training. Having spent a large amount of money over the years training for my PPL, CPL and lastly my ATPL, I would still like to be **paid to fly, not pay to fly!** Also, the ever increasing security requirements have made it virtually impossible to take a friend for a flight, look around an aircraft at an airfield, or use your initiative in any way. A lot of what I have managed to describe in the book would be impossible today. Being able to go on the flight deck of an airliner gives interest and inspiration to young people wishing to take up a career in flying, either as a military pilot or in the airlines, but that is now impossible; even if the person is known to you.

Being out of work gave me the opportunity to write the book while attending a free "Return to Work" course at the Aspire Centre, Burford, near Tenbury Wells. I am deeply grateful for being able to use their facilities while writing the book and learning about computers along the way. They took a very nice photograph of me sat at my computer desk which is shown here.

This college campus is part of the Walford and North Shropshire College where it has excellent facilities for both computer studies and practical engineering training. It certainly kept me out of mischief for a year! Sadly, funding for the college course I did is no longer available so I shall not be doing any more computer studies there, but the facilities are excellent and high quality engineering courses for apprentice engineers are held there on a regular basis. I certainly got the motivation to write this book which I have successfully done. I am not sure what I will do in the future if I am unable to return to full time flying and regretfully, I have little other practical knowledge, skills or experience since all I have ever done is FLY. If this book is a success I might become an aviation writer or get involved in ground school teaching again. Who knows what might be around the corner; I could become a professional dog walker?

Wendy, my partner, has had to continue working during this time despite being over 60 but I have helped by regularly walking the three dogs we now have. She has found it difficult to cope having me at home all the time whereas when I was working, I was away most of the time. We have however managed a trip to France and Andorra to see Bob Watts who was one of the flying club directors at Cardiff seeing some of her own friends as well; and while working for Air Contractors, we both spent a week in the States. We also had a day out with the Red Arrows at RAF Scampton in April of 2009 as members of a Flying Farmers Association visit there. Despite threatening weather, we were all treated to a full display routine in clear skies and I was able to attend the de-briefing session afterwards during which a review of the previous display, which is always filmed, was made.

Isobel and Jenny the two Terriers have been with us for some time but we both inherited the Shetland Sheepdog Carly after Wendy's mother died early in 2010.

I am particularly thankful to several people for helping me on my way. Firstly there are my parents who were happy for me to pursue a career and interest different to farming. Then there was the owner of Shobdon airfield David Corbett, who helped me financially, told me off a few times and helped get me the Flight One job at short notice. Also, there was John Penny, a club member at Cardiff who urged me to take up the opportunity to go and work for the army when I had never been abroad before; and the management of BAC Express decided to keep me on after I had burst two tyres! The North Atlantic ferry flight was my most cherished memory. The most satisfying job was probably the Brymon job based at Birmingham flying the Twin Otter due to its routine and stability.

Unfortunately, Wendy is not a keen aviator, especially when flying in a light aircraft. I did take her up in Rachael Well's Jabiru G-CCAE for a short flight but she did not enjoy it even though she was still smiling when the photo was taken after the flight was over.

I do have some regrets as well. Not buying the Auster G-AIPW when it was offered to me for just £400 was one. Another was not

217

deciding to stay with Loganair after I had made my mistake as I liked Scotland and would inevitably have gone to live there. If had done that, I might not be currently out of work, writing this paragraph now and walking three dogs daily to keep fit. I also remember, somewhat wistfully, the day I did not succumb to the temptations of a particularly attractive lady when at Shobdon; despite her advances! Unfortunately, my loyalty to work meant that I had to go; otherwise it could have led to something more? Perhaps I should have rung in and reported sick? Leaving Flight One Ltd when I did in 1986 was another error as had I stayed another month or so, I would have got some redundancy money as they went out of business a short time later.

My biggest annoyance was having one persistent objector come to live close by the farm and airstrip. His constant complaints, which I am told, continue to this day, made both my life; and that of my parents difficult. I would like to give you a name but dare not to! The NIMBY culture of "Not in my back yard" will inevitably lead to opposition to any kind of airstrip development, however harmless it might be. At the planning enquiry into a proposed nearby airstrip at Hanley William, which unfortunately was lost, I asked the local council concerned, (who were opposed to the application), WHERE in their area of responsibility would they allow an airstrip to be developed for the use of their local rate payers who fly? They either would or could not answer my very sensible question!

I have made a few observations over the years and have a number of comments to make about flying in general. Once, someone who had built a microlight at Milson wondered why, when he was doing fast taxi runs up and down the airstrip prior to a planned first flight, it kept going the opposite way on the ground. Closer inspection revealed that the rudder control cables were crossed as they passed down the open fuselage. Numerous inspections and a final inspection by the local LAA inspector had failed to notice it. You do sometimes see what you want to see rather than what is actually there.

As a LAA coach and instructor, I have become aware that the altimeter and magnetic compass accuracy can be very poor on many home built light aircraft. I once went and checked the altimeter readings on a number of aircraft all parked on the same level location and they had up to 5 millibars of pressure difference when set to read zero on the ground. As for the aircraft's compass, if they are not correctly swung, and it is a complex task to accomplish a swing, the reading can vary widely on different headings due to

218

deviation caused by the magnetism and electrics within the aircraft. Never for example try and read a compass while transmitting on the radio and beware if you put any metallic object near to the compass.

Over the years I have written and used many types of checklist, some good, some bad but NO checklist is ever perfect. You will always find that something is in the wrong order or that someone thinks something should be done differently. That is why in commercial flying you have an agreed set of Standard Operating Procedures (SOP's), which you must use. This ensures a flight can be carried out safely whether you are flying with your lover or with someone you cannot stand the sight of. In most light aircraft you can get away with just doing a logical check around the cockpit but you should still have a printed final checklist to check and re-check with, rather than relying on memory. That said, military pilots are required to know all their checks on a particular type by heart before flying solo as they need to be able to fly semi-automatically when carrying out a military task possibly under fire. I mentioned a take off check list in an early Chapter but for a typical light aircraft, **"Test The Mags For Firing Or I Haven't a Chance"** can remind you of the **T**rim, **T**hrottle friction, **M**agnetos on, **F**uel on and correct tank with pump, **F**laps, **O**il temps and pressures, **I**nstruments , **H**arness and hatches and finally, **C**ontrols full and free.

Glider pilots are generally good at understanding the weather, but you must think wind when flying and plan ahead in your mind where you want the aircraft to go. Smooth and co-ordinated flying usually results in a good approach and landing but rash sudden movements and ill thought out actions can lead to a disaster. Remember also that if the **routine** is interrupted things can get difficult or mistakes can be made, so never assume, always check.

Two rule changes would be helpful, you can fly both a microlight and an aircraft but only flying an aircraft counts for the renewal of an SEP rating. This is absurd when the type and handling characteristics are sometimes almost the same, such as types like the Kitfox, Jabiru and the Eurostar, where only a weight difference makes the distinction. A microlight administered by the LAA with a "Permit to Fly", should in my view be acceptable. Also, an instructors test is not a flying licence check yet you are flying the aircraft throughout. I fell foul of that rule once and had to do another test to re-validate my pilots licence when the error was revealed.

I would like to emphasise to the reader that it is not just the idle rich who fly, although it does help if you have unlimited funds. When I was an instructor at Shobdon in the early 1970's I sent a student solo was still learning to fly TEN years later. That particular gentleman had no desire ever to get a full private pilots licence; all he wanted to do was to be able to fly around his local home area on his own on a nice day, when he could afford it. He was a local farm labourer with a poor education but he just enjoyed flying. I also met a young lady at Shobdon who had a clapped out motor car with bald tyres; she was a check out girl at a local Tesco's supermarket who was spending almost all her earnings learning to fly helicopters! When I suggested to her that she try flying light aircraft instead as it was much cheaper she said she had already tried that but was frightened of getting lost when flying on her own. She said that in a helicopter she felt much more relaxed; "If I get lost, I can land and ask the way?" Flying for pleasure attracts all kind of people, both rich and poor. It is very wrong for those who object to so called "noisy" aircraft, jealous of the fact that someone else is flying around defying the ground; when they themselves cannot hear themselves speak because of the noise of a local nearby motorway or railway line. No one at Otherton Airfield near to Stafford can fly before 10 am on a Sunday yet the M6 motorway is just a few yards away with almost continuous traffic noise. What hypocrisy?

Finally, when landing once at Inverness in the "Shed" I once had nine radar transponder blips come up on my TCAS readout on the VSI, approaching from behind just as I was about to touch down on Runway 23. The RAF **"Red Arrows"** flew directly overhead for a running break to land and came in to land behind me. Unfortunately I did not have my camera with me; you never do when something like that happens unexpectedly! Take care, think ahead, and safe flying, if you are thinking of trying it?

The photograph shows both Wendy and I at a function for a family friend, taken in 2009 shortly after I had been made redundant.

I hope you have enjoyed the reflections of a lucky civil pilot, who achieved his ambition to fly, against the odds!

Safe flying; **"never assume, always check"** was my alternative title for this book.

Wings of Death!

MOD in their wisdom sent, a pilot for the
regiment,
The one that came by name was Hugh
But there's one thing they did not do,
One small error in the halls of fame
As unfortunately they mislaid his brain.
He bumbles through the sky it seems, and
oblivious to the tortured faces,
Puts the Beaver through its paces.
Our CFI has had his fill of hurricane Hugh and
his need to kill,
But hurricane Hugh will not relent, to kill more
cars he is hell bent.
With hawk like eyes he scours the ground, until
at last his victims found;
Nose dips earthwards and down he flies, a glint
of fire in his steely eyes,
Swoops across his victim's path, no one can
escape Hugh's wrath.
The tails flicks down, the wheels dig in
With eagle like talons piercing the skin;
But this is just a game he plays, I don't get bored
is what he says,
God forbid is what we cry,
For he wants the job of CFI!

Anon

Statistical Facts.

During the course of writing this book, I have gradually transferred my 23 small log books on to the computer in order to check the accuracy of my hours and to give some vital statistics about my flying history. Listed below are all the various aircraft types which I have flown either as Captain and/or Co-Pilot; or as Co-Pilot or First Officer only. The various companies I have worked for can be best illustrated by copying part of my current CV. As I write this book, I hope that I will be able to continue flying for some time to come using the proceeds of this book to fund my flying for pleasure? Wishful thinking perhaps!

Aircraft Types Flown as Captain (Solo) or Co-Pilot/Dual.

Aero Commander 200 (single engine)
Aeronca L7 Grasshopper/Chief/Champ
Auster J1 Autocrat/Anglet
Acrosport Biplane
ARV Super Two
Avid Flyer
Beagle Terrier
Beech Musketeer/Sierra
Britten Norman BN2a Islander
Cessna 150 Tailwheel Conversion
Cessna 150/152
Cessna 172
Cessna 182
Cessna 185
Cessna 206
Currie Wot
De Havilland Beaver
De Havilland Chipmunk
De Havilland Twin Otter Series 300
Denny Kitfox
Druine Turbulent
Fournier RF4 Motor Glider
Glos Airtourer
Jabiru; both versions
Jodel D112/D119 Mascaret
Luscombe Silvaire
Motor Falke

Noorduyn Harvard
Piper Apache
Piper Arrow T Tail
Piper PA12 Super Cruiser
Piper PA18 Super Cub
Piper PA23 Aztec
Piper PA28 Cherokee 140/180
Piper PA34 Seneca
Piper PA38 Tomahawk
Piper Comanche
Piper J3 Cub
Piper Tripacer
PN68 Partenavia
Piston Provost
Rallye Club
Rallye Commodore
Rans S-10
Robin Knight/Regent/Royal
Rollason Condor
Scottish Aviation Twin Pioneer
Shaw Europa (monowheel)
Shorts SD 360
Streak Shadow
Sipa 903
Slingsby Firefly, civil and military
Stampe
Taylorcraft

Aircraft Types Flown as Co-Pilot/Dual only.

Antonov AN2 Biplane
Boeing Stearman Biplane
De Havilland Tiger Moth
Handley Page Dart Herald
Shorts SD 330
Zlin (Two types)

I also flew with the military as a passenger in an RAF Hastings, VC10, a Bell Huey (Vietnam style), Westland Wessex, Gazelle, Bell 47 Sioux, Scout and Squirrel helicopters, and a Hercules when I was able to stand on the rear ramp during the flight (with a safety strap on to prevent me from falling out).

223

Log Books Grand Total at Print of Book in September 2010.

Grand Total of Flying Hours with Individual Log Book Records, which is still increasing!

No	From	To	Flights	T/O & Lnds	Single P1 Day	Single P2 Day	Multi P1 Day	Multi P2 Day	Single P1 Night	Single P2 Night	Multi P1 Night	Multi P2 Night	Instruction	Lifts	Tows
1	16/08/1969	12/08/1970	556	869	329.00	69.15	0	0	2.75	5.55	0	0	131.30	28	20
2	13/08/1970	11/02/1973	567	1040	355.4	1	0	0	14.9	3.5	0	0	334.45	17	21
3	13/02/1973	13/07/1973	560	1008	345.6	2.65	0	1.4	4.9	0	0	0	309.3	6	34
4	14/07/1973	12/01/1974	577	1070	325.8	5.95	2.85	5.1	4.05	2.6	0	0	295.55	8	56
5	14/01/1974	31/07/1974	599	957	353.15	6.1	0	0	10.4	1.8	0	0	330.35	4	19
6	01/08/1974	13/03/1974	565	1071	379.7	1.3	0	0	38.55	0	0	0	385.35	15	0
7	14/03/1974	26/07/1975	475	904	349.1	0.6	0	0	2	0	0	0	309.75	465	7
8	26/07/1974	03/01/1977	599	1250	396.85	6.55	270.95	2.65	23.35	0	0	0	209.95	1005	37
9	03/01/1977	05/03/1978	620	1679	236.85	10.85	9.9	6.4	27.55	0	5.65	0	209.1	17	0
10	05/03/1978	10/12/1978	558	1118	450.8	16	1.3	0.4	26.45	0	0	0	431.85	0	0
11	11/12/1978	10/11/1980	560	820	234.35	12.5	555.15	121.45	22.15	0	0.75	57.95	207.45	76	0
12	10/10/1980	06/05/1984	568	694	99.75	2.35	244.6	46.6	3.3	0	2.45	62.45	6.95	0	5
13	10/05/1984	28/05/1987	554	701	194.45	38.7	0	14.75	1	0	200	1.8	130.1	0	0
14	28/05/1987	15/06/1988	557	565	0	0	243.35	12.75	0	0	408.25	2.5	0	0	0
15	16/06/1988	16/06/1988	571	580	6.7	0.5	564.7	2.25	0	0	48.1	0.25	0	0	0
16	23/05/1989	21/05/1990	615	621	7.65	0	557.75	46.3	0	0	51.7	7.7	0	0	0
17	21/05/1990	15/09/1996	581	709	221.25	23.7	3.35	179.85	2.4	1.4	2.6	26.9	54.6	0	0
18	23/09/1996	15/07/2001	1278	1694	286.9	13.5	0	120.85	5.9	0	0	630.85	167.75	0	0
19	15/07/2001	26/01/2003	556	595	78.5	1.3	0	41.45	0	0	0	329	23.75	0	0
20	26/01/2003	13/08/2004	550	680	71.2	2	0	76.3	0	0	0	465.75	51.65	0	0
21	16/08/2004	02/01/2006	548	670	62.55	1.8	0	65.85	0	0	0	488.45	48	0	0
22	04/01/2006	16/11/2007	676	773	41.05	0	0	170	0	0	0	493.5	26.45	0	0
23	17/11/2007	30/07/2010	582	721	69.45	5.45	71.4	127.3	0	0	172.95	103	48.8	0	0
Column Totals:-			13872	20789	4896.05	221.95	2525.3	1041.45	189.65	14.85	892.45	2670.1	3712.45	1641	199

Grand Totals at Book Print:- 12451.80

Log Book No 18 had twice the pages to all the others!

224

Companies worked for over the last 40 years, showing my last job first, are:-

     1. **HD Air Ltd** (Previously BAC Express Airlines and Air Contractors) SD360 First Officer since 1998, Captain since July 2008 flying UK and European routes for Fed Ex. This was mainly night and royal mail flying until recently.

     2. **Oxford Air Training School,** from 1997/8. Ground school instructor for one year teaching mainly navigational subjects.

     3. **Aviation Defence International** in 1997. Security Officer at Birmingham Airport for about three months in early 1997.

     4. **Brymon Airways** from 1988 to 1991 (Based at Birmingham airport). Twin Otter Single Crew Captain from 1988 to 1990 and then as an SD330 First Officer for three months prior to being made redundant early in 1991.

     5. **South East Air Ltd** in 1987 (Based <u>London Heathrow</u> and Southend airports). Single Crew Captain on Twin Otter flying night freight to Europe during 1987, mainly Maastrict and Brussels. Made redundant when company ceased trading.

     6. **Loganair Ltd** for One month in 1987. (Based Glasgow airport). Twin Otter Captain for one month but left due to aircrew error. Was offered alternative position on F27 but declined and returned to previous employer.

     7. **Hubbardair Ltd** in 1986 and again in 1987. Based Cardiff & Southend airports. Single Crew Twin Otter Captain flying night mail and freight flights within UK.

     8. **Flight One Ltd** from 1981 to 1986 (Based at Shobdon and Gloucester airfields). Single crew captain flying ancient Scottish Aviation Twin Pioneer on Survey and other research duties for 5 years. Left for a career change and more flying.

     9. **Channel Express in 1980** (Based Bournemouth airport). HP7 Herald First Officer for 9 months but made redundant due to financial difficulties. This was my first airline job away from light aviation and flying instructing etc.

     10. **Note** that between jobs and during periods of unemployment, I developed small farm and private airstrip at **Milson,** west of Birmingham in England. During these times carried out part time flying instruction with local flying clubs etc, but was not fully employed.

     11. **Prior to 1980**, I flew mainly light aircraft as a flying instructor at Cardiff and Shobdon. I was also a parachute dropping and glider tug pilot over a 10 year period from 1970 after I had first

learned to fly. This included a period of two years flying a DHC-2 Beaver in Cyprus and the BN2a Islander in West Germany with the British Army in 1976 and 1977.

12.   Before beginning an aviation career, I worked on Parent's farm after leaving school. I have a good general knowledge of farming activities, machinery, and tractor driving.

Postscripts to the written text:-

G-AWAW which in the book ended up in the Science Museum was withdrawn as a public exhibit several years ago and re-located to the aircraft store at Wroughton Airfield near Swindon. It has since been acquired by the Cessna 150/152 Club in the United States where it is to be restored and possibly returned to flight, so it is on the move again.

Finding a job is becoming increasingly difficult.   As a professionally trained pilot I am seeking to find work and be paid for doing it but as I have already said, the current state of the industry in 2010 is such that people are now prepared to "pay to fly" rather than being "paid to fly! What a turnaround in fortunes for employers and airlines alike.   One job I was interested in recently had over 200 applications in just 24 hours; and some of those pilots had current ratings on the aircraft type already, with a valid I/R as well.

John Ruskin's Quote seen at Moreton in Marsh.

This can be seen if you look to the left just after you have turned towards Oxford on the A44 trunk road in the centre of the town.   This print was taken from the "Google Streetmap" off the internet and is my chosen quote at the start of the book about my flying career.

The creation of Milson airstrip, my "Legacy to Aviation", is the reason why I thought it an appropriate quotation at the start of the book.

Emergency Landing for Pilot after Engine Fails.

A former South Shropshire airstrip owner was forced to make an emergency landing in a field after his plane cut out at around 2000 feet. Private pilot Hugh Thompson from Ludlow came down in a field near the Market Drayton Muller factory at around 10am today after his Kitfox plane suffered an engine failure.

Hugh Thompson is the former owner of Milson airstrip which is near to Cleobury Mortimer in the heart of the south Shropshire countryside. The stricken plane made a Mayday call which was picked up by RAF Ternhill. Controllers then diverted a nearby helicopter from RAF Shawbury to investigate.

Top instructor Squadron Leader Tim Whitcombe and trainee instructor Flight Lieutenant Harry Palmer rushed to the scene and found the small aircraft in a field around one mile from a nearby emergency landing strip. They landed and went to offer assistance but found Mr. Thompson unhurt and his aircraft undamaged.

Fly Lt Palmer said today: "We were about three miles north of Market Drayton doing some training when we heard his radio call. We flew over and saw him there. We made a landing a little distance away and I walked across to him to see if he had been injured or jarred his spine. He seemed pretty organised and had phoned his support team to come and get him". He added: "Every pilot fears an engine failure and most civvies don't come off as well as this guy. He must have done a great landing".

Note: This report is slightly inaccurate about facts, as are most newspapers, but it is re-produced as written. I was to meet Harry Palmer again about 4 years later when I went on an arranged meeting to the Defence Helicopter Flying School. I knew the face but could not recall when I had last seen him until I checked this newspaper report.

Appendix Two. National Farmers Union
Article printed in November 1954.

Shropshire Farming Series. Mr. and Mrs. GMH Thompson, New House Farm, Milson.

In Shrewsbury and in Wellington, "New Street" evidently means "just a little less old than the most ancient streets". At Milson, "New House Farm" means what it says for in 1947 when newly married Mr. and Mrs. Guy Thompson took over the 103 acres of land previously run as an off farm from Eastham, Worcestershire, there was no house at all on the land and only a very small amount of buildings of any sort. For two and a half years the Thompson's lived in a rented cottage near to the farm and began a paper battle with the authorities to obtain the necessary license and material permits for the building of a farmhouse on the land. The "Snow-Cem" finished "New House" now facing the afternoon sun is a very serviceable and well appointed homestead with its own water and home supplied electric light. The original cost of the bare dwelling was £2050, but some hundreds of pounds have been added for road making, fencing, gates, and the like.

A water supply was an essential requirement. This was provided by a borehole and overhead tank at a cost of something over £400, subject to grant aid. It was fortunately possible to keep this cost to a minimum by avoiding piping to fields because most of the farm is naturally watered by a good running stream. It has been said the Shropshire is particularly noted for its generous supply of Dutch barns. Few counties seem to value them more highly. Though there was and still is little permanent building on the farm a Dutch barn was regarded as essential and was erected in 1952 at a cost of just under £700. One bay of the barn has been sheeted down to become a store house. It is proposed to put a wood ceiling to this section and to form an upper storey. On the "weather" side of the barn a wide lean-to has been constructed for further fodder and general storage accommodation.

The land as purchased in 1947, without the fixed equipment, cost £3000. At the end of March 1952 valuation, machinery, implements, and vehicles were valued at £1960 and live and dead stock at £2345. The original capital brought into the business by the partners, Mr. and Mrs. Thompson. was under £600. The whole of the further capital required for the buying of land, buildings, livestock etc, was borrowed and substantial interest payments have to be made. Considerable enterprise and courage were needed for young people to face the financing of such a project. The accounts show that for the years 1949-51 quite useful profits were made, a

ii

large part of which were ploughed back into the business. Some £1330 worth of timber was sold and converted into working capital.

In the year ending March 1952, the profit was unsatisfactory. This result seems to have followed directly from temporary lower sales of milk and livestock produce with higher expenditure on seeds, fertilizers, cultivation costs and wages. Normally one full time man is employed plus a little casual labour as Mrs. Thompson also works regularly on the land.

Indeed it might be said that so does the fourteen month old baby boy, for each morning this summer, he has been at the milking bail in the open field immediately after the seven o'clock news.

There are seventeen mixed attested dehorned cows, and forty cattle in all. Use is made of the AI sub-centre in Bridgnorth to cross the best milkers with a Shorthorn bull and the others with a Hereford. The land is fairly strong and well suited to both milk production and cattle rearing. In winter the portable milking bail is brought to the homestead and stood on a concrete base. The cows have an open yard within the original old buildings to give some loose shelter and fodder space. The considerable amount of conserved grass silage and the six acres of root and kale are fed on the fields.

In 1951, 24 cross bred ewe lambs were brought and run with the ram. They produced 19 lambs in 1952 and 5 non breeders were graded. In February 1953, the 19 yearling ewes produced 27 lambs and 23 were graded in June for an average price of £8 10 Shillings. No corn was fed to either the ewes or lambs. Two breeding sows give satisfactory returns.

iii

The 9 farrows recently sold at 9 weeks old and one of them realized £7 10 Shillings a piece.

The cropping this year has been: Hay 26 acres, Silage, 5 acres cut twice plus 4.5 acres cut once, Oats 8 acres, mixed corn 6 acres, Wheat 2.5 acres, and potatoes 2.75 acres. All the crops are for consumption except the potatoes which are earlies and had failed to find a market, so the Ministry guarantee was invoked and they were expected to be moved in October.

Free market conditions are not necessarily the panacea for all ills at New House Farm. Some 10-13 years ago, about 9 acres of land were planted with standard Damson trees and a few Plums. The usefulness of Damsons as a cash crop has been varied. The past three years have given the following results: 1951 just over 4 tons sold at £80 a ton for £330, 1952, 8 tons picked realized just £80, about the cost of picking at 1 penny a Lbs with at least 4 tons rotting on the ground, 1953, 56 chips at 4 shillings a chip brought £11, 4 shillings as the sole return because of the lack of a crop. It should perhaps be added that these are grass orchards with livestock running under except when the fruit is on the trees. This kind of experience has been common to a great number of growers in the country south of the Clee Hills and elsewhere.

(Please note that this article was re-written with some minor grammatical errors corrected before this book was prepared for print).

Appendix Three. Navigational Competition at Shobdon.
(Note that I got 25 Bonus Points)

**Appendix Three. Herefordshire Aero Club
Navigational Competition. 26th April 1970**

Aircraft	Pilot	Time	Early or Late	Line Of Approach	Cottages	Hangars	Number	Colour	South West	North East	Penalty for Wrong Letter	No of Jumps	Total Penalties	Secret Check	Straight Approach to Check K	Final Score	Final Placing
Possible Number of Penalties		1 per Sec		25	10 or 20	10	10	10	10	10	25	25		25	25		
G-ATOR	L Thomas P Taylor	11	Late										11	25	25	+39	1
G-ARIV	J Hitchings	17	Early										17	25	25	+33	2
G-AXIX	D Miles	32	Early										32	25	25	-7	3
G-ATIE	Mrs Turner	20	Late								25		45	25		-20	4
G-AJRK	G L Cross	1	Late								25	25	51	25		-26	5
G-AKEL	F B Miles	67	Early					10	10				87	25	25	-37	6
G-AXJH	R Gaskell	38	Late										38			-38	7
G-ATWE	R J Hale	15	Late					10	10	10	25		70		25	-45	8
G-AXHX	P McGregor	54	Early								25		79			-79	9
G-ATLV	B H Lewis	114	Early				10				25		149			-149	10
G-AVAW	G V Blakeway	111	Early				10	10			25		156			-156	11
G-AUZ	**Hugh Thompson**	178	Late			10	10	10	10				208		25	-183	12
G-AREZ	C Roberts	188	Late					10	10	10	25		243			-243	13
G-AWMP	J Williams	226	Early								25		251			-251	14

Note I am third from bottom but did correctly identify the letter at Check "K" and got 25 bonus points for straight approach to Check "K". Not bad for a Student Pilot having to fly on his own..

V

Appendix Four, Part One. CAA Hearing Consultations in 1978 Prior to Issue of Commercial Class One Medical in 1979.

Air Commodore King
Central Medical ... nt
Royal Air Force
Kelvin House
Cleveland Street
LONDON, w1   3 November 1978

Dear Air Commodore King

Re: Hugh THOMSON 26 years PRIVATE PILOT/INSTRUCTOR

I would be grateful for your opinion on the above pilot who has
re-applied for a Commercial Pilot's Licence after being turned
down in 1973 on grounds of a long standing hearing deficit.

He was first seen in 1956 when he was 13 years old by Mr J L Godden
an ENT Surgeon at the Hereford General Hospital. The diagnosis of
bilateral high tone perceptive deafness was made at that time but
we have no record of his audiogram.

In 1973 he was assessed unfit for a Commercial Licence on the
grounds of High Tone Hearing Deafness and his audiogram is as follows:

Right		Left
60	3000	65
60	2000	70
20	1000	15
20	500	10

We have another audiogram carried out in 1975 and it is unchanged.

Since he was assessed unfit for a Commercial Licence he has demonstrated
considerable ability as a Private Pilot and Flying Instructor. He has
now logged over 3,000 hours including flight to Europe and the Mediterranean
and he is now asking whether we would re-consider him for a Commercial
Licence. We would like to have your opinion before we make any other
arrangements for medicals.

Many thanks for your assistance.

Yours sincerely

FILMED

DR E A DE LA MARE
Medical Assessment Board

This letter was sent to the RAF Central medical establishment in November of 1978 seeking an opinion on whether or not to issue me with a commercial pilot's medical certificate. The response is given overleaf.

Air Commodore P E King OBE FRCS(E) DLO MRAeS RAF

⑤

Consultant Adviser in Otorhinolaryngology

Central Medical Establishment
Royal Air Force Kelvin House
Cleveland Street
LONDON W1P 6AU

Tel: 01-636 4651

FILMED

6 December 1978

Dr E A De La Mare
Medical Assessment Board
Civil Aviation Authority
Space House
43-59 Kingsway
London
WC2B 6TE

/id 8/12/78.

Dear Dr De La Mare

RE: MR HUGH THOMSON 26 YEARS PRIVATE PILOT/INSTRUCTOR

Thank you for asking me to see Mr Thomson today, who is a candidate for a
CPL. He is a private pilot and instructor of some years' standing, and has
flown in this capacity for the Army in Cyprus. He has notched up over
4,000 flying hours. He is a known case of high tone hearing loss and
essentially my audiogram, a copy of which is shown below, is not really much
different from that which you sent me.

By audiometry he falls below the standard of hearing requirement 1. On the
other hand he has a fair amount of flying experience so that one could apply
the let-out clauses which relate to those with hearing worse than the
profile for the hearing requirement.

He easily hears a conversational voice at 2 metres with both ears open, and
I think if he passed a test of simulated material which is operated by the
CAA, one could consider him for a CPL.

With all good wishes.

Yours sincerely

LOSS DECIBELS		
R EAR	FREQUENCY	L EAR
80	8000	85
60 65	4000	70 45
55	3000	70 55
60 50	2000	70 60
20 15	1000	15 5
10	500	10
10	250	20 85

FILMED

vii

Appendix Five. First VFR Trip into Europe.

Ever thought of flying yourself around part of Europe on holiday? Well, this summer one club member decided to do just that, using a Cessna 172 G-CLUX, which had a full compliment of radio equipment including R Nav. That, for the uninformed, is a complicated electronic gadget enabling you to move your VOR/DME beacons to where you want them; i.e. on direct tracks between airfields or turning points. Nearly 13 hours were flown over a 10 day period where a 2 night stay at each stopover was planned. The trip began from Compton Abbas, a delightful grass airfield in Dorset: well worth a visit if members are planning a cross country.

First stop was at Amsterdam's main airport at Schiphol after first clearing customs at Southampton. The landing fee there was expensive at £10.35 but was pleasantly offset by a charge of only £12.50 at Schiphol for the initial landing and 2 days parking. Although up to Heathrow standards with 6 runways, it is relatively easy to fly into by following a specific VFR routing procedure and good pre-flight planning which is essential. It may not be appreciated by pilot members that a free service for overseas flights is available from the Aeronautical Information Services (A.I.S.) where, on request, they will send you mainly photo-copies of any necessary documents/routes etc. They will, even take the trouble to underline any important points for you. You must however, provide your own up to date maps and Radial Nav charts, frequency books etc

Next stop on the tour was Wilhelmshaven in Northern Germany where the landing fee and parking came to only £5. Fuel however required payment in cash which is usual at small light aviation fields so one must be prepared to visit the bank! The main reason for going there was to visit an ex-instructor member of the club; Alan Munro. Alan, Who is still in the RAF and currently working for NATO, and his wife Wendy, send their regards and best wishes to club members who remember their time at Shobdon.

After a two day stay, a long flight across Germany, Holland Belgium and France was made at FL 45; VMC on top for most of the way. The rules for VFR overseas allow this; even in the airways up to certain levels but once again good pre-flight planning is needed to ensure you stay legal all the way, as the rules vary from country to country and there may still be specific restricted or danger areas to negotiate. The destination was Beauvais, north of Paris, where there is a large Gothic cathedral.

When preparing to leave Beauvais for Guernsey, it was discovered that at Rouen, directly on track, an air show was being held. It was decided to visit the show where an enjoyable PFA (Now LAA) type light aircraft meeting took place. This particular day was very hot and dry and resulted in a blocked pitot on departure for Guernsey. Initially there was no airspeed at all but after 30 minutes or so an incorrect reading was given being about 20 knots slower for the rest of the holiday. This, as one can imagine, is more dangerous than having none at all, but with the aircraft being flown only in good weather, it was acceptable despite only showing 40-50 Kts on approach.

The arrival at Guernsey was via the usual VFR route from Cap-de-Flamanville and being under special VFR within the Jersey Zone could be refused by A.T.C. Pilots are therefore advised, in fact required, to ring Jersey before flying to the Channel Islands and could save themselves an embarrassing abort or diversion. (Read the Air Pilot in the clubhouse for the details). Guernsey is a good place for a flying visit. Food is good, accommodation cheap with no VAT, the landing fee for a Cessna 172 only £5.25 and you get unlimited parking free.

The final, flight was a return to Compton Abbas routing via Exeter for customs where a surprise landing fee of only £3.45 was charged; rather different to £10.35 we had to pay at Southampton. On arrival at Compton, the A.S.I. was rectified, the culprit being a Mudfly Beetle, It is no coincidence that several aircraft have had ASI problems during the hot dry weather, therefore if a cover is available, ensure it is put on during hot dry weather while parked.

To conclude, an enjoyable 10 day trip to 5 destinations in 4 countries, in a little less than 13 hours. The aircraft's radio gear Including the R Nav was exciting to use particularly routing into Schiphol and Guernsey as it provided accurate track guidance. To other club members, I say such a trip is recommended. Cost sharing will make it cheaper than you think, and you only have yourself to please and experience to gain. For Deborah Wright and Hugh Thompson, it was a success with a very good aircraft and ideal flying weather giving excellent visibility.

Note that this report was written in the autumn edition of the Herefordshire Aero Club newsletter in 1984, hence the price differences and there is no mention of GPS which wasn't invented then! The facts are correct for that date.

Appendix Six.
"Linkman Hugh Keeps Things Going."

A big thank you was on its way today to a 22 year old flying instructor who linked the control tower to aircraft during communications problems at Glamorgan (Rhoose) Airport. Hugh Thompson, the Chief Flying Instructor with the Pegasus School of Flying had just taken off in his light aircraft when a power cable was cut through during work on the airfield.

Part of Job:- Radio communications was hit and emergency procedures were brought into force. Hugh landed, moved off the runway and sat listening to find what was happening. "I took over relaying messages because I was the only one able to hear air traffic control properly", he said today. During the ten minutes he acted as linkman, three aircraft including a Viscount and an HS 125 jet were brought into land.
"Somebody had to do it, and it happened to be me", said Hugh. "I did not become air traffic control, but merely passed on instructions". "It is all part of the job". Hugh, the youngest chief flying instructor in the country has been with the Pegasus Club for six months. Mr. Keith Mack, the Civil Aviation Authority chief officer at Rhoose said the emergency communications system had had a much sorter range than intended due to flat batteries. We were having a little difficulty speaking to some of the aircraft.

Grateful:- Mr. Thompson was sitting in his aircraft on the other side of the airport. We gave normal air traffic control instructions over the emergency radio and he was simply passing on the messages for us. "This is the sort of thing which happens from time to time; sometimes in the air. We are very grateful for what he did and we will be relaying our thanks to him", said Mr. Mack.

Explanation:- The Incident occurred while I was in Cessna 150 G-AYRP, and reported in the South Wales Echo Newspaper in October 1974. My aircraft appeared to be the only one able to hear the control tower after the main power cable to ATC was cut and it was found that the emergency batteries were almost flat!

Appendix Seven. Daily Telegraph Sales Article.

Sheep may safely graze during take-off. Buy Little Down Farm and you'll be able to fly home, says Chris Arnot; and you could get a tractor thrown in free?

Taking off: Little Down Farm is a paradise for sheep; and pilots!

SHEEP may graze safely in large parts of Shropshire without being disturbed by much more than the occasional tractor or Land Rover. After all, this is one of England's most under populated counties. But the sheep that crop the grass on some of the 62 acres at Little Down Farm, just south of the sparse and brooding Shropshire Hills, have become used to traffic. Aerial traffic, for the most part. RAF helicopters drop in twice a week, and land on an aluminium pad right in their midst. Traffic flow on the adjoining airstrip is rather less predictable. Planning permission has been granted for up to 10 flights a day for small aircraft and microlights. No wonder my Rover 25 causes hardly a ripple of apprehension among the grazing flock as it bounces alongside them, down a long, rutted track towards the house on the horizon.

It turns out to be a surprisingly modern house at close quarters. "Compact", too, to use estate agents' vernacular. Or perhaps that's just an illusion created by this great sweep of spectacularly hilly countryside in which it was built 10 years ago. Certainly, the building seems big enough inside.   There are three decent-size bedrooms (one en suite) and a spacious, handsomely tiled kitchen with an oil-fired Rayburn. The views from every room are stunning, but it is the foreground that makes this sale intriguing. "This is the only small, private airstrip in south Shropshire with planning consent," says the owner, Hugh Thompson, as we take a stroll down the strip.

A few molehills provide the only deviation from the horizontal for 1,500ft where the land begins to slope upwards again. An electric fence keeps the sheep at bay. "Otherwise we'd have droppings all over the planes," he continues. "I keep the grass down myself. I'm prepared to throw the tractor in with the sale of the house and land to someone who wants to keep the strip going.

"I haven't worked on this for nearly 30 years to see it disappear. It's not commercially viable, but it would be ideal for an aeroplane enthusiast who wants to park on his front lawn and take a flip on a nice summer's day." Mr. Thompson has been an enthusiast since he was a teenager. His farming father had sent him to a boarding school in Herefordshire that happened to be almost next door to Shobdon airfield. "I used to hang around there at weekends, doing odd jobs and being rewarded with the occasional five-minute flip," he recalls, fondly.

By the age of 19, he was already a flying instructor and evidently not inclined to follow in father's wellie-prints on the farm. "I wanted to join the RAF," he admits, "but my eyesight and hearing wasn't good enough." So he became a contract pilot instead. He now flies freight, including the Royal Mail, between Bristol, Stansted and Norwich, and needs to move closer to his starting point, hence the sale. Included in the price are two tubular structures with steel frames. They could be put to agricultural use but, right now, they are acting as aircraft hangars.

Other enthusiasts park their Kitfoxes, Streak Shadows and Turbulents here. What is more, they pay rent for the privilege. The new buyer could look forward to an annual income of more than £4,000 from this source. "That's not to be sniffed at," Mr. Thompson suggests, "at a time when farms have to diversify to increase revenue". Little Down also receives £5,000 from the farmer who grazes his sheep on its land.

The arrangement with the Defense Helicopter Flying School is less lucrative. In fact, this frustrated would-be air force pilot lets them use his pad for the price of a day out at RAF Shawbury once a year and a slap-up dinner in the mess. "I believe our armed forces should be supported," he says. "The helicopters are only here for about 10 minutes, twice a week." That's rather too long for one of his neighbours, who evidently disapprove of the noise emanating from both the helipad and airstrip. As a result of his complaints to the local authority, no flying is allowed on Sunday afternoons in the summer. Mind you, "neighbours" in these parts hardly live on top of one another. Little Down lies nearly four miles from the handsome town of Cleobury Mortimer and about a mile from the hamlet of Milson. And the nearest house is at least half a mile away, at the far end of a rutted track and beyond many, many sheep. Published by Chris Arnot: 12:00 am GMT 18 Nov 2000. This property sales report was published in the Saturday edition of the Daily Telegraph newspaper when the farm was first put on the market.

Appendix Eight.
Personal Reflections on Flying the Monowheel Shaw
Europa Aircraft.

After becoming a PFA Coach Pilot in 1996, I had the opportunity to get checked out on the Shaw Europa (Monowheel) version and after an interesting hour with John Brownlow in August 1998, soloed on type. Being a tailwheel trained Auster pilot in my early days, I did not find it difficult but must state right away that as this type of Europa is unique to itself it should not be a problem if you have never flown any tailwheel types before. It is similar in its undercarriage design to many gliders, like the Motor Falke, and Fournier RF4/5 aircraft. One comment about the airfield used was that it was one of the roughest grass strips I had ever experienced up to that time. Sadly I have to report that it was at Cambridge but I am told that previous dry summers had caused the ground to dip in places. Similar problems also occur at Barton (Manchester) which is why it is an on going problem to try and level the grass runways there. Repair one bump and another appears!

Since then, I have carried out a number of type conversions on to this aircraft, one of which resulted in an accident due to a lack of experience and complacency; using both grass and hard runway surfaces. To date, I have flown just over 160 hours during 260 logged flights with up to 1000 Landings and Take Offs. Personally, I have found grass much more forgiving and helpful if it is smooth enough, but if you can master the art of keeping it straight on a hard runway after you have landed the aircraft, so much the better. More on take offs and landings later.

The Europa is an excellent aircraft to fly when airborne and if equipped with a variable pitch (vp) and/or constant speed propeller flies like a small fighter aircraft. Lookout is perfect, handling is crisp and lively with a good roll rate and it can be safely flown clean or with the gear and flaps down, but at a much reduced speed. It does take some time to get used to flying it especially if you have a variable pitch propeller, and a lot of practice is needed at raising and lowering the gear/flap combination without violently pitching about as you move the lever! You have to get used to holding an attitude in pitch visually while you raise and lower the gear/flap.

If you have not flown a variable pitch propeller aircraft before, it is important to have a good understanding of the principles before trying it. Basically the power output is indicated with a manifold pressure gauge and the RPM is dependent on the pitch setting. Some aircraft will have a pitch setting indication only, others only a manifold pressure gauge, and some, both; depending on the individual builder's choice. When increasing the engine power output advance Pitch or RPM before the throttle or manifold

xiii

pressure and when reducing power, reduce the manifold pressure first. It is worthy to mention, that if you do have a vp/constant speed prop, any carburettor icing will be indicated by a gradual drop in manifold pressure rather than engine rpm. One student of mine who had some difficulty understanding both the aircraft and propeller at the same time suggested that early on you simply set the propeller in fine or nearly fine pitch, and simply leave it alone, treating the aircraft as if it had a fixed pitch propeller; which is the case on some Europa's anyway.

Flying the Europa in the air is hard work initially due to its increased speed in the cruise; you need to think ahead and give yourself plenty of room to slow down before lowering the undercarriage and flaps at 83 Knots or less. If you have a vp prop reducing the blade angle, i.e. making it finer, helps to slow you down as the prop acts as an airbrake. Also, remember that power plus attitude gives you performance so it is important to hold the pitch attitude constant when lowering or raising the gear. As every homebuilt Europa is different, I cannot give specific details on speeds, power settings etc but a typical cruise speed with a vp prop is about 120 Knots, best climb and descent speed is 75 Knots (if gliding with the flap/gear up) and around 60 Knots with the gear/flaps down; such as during a forced landing. In reality however, you would normally establish both a cruise climb and descent when flying on a cross country to give yourself maximum endurance and range; once a safe height after take off has been reached.

As for taking off and landing, both a difficult task initially for a newcomer, especially if they have had no previous tailwheel experience, on balance I think the Take Off is more challenging as you have full power applied! It does not matter if you do not have any previous tailwheel experience although any flying experience helps, as the aircraft in unique in its handling characteristics. Keeping it straight is the difficulty so you must have foot pressure applied to both rudder pedals, look ahead and outside the cockpit while you apply power and initially keep the stick fully back to ensure you have directional control. Early in the take off roll you will have no aerodynamic effect on the control surfaces unless there is a very strong headwind. Only when you reach 30-35 Knots on the ASI can you relax the back pressure on the stick and if it is then kept almost neutral, the aircraft will leave the ground on its own depending on the position set on the trimmer. This depends on the amount of fuel and baggage carried but I tend to trim it slightly nose down to ensure the aircraft does not pitch up sharply as it gets airborne. Do not physically put the stick forward to raise the tail like you would do on normal tailwheel aircraft; this will almost certainly lead to a loss of control especially at the lower speed early in the take off roll. It is also important to get full power applied smoothly and quickly. Trying to take off with less than full power will only prolong the agony of trying to keep it straight. Finally, as you get airborne ensure you have a safe airspeed before allowing the aircraft to climb away. I would like to make one final note about taking off. When you have plenty of experience and know your own aircraft, it is possible to concentrate on keeping it straight only and holding the ailerons neutral, simply allow the all moving tailplane to move itself providing the trim is correctly set. If you look at your aircraft you will see that it is already sitting in the required take off attitude so there is no need to try and raise the tail at all!

Raising the gear/flap combination after getting airborne can cause problems until you get familiar with it. Spectators often wonder why monowheel Europa pilots appear to lose control at about 2-300 feet. This is when you pitch violently up and down when trying to raise the gear and push the level into its recessed up position. You must concentrate on keeping a constant attitude by looking outside at the natural horizon while moving the undercarriage lever. This is easier said than done when you first try it but practice will soon make the manoeuvre easy to accomplish.

Landing the aircraft is potentially more difficult as it is very possible to ground loop it after touching down and you think the landing has been successful! In any tailwheel type aircraft no landing is ever complete until it has come to a complete stop. You must not relax your concentration or stop looking ahead until you have virtually stopped moving. It is no good making a smooth landing and then looking at your passenger with a smile or trying to find the brake lever only to subsequently ground loop it, yanking on the brake and either tipping it on its nose or scraping the wingtips!

You cannot make a good landing unless you first make a good circuit and a nice trimmed out approach at the correct airspeed. The Europa manual suggests 60 Knots as the final approach speed but, subject to the weight of your own aircraft, feel that about 55 Knots (Vat) at the runway or touchdown threshold is about right; as you do not want to prolong the float and when it does land, it is desirable to stay on the ground rather than get airborne again. Believe it or not, some Europa pilots, even experienced ones, have managed to land it with the gear and flaps up, especially when there is a strong headwind and the approach attitude looks normal. The difference approaching to land with the gear up is the Airspeed indication; it will be at least 10-20 Knots faster than normal. During training I get all my students to deliberately make an approach with the gear up just to impress on them how easy it is to forget it. So far, I have remembered to "Go Around". You may think this will never happen to you; but it might?

Apart from keeping it straight after landing, and this is the difficult part for most pilots, it is important to attain the correct attitude in pitch when checking the rate of descent and holding off. If this is achieved correctly, it will land when the speed dissipates. If a small bounce occurs which often happens, just hold the attitude? Do not relax the back pressure on the stick or put the nose down. If you achieve a touchdown before you get the stick right back, continue to do so and make sure the throttle is completely closed. As far as the attitude is concerned, keep whatever seating position you are used to so as not to change the apparent attitude for your aircraft. Someone else's Europa may be different so before getting airborne take a moment when you line up to study again what you're particular landing attitude happens to be! It is highly recommended that you sit as high as possible; using added cushions if necessary.

Throughout the landing you must concentrate on looking ahead out of the cockpit and working the rudder to keep it straight. If there is a crosswind you can only keep the wings level and maintain the runway centre line with the rudder, straightening it just as you land. Only then can you use the ailerons to lower the upwind wing. If you try the wing down method then it is possible that the outrigger wheel will make contact with the runway surface first causing a swing. It is perfectly possible to bounce it a little as all the weight is on one main wheel but I find that on grass this rarely happens; unless it is a really bad arrival. If you have a choice, a grass landing is much more forgiving on the aircraft, if it is a smooth airstrip; and it is much easier to keep it straight as you slow down. In my one accident, directional control was lost late in the landing run and the aircraft ground looped on a hard surface. Unfortunately both the student and I applied the brake which resulted in the aircraft tipping on to its nose. If you are confronted with a ground loop, keep the stick back, switch off the ignition, and do not apply the brake. You may then get away with it, if you are lucky!

During the flying I have obtained on the monowheel version of the Europa, I have gained some valuable tips on various items. One of these is the fuel tank. As it is made of a glass fibre or plastic material and moulded together when built, it takes some considerable time to get all of the very fine debris out of the system. On one occasion after we had flown about three hours on a newly built aircraft, I advised the owner to check the fuel filters. He forgot to do so, and on our next flight we lost power during the take off and initial climb. On reducing power the engine ran smoothly again. I immediately asked if the filters had been checked. Being given a negative answer, I knew what the problem was. If rough running does occur, change to the reserve; part of the same tank in practice but with the fuel now coming via a feed line which will have had much less use and a fresh filter! Also the capacity of around 70 litres can vary from tank to tank especially if venting of the air in the sealed tank is a problem. Some owners are often unsure whether their fuel contents gauge is with or without the reserve content of about 12-15 litres.

When I went to fly with a new Europa owner who was an experienced Ex RAF and British Airways pilot, we got in and he wanted to start with the MAIN tank selected. I advised him to always start on the RESERVE to check that fuel line is working ad is not blocked, then to do the engine run up and checks on the MAIN. We did this, and the engine soon stopped. Try starting it with the fuel OFF I suggested which it did! The previous owner and builder had connected the fuel pipes incorrectly and the fuel was in fact off when reserve was selected and vice versa. The previous owner had always selected and left in on the MAIN. Apparently, it must have also been missed during inspections and during air testing, so never assume, always check.

The PFA appears to be very concerned about the provision of stall warning devices on the monowheel type of Europa requiring all aircraft to have a 4 to14 Knots warning of the stall. I personally think this is unnecessary if you have been trained properly and remember what the true symptoms of an approaching stall are. I know of some owners who simply disconnect the warning as it distracts them from concentration during both take off and landing. There is no harm done having some kind of warning but when I leant to fly they did not exist; on the Auster. Having said that, there was a more pronounced natural buffet on older types of aircraft than there are today's more modern designs.

As there is only one main wheel and no differential braking, the turning circle of the single wheel Europa is a fixed radius. This can cause problems on narrow taxiways and runways. You must think ahead and use any crosswind component to your advantage. Accelerating a little prior to a turn can give you more momentum but do not be surprised if your passenger, if you have one, eventually has to get out and lift the tail round one day. Only by experience can you get an appreciation of the possible difficulties.

One very good tip if parking for long periods on a grass surface is that prior to getting in and starting, always move the aircraft slightly by hand. As all the weight is effectively all on one wheel, it can sink into soft ground making it virtually impossible to move, except with full power; which with a possible cold engine is not a very good idea. With even a hot engine, a high burst of power could end up putting the aircraft on its nose; an event I have witnessed at least once and heard about many times.

There are two modifications I would like to see on the aircraft. Firstly, the one landing accident I had was possibly caused by the port outrigger wheel not locking down correctly. On an earlier flight we had had a ground loop in the same direction as a result of the port wing lowering. On that occasion we got away with it but sadly not the next time. I do remember that on one aircraft you could hear the outrigger wheels clicking into position about 10-15 seconds after the gear and flaps had been lowered. To ensure the outrigger wheels are down, I would like to see a modification done so that when they extend fully a small pinhead painted red (or some other colour) would protrude slightly above the upper wing surface. As you cannot see these small extended wheels in flight, there is currently no way of knowing if they have fully extended! In feedback prior to publication of this article, the owner has confirmed to me that tests proved that the port outrigger wheel was not locking down correctly!

As far as the accident was concerned, the owner decided to convert his aircraft into the Tri-Gear version, so regrettably he never achieved his aim of flying it solo as a monowheel. This was a pity. Unfortunately he subsequently suffered a nose wheel failure as well and ended up selling his aircraft.

The second modification also concerns the undercarriage. On two occasions in turbulence, I have had the gear come down inadvertently at cruising speed; nearly taking the end of my finger off the second time. It would be nice to see a secondary up lock incorporated to prevent the main gear lever coming unlatched unless deliberately intended. However, this event appears to have been an isolated case on one aircraft but nevertheless would be a useful additional safety aid. This would be similar to the fitted down lock safety catch which all monowheel Europa aircraft are required to have.

Based on all the experience gained to date, I have prepared a basic list of good advice for any monowheel Europa owner. I have found some conversions easy to accomplish, whilst others have been more difficult. As an instructor, I cannot teach anyone to fly the aircraft; they have to do it themselves in the end. What I can do, is demonstrate, advise where they are making errors, and suggest ways of overcoming any difficulties. My list, which applies to the monowheel version only, is given below:-

1. Landings are not finished until it comes to a complete stop. As you slow up, directional control becomes very twitchy as you lose any aerodynamic effect and tailwheel becomes the only way to keep straight.

2. Keep Foot pressure on both rudder pedals to ensure positive control and feel. Anticipate application of right rudder as you get airborne to keep straight; depending of course on the wind and engine fit.

3.   Aircraft is more difficult to Take Off and Land with NO wind. Best conditions are a gentle light headwind of say 10 Knots. No wind makes one complacent and ground loops often happen when you least expect them.

4   On Take Off keep stick fully back until you are conscious of a positive forward movement, either by outside reference or noting airspeed at end of yellow arc at 30-35 Knots on some ASI's. As you become airborne you need to prevent the nose pitching up to ensure a safe airspeed then climb away. Look well ahead at all times.

5.   On landing speed control is essential. Aim for 50-55 on round out and do not over rotate and get nose too high. There is a tendency is to check a little on the high side. Make sure Stick is moved fully back and throttle is closed. If you make a small bounce do not let stick go forward just hold it steady. The Aircraft manual says 60 Kts as the final approach speed with touchdown around 45-50 Knots; but my experience suggests that is a little fast! However, for a heavier Europa, 65 Knots may be a better speed.

6.   As you slow up on landing do NOT look for the brake lever, you may lose directional control. Apply brake only if need be, gently. Keep looking ahead.

7.   On Take Off be positive. Start from a FULL Stop if you can and look and study attitude as a reminder. When applying full power, do so quickly and smoothly. Remember to hold the stick back initially while applying the power.

8.   Do not find yourself high and fast on approach. Give yourself plenty of room to slow down. In any light crosswind, keep wings level on approach and use rudder to maintain the centre line. Work the rudder throughout the approach.

9.   Aircraft prefers grass for both Landings and Take Off's rather than tarmac or concrete, if you have a choice, and it is smooth enough!

10.   Since we all fly for pleasure, if the wind is not right, leave it for another day!

11.   Always start engine on the "Reserve" tank selection and change to Main" prior to engine run up. This will ensure both fuel lines are clear and working correctly.

12.   80% of all accident, incident, and insurance claims are ground related. If you are ever in any doubt, stop, shutdown, get out, and move the aircraft manually; otherwise you might end up with a bent propeller or damaged wingtip.

Prior to publication, I sent a draft of this article to all the Europa Owners I have flown with, and the manufacturer. Very positive feedback was forthcoming and a number of changes have been made as a result, including my spelling mistakes. One comment was that I should consider seeking a commission from the Europa manufacturer for all the Tri-Gear conversions I might induce as a result. There is however a great degree of personal satisfaction to be gained from a successful monowheel conversion which will give any pilots a great degree of confidence when flying other types of tailwheel aircraft; including a Spitfire if you were so lucky!

I have also learnt as a result of the feedback I received, that the LAA now require a manifold pressure gauge to be fitted to all variable pitch propeller aircraft. This may have been the result of one of my reports when I expressed surprise that there was no indication of the power output on one aircraft. During air testing of that particular Europa, I had a nasty scare when I was mis-informed about the propeller pitch setting; which I was told had been adjusted! I made a take off with the fine pitch setting too fine and was barely able to stay airborne, right on the stall, until I had the presence of mind to increase the blade angle; i.e., make it coarser. The engine rpm was also exceeded by a wide margin and my first action was to reduce the power. Another important point is that if you are doing fast taxi runs prior to an intended first flight always secure your harness fully and close both canopies; just in case you inadvertently get airborne. As I understand it, there was once an unfortunate fatal accident (which was not witnessed) at a private grass strip where the owner probably did not intend to fly, yet got airborne without being strapped in.

Finally, as a summary, can I say that the standard monowheel Europa is an excellent aircraft, handles very nicely in the air like a small fighter, but it can be a handful during both take off and landing. Good training is required to ensure a safe operation and you must expect problems at any time; especially when there is no wind, when you may become a little complacent! My aim in writing this article has been to promote increased awareness and flight safety when flying this particular aircraft which has, in the past, gained a bad reputation as a result of the number of accidents which have occurred; particularly during landing.

Appendix Nine.
Instrument Flying Summary.

The purpose of this article is to summarize how to fly a light aircraft on instruments, both using a full and limited panel. The information has been obtained from many flying training manuals and personal experience but cannot be guaranteed to be the only correct way to safely fly an aircraft on instruments. You cannot beat experience so, even if you knew all this by heart, proper training and constant practice is a must if flying IMC or "Under the Hood" is to become a natural activity like driving your car.

The first thing to be said about flying on instruments is that is **exactly** the same as flying visually with a good natural horizon, the only difference being that you cannot see it due to cloud, heavy rain, or haze. The natural horizon has, on a full panel, been replaced with an artificial horizon (A/H) also known as an attitude indicator (A/I). The problem is that the pilot is usually more tensed up (naturally if in bad weather conditions), and has a tendency to over control the aircraft; i.e., he or she is not relaxed and incorrectly in trim.

When first experiencing the need to fly on instruments, the complexity of the instrument panel in front of you might look daunting. However, as we shall see, there is no need to try and look at all of the instruments at the same time. In fact, the key is to establish the correct radial scan of a selected number of instruments depending on what stage of the flight you are carrying out; whether climbing, turning, descending, or indeed flying straight and level. On modern displays, some of these instruments may be combined in which case the appropriate scan of the instruments will be different.

The Instrument panel of modern light aircraft can vary markedly due to the types of instruments and equipment fitted; such as a GPS moving map display etc. However, all must have an airspeed indicator, altimeter, some kind of turn and/or balance indicator, a compass, and engine rpm or power output. The compass and engine power instruments are elsewhere on the aircraft, as are the Flaps which change the wing shape to create more lift and/or drag at lower speeds. Those intended for instrument flying also have other instruments fitted such as an attitude/artificial horizon and a directional indicator. In a normal light aircraft used for training, these instruments are normally laid out in a standard manner to give what is called a full "T" panel but more modern aircraft can combine several instruments into one presentation. The conventional T layout, found in most club aircraft today is illustrated on the next page:-

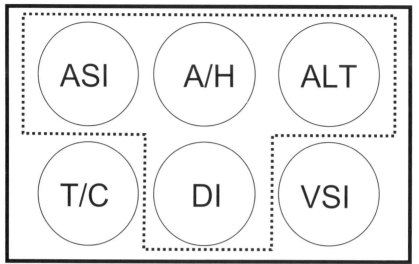

Shown are the ASI Airspeed Indicator, A/H Artificial Horizon or Attitude Indicator, ALT Altimeter, T/C Turn Indicator or Turn Co-ordinator & Balance Ball, DI Directional Indicator or Gyro Compass,
and the VSI Vertical Speed Indicator

The layout shown is the one used on all small training aircraft. In the military the "T" is prominently shown by a white outline and they only use a standard turn indicator. The reason for not using the more modern turn co-ordinator is that this instrument shows both a rate of roll and turn, which is not acceptable for flying aerobatics. Note that I mention the flaps; this is because if lowered slightly they change the characteristic of the aircraft's wing, producing slightly more lift and much more drag at lower speeds. This will change the amount of engine power required to maintain a particular airspeed when flying with a selected pitch attitude.

When flying on a full panel of instruments, only **three of the six instruments are needed** at any one time but all should be scanned from time to time. The important thing is to know which are more important depending on what stage of the flight you are flying. Also, I have always found it helpful to remember that "Power plus Attitude gives Performance"! The directional indicator (D/I) is also dependent on being set to read the correct compass heading; otherwise you could be flying in the wrong direction. I recall a student landing at an airfield once having flown 50 miles in the opposite direction to that intended; and he was flying VFR as well!

It is best to start by examining which instruments are needed to fly straight and level, something you will do for most of the time if going somewhere.

The three main instruments of importance are the Attitude indicator, Altimeter and Directional Indicator. Note the airspeed, whilst important, is not one of the primary instruments as the speed shown will depend on the power selected and attitude being flown; with or without any flap selected. The correct <u>Radial Scan</u> for Straight and Level Flight is shown below:-

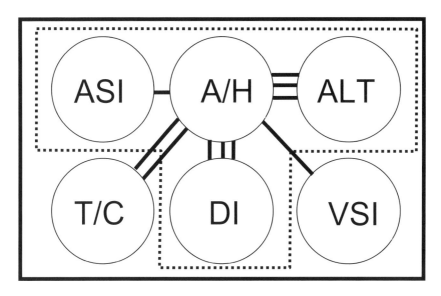

This is the correct scan for Straight and Level Flight using the Artificial Horizon or Attitude Indicator as the <u>main</u> instrument with both the Altimeter and Directional Indicator or Gyro Compass of equal importance with aircraft with conventional instruments.

If we think about our requirements for a moment we will see that the ASI is useful but not essential as we are trying to fly straight, i.e. DI and Level, i.e. Altimeter. The balance part of the Turn indicator is needed to ensure fine balance but remembering basic flying, provided the wings are level and the aircraft is on a constant heading, the aircraft will be in balance. The Vertical speed indicator is not required but is useful to see if there is a trend developing in which case the attitude and/or power should be adjusted slightly. However, flying on instruments will be made much more difficult if the aircraft is not in Trim. It is essential to get the aircraft in trim, particularly in pitch but on some aircraft where you can trim out the aileron and rudder so much the better.

When carrying out a constant turn, surprisingly the D/I is not required as we know we are turning; it is only needed when you are required to roll out on to a particular heading! Having the aircraft in Balance is important so the Turn Indicator or Turn Co-ordinator becomes one of the primary instruments. Also, most instrument flying turns are limited to about 15 degrees of bank angle (or a maximum of 25 degrees) depending on the true airspeed; giving a Rate One turn. That is three degrees per second or 180 degrees in one minute. For most light aircraft, 15 degrees is the accepted bank angle and the turn indicator is designed to accurately show a "Rate One" turn. The correct <u>Selective Radial Scan</u> for a balanced turn is shown below:-

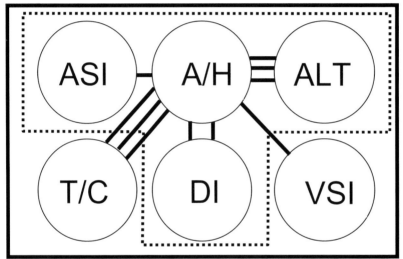

Once again, only three of the six instruments are actually needed when in a turn. The D/I become important when you are required to roll out on a particular heading. The turn indicator or turn co-ordinator becomes important to maintain balance using the balance ball.

When climbing or descending the airspeed does become important as a way of confirming the correct pitch attitude is being maintained on the A/I. Also the VSI will have to come into the scan if a particular rate of descent is required in which case the engine power may need to be adjusted. We very rarely descend with the throttle fully closed these days unless in a pure glide as slow powered descents are often made during a cross county flight, hence the need to consider the engine power during a descent on instruments. It is assumed that any normal climb will be made on full or climbing power and any rate of climb which results is accepted. Like during a turn, the altimeter is not required until we are required to level off at a particular level, altitude or height (depending on the datum setting being used) The desired selective radial scan for both a straight climb and descent is shown on the next page:-

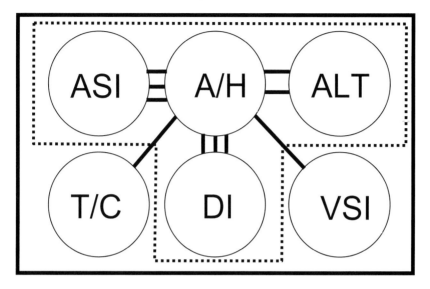

While climbing or descending the ASI <u>does become</u> one of the three primary instruments. The Altimeter and Vertical Speed Indicator become important if a particular height is required on completion or a specific rate of descent is required. Note that the engine power comes into the scan this time! This is either the actual RPM or the manifold pressure reading if using a variable pitch propeller.

The final selective radial scan scenario is that for carrying out a climbing or descending turn. You should now be able to work out which are the three important instruments of the six on a full panel but just in case, it is shown here:-

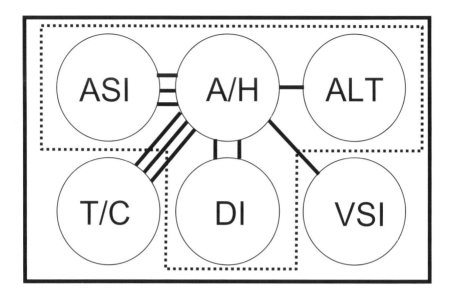

When in a climbing or descending turn, the altimeter and directional indicator assume equal secondary importance if you are required to roll out on a particular heading or level off at a particular altitude/height. Once again the actual engine power is part of the scan if you are required to descend at a particular rate such as during a radar approach.

Now we know the required scans, what are the problems? Firstly, most pilots get very tensed up and try too hard, often over controlling the aircraft. It is very important to get the aircraft in trim, relax, and not to grip the control column or stick tightly. The actual flying is the same as when flying visually, but the relatively small attitude indicator has to be trusted and believed. Relatively small pitch movements on the A/I reflect rather larger movements externally, so when you first start instrument flying it should be done in good visual conditions so you can compare attitude changes both inside and outside the cockpit. For whatever reasons, pilots often suffer from false illusions of movement when flying on instruments until it becomes second nature. You must believe the instruments. One common feeling is that of turning when in fact you are flying straight.

You should know your aircraft performance criteria well before trying to fly on instruments. For example, a particular Cessna 152 might fly straight and level at 85 Knots with a power setting of 2300 rpm. Small airspeed reduction changes are acceptable when turning, so concentrate on the attitude indications rather than get fixed on the ASI or any other instrument. A good helpful phrase which is more suited for limited panel flying (more later) but which applies just as much when flying with a full panel is **"Change, Check, Hold, Adjust, and Trim"**. Always give the instruments time to settle down after a change has been made, and most important of all, do not chase the needles like the Airspeed or Altimeter. Remember that there is a lag in the Vertical Speed Indicator in particular, so do not be tempted to chase the needle one way or the other.

It is a common fault to get fixed on one instrument and allow your correct radial scan to fail. You must keep up a **constant scan** of all six instruments, of which only **three** are important ones at any one time but do not forget to check the other aircraft instruments, such as the compass and D/I for example from time to time; together with the fuel gauges, oil pressure, ammeter, carburettor icing, and so on.

There is one final useful tip if making an instrument approach. An ILS or Radar approach is normally based on a nominal 3 degree glide slope. The Groundspeed X 5 gives the correct Rate of Descent, so the VSI can be a useful aid when carrying out an I/R approach.

Unfortunately, instruments can fail in flight. That is why we also have to consider flying on what is commonly known as a "Limited Panel". This is obviously harder to accomplish and lots of practice is required to avoid over controlling the aircraft. There are various types of failure possible.

In most light aircraft the airspeed, altimeter, and vertical speed indicators are all pressure operated instruments taking an air pressure reading of the "static" outside atmospheric pressure. As this can become blocked, there are usually two external static source sensors or alternatively an Alternate Static source which can be selected if required. In addition, the ASI also requires a reading of the dynamic pressure through a pitot head; caused by the forward movement of the aircraft. This too can become blocked either by ice if there is no pitot heater fitted or debris such as insects during the summer months. This happened to me once when I had a partial reading which was even more difficult to ignore, so I covered it.

The Attitude indicator (or Artificial Horizon) and directional gyro are normally operated by suction on light aircraft, either from an engine driven vacuum pump or an external Venturi tube; in which case they will NOT work until you have been airborne for about 5 minutes. Although electrical ones are now available, the usual assumption is that they are vacuum driven and limited panel flying training is usually based on a failure of these important two instruments.

The Turn Co-ordinator usually found in light aircraft these days is electrical and senses both roll and yaw but an older type turn Indicator which only shows yaw can be either electrical or suction operated. The basic magnetic compass is the only instrument **not** reliant on any external power source and is self contained but it can be affected by deviation errors, either known and tabulated on a Deviation Card; or unintentional, as when a metal object is placed close to it, or the radio transmitter is still radiating! In effect if all else fails the basic compass, despite all its errors, should find you a way home and can be used to descend through cloud on a southerly heading in the northern hemisphere, a heading on which it is extremely sensitive.

The next diagram shows the basic **Limited Panel Scan** used when the A/I and D/I have been lost. Note the equal importance of nearly all, the VSI being useful as a trend instrument only due to its ability to lag markedly when making any attitude changes. The compass is also required to ascertain your heading.

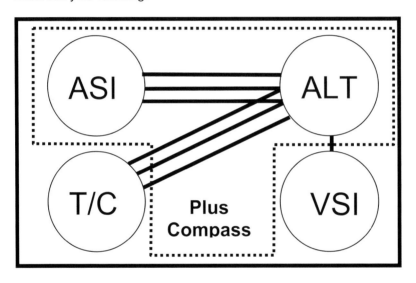

As the Turn Co-Ordinator senses roll, yaw, and balance, it is the primary instrument for maintaining the wings level, and hence continuing to fly in a constant direction. It is also used when making rate one turns (3 degrees per second) in conjunction with a **STOPWATCH** as it is not reliable to scan the basic compass while in the turn due to its inherent errors particularly during turns to/from North or South. Remembering that **"power plus attitude gives performance"** when flying on limited panel, gentle movements of the control column or stick are required allowing the instruments to settle down. There is often a lag on both the altimeter and vertical Speed Indicators so in effect the airspeed probably gives the first indication of a pitch attitude change. When changing pitch move the control column or stick enough to get a 5 Knots change of speed then hold it, let it settle down, and trim. Do not over control the aircraft or try and chase any of the instruments, as a PIA or Pilot Induced Oscillation will begin. The **"Change, Check, Hold, Adjust, Trim"** method of control applies! As far as turning is concerned, no more than a rate one turn should be attempted. Knowing that this is 3 degrees per second, time any turns, i.e., 30 seconds for 90 degrees, 10 seconds for 30 degrees and so on, keep the turn co-ordinator or turn indicator showing a rate one turn and ensure the balance ball is centred. It is possible after a prolonged turn to feel as if you are still turning when returning to level flight again; you must trust your instruments!

Particularly when flying on a limited panel, it is possible to loose control especially if you have been distracted by the radio, looking at a chart, trying to read the compass etc. If this happens, then we have to consider a "Recovery from Unusual Attitudes" scenario. These are characterized by a reducing or increasing airspeed, and usually a high rate of turn, the spiral dive being the most probable result! To recover, you must follow the following procedure, power on or off, needle, ball and airspeed; in that order! Firstly, if the airspeed is increasing, reduce power; if it is reducing, increase power. Then looking at the turn co-ordinator, (or turn indicator) roll the aircraft until the needle centralizes, and check the balance ball is central using rudder to do this. Finally, make a pitch change to either increase or decrease the airspeed by about 5-10 Knots only. Then let it all settle down, otherwise you will be over controlling the aircraft and making matters worse. It is surprising that just a small paragraph explains it all, but only good training with an experienced instrument instructor will suffice. Practice makes perfect.

As I have already said, other types of failure can occur such as a loss of airspeed but if you have the Attitude Indicator, it should not be a problem as you know that at a certain pitch attitude and power setting, the aircraft will fly at particular airspeed, depending on any flap setting which might be selected. This is similar to flying in very rough air when the airspeed indicator, altimeter, vsi, and compass are all over the place; you must just fly attitude with a sensible power, trimmed out, and try and relax!

Finally an important note of caution for PFA/LAA type "Permit to Fly" aircraft. These are NOT to be flown in IMC or at night, you must fly VFR so legal instrument flying is not allowed. However as many types are now fitted with a full set of instruments, it is wise to have some instrument flying training and knowledge; just in case. Also, some aircraft have instrument panels which are not laid out in the standard "T" pattern, so you would have to modify your scan to suit your own aircraft. Please note this has only been a summary of general instrument flying so other reading material is recommended for a greater understanding.

Appendix Ten. Part One. Twin Pioneer comes to Samlesbury.

People at Samlesbury might have wondered what a Twin Pioneer aircraft was doing there for three weeks during January. The answer is that the aircraft was carrying out airborne proving trials of some new sensor equipment. We visited Samlesbury to find out what was going on.

We were told that four consortia, made up of companies from America, Germany, France, and Great Britain are bidding for a 400 million dollar development program to up date the Nato Artillery Multiple Launch Rocket System (MLRS to a Mark 3 version. This development program will run for approximately 86 months before the new MLRS goes into production. The Mk 3 version which is being funded by the four countries has to "detect and destroy tanks at long range". Each consortium has until 1st April to submit its proposal for evaluation.

One consortium is made up of General Dynamics and Sperry in America, Bae Bracknell and Scinon in the UK, Dynamit Nobel of Germany and Sep of France. In January a team of people from General Dynamics, Sperry, and Bae Bracknell came to Samlesbury to carry out some special airborne trials using a Twin Pioneer aircraft. The trials were set up by Bae Bracknell at the request of Sperry who were anxious to do airborne trials with their new sensor

Because Bracknell knew the Advanced Technology Group at Warton had experience of testing their millimetre wave radar sensor equipment using a Twin Pioneer aircraft they asked the Warton group for assistance. Although they didn't participate in the trials in any way the Warton Group organised the facilities at Samlesbury.

Rick Rome from General Dynamics told us that the team is working on a second generation warhead and that General Dynamics is involved with integration of the sensor system and instrumentation. The radar sensor equipment has been developed by Sperry and Tony Leotta from Sperry says that before bringing it to Samlesbury for airborne testing the new sensor had been ground and tower tested Florida. One of the primary aims is to demonstrate the effectiveness of this sensor with tanks and targets of interest in the snow. So after proving flights from Samlesbury over a marked out target zone and over some armoured vehicles from the Territorial Army Unit at Chester the equipment was being taken to Germany for extensive airborne trials over snowy terrain using the Twin Pioneer aircraft. David Hughes from Bae Bracknell told us that Project Leader Tony Aked and two technicians set up their equipment in the aircraft. Bracknell's involvement with the airborne trials was to get a stable 3-axis platform to mount the sensor on; so that no matter what the aircraft does the platform will stay solid end will act as a good reference point as it's always in the same direction. A TV camera is mounted next to the sensor so that simulated targets can be seen and identified. "Once there is a valid control system we will drop out for a while" David said. "There is no intention for people from Bracknell to go to Germany, but if anything goes wrong we will be supporting the trials. If we get the proposal through we will be involved with general control electronics".

The team stayed at Broughton Park Hotel during their visit and we were told that the support they received from Samlesbury was "outstanding". When Chris Spacone from Sperry celebrated his birthday during the trials Canteen Manageress, Jo Easton, arranged for a birthday cake to be made by her staff to make him feel at home.

John Boad from the Flight Test instrumentation Department at Warton looked after the visitors at Samlesbury and Liaised with staff at Samlesbury. The team worked closely with Len Asher Superintendent in No 2 Shed where the Twin Pioneer aircraft was housed and with foremen Roy Butcher and fitter Fred Moorcroft.

Fred Moorcroft from 387 Shop normally works on the ground staff where he is involved with engine runs, preparation for flight and flight snags. During the special trials at Samlesbury Fred has been involved with installing racks into the Twin Pioneer. He told us that the Americans saw the aircraft briefly in September and took measurements for the equipment to be made back home. But when they came to fit them into the aircraft, the racks didn't quite fit, so Fred helped with modifying them so that they could be mounted in pairs inside the aircraft. "I also made a table for the gyro" he said.

Ground staff foreman Roy Butcher has been involved with the exercise since the Twin Pioneer arrived on 4th January. "I've been generally looking after the team" he told us "and I also made arrangements for the team to have wet weather clothing because the weather has been very rough".

All the Shipping arrangements connected with the trials were handled by Frank Williams and his staff, from the Shipping Department at Samlesbury.

We were told that they worked very hard to make sure all the paperwork needed to get the equipment to Germany and back to the United States afterwards was ready on time.

The weather at Samlesbury was rather wild when the team involved with the trials was photographed with the Twin Pioneer

I am seen looking from behind (with cap on) fourth from the left of photo.

From left: Tim Kirchoff, Les Cookson (Shipping), Ian Forrest (Shipping). Hugh Thompson (pilot), Frank Williams (Shipping), George Gurran, Keith Ex, Tony Leotta, Gary Schmitr, Fred McCord. John Boad (FTI. Warton), Ernie Harris (Bracknell), David Stephens, Ghris Spacone, David Hughes (Bracknell), Rick Rome. Dick Noblett (Samlesbury. Sid Crabtree, Roy Butcher (Samlesbury) and Fred Moorcroft (Samlesbury) John Miller (General Dynamics). missing from photo.

Appendix Ten.

Part Two. JUNE1983. TRIALS IN NORWAY.

*Pictured with the Twin Pioneer aircraft at Warton are, from left: Ron Evans, Jack Allinson, Julian Thomas, Peter Studdart, who helped out prior to flying to Norway, Tony Archdale, **Hugh Thompson**, the pilot and Mike Everett, (Geoff Salkeld is missing from the photo,)*

A 5-MAN team from Warton visited Norway in March to carry out some special trials for the Royal Signals and Radar Establishment (RSRE) to measure back-scatter from snow using our millimetre wave radar sensor equipment. This equipment, featured in Intercom in October. 1981, is amongst the most sophisticated anywhere in the world. It operates at wavelengths of only a few millimetres, which enables very accurate measurements to be made.

The Warton team involved with the trials was made up of Tony Archdale, Geoff Salkeld, Julian Thomas, Mike Everett and Ron Evans, and they were accompanied by three people from RSRE and one person from the Norwegian equivalent, NDRE. Tony, who is Project Manager for the millimetre wave radar program, told Intercom that the trials to measure radar return from the snow were carried out using a Twin Pioneer aircraft, hired from Flight One. "This aircraft, built in 1953 as a troop carrier by what is now BAe's Scottish Division, saw service in Malaya with the RAF, and is one of only three left in a flying condition. Now modified for aerial survey work with two 18 inch diameter holes in the fuselage floor, it makes an ideal platform for our radar. The radar protrudes through the more central hole and two benches on either side carry the supporting equipment. The aircraft was piloted during the trials by Hugh Thompson with Jack Allinson navigating".

Julian and Mike drove to Norway in a Range Rover towing some of the equipment in a trailer behind them. The rest of the team flew out in the Twin Pioneer to the half military, half civil base at Gardermoen (about 30 miles north of Oslo); which was the centre for the trials. "While we were making measurements from the air, the RSRE team was making ground measurements of the snow's characteristics. To carry out the radar trials we had to fly at 200 feet and local residents were told about our special trials by a local newspaper". Tony told Intercom; "We identified two routes to fly, which were each about 6 km long. The idea was to fly these routes with different radar depression angles and to repeat the trials at different times of the day when the solar loading would be different". Over a 3-day period 8 flights were made; 7 along the chosen routes and one over a frozen lake that had a covering of snow on it. With the measurements from all these sorties, the team was able to set off for home after successfully accomplishing everything that they had set out to do.

"The exercise went very smoothly", Tony told us, "Thanks to the help we received at Gardermoen, especially from the Chief Air Traffic Controller, Arnfinn Taalesen. The equipment worked exceptionally well after having traveled so far. On return to Warton the data was analyzed by computer and RSRE are very pleased with the results".

Appendix Ten.

Part Three. "Eye-in-the-Sky" looks for energy losses.

BAe News generates a little "heat" among its readers occasionally, but we never thought we would cause an organised hunt for heat

AN AERIAL SURVEY has been carried out with BAe heat-detecting equipment over Aircraft Group factories in the company's campaign to save energy. Results of the survey in March are still being analyzed but are expected to yield valuable information pointing out where oil, gas, coal and electricity savings can be made.

Linescan infra-red equipment loaned from the maker, Hatfield Dynamics, was taken aloft In a Twin Pioneer aircraft and flown low over Hatfield, Kingston, Dunsfold, Hamble, Chester, Woodford, Chadderton, Preston, Samlesbury, Warton, Prestwlck and Brough. The Linescan equipment was originally designed by Hatfield for military and policing purposes to "suss out" hidden enemy vehicles or ships engaged on illicit activities in darkness or poor visibility. But the system's ability to detect the infra-red in the tiniest emissions of heat and produce a thermal "picture" of the scene has a number of civil applications.

This was proved in trial surveys of the Hatfield and Bristol sites in 1981. The aerial picture obtained showed just where heat was being lost from the buildings and Installations which were easily Identifiable. The picture was published in BAe News In June 1981 with a report on what was being done within BAe to conserve energy. Among those who read the feature with special Interest was Aircraft Group's resources engineer Mr. Fred Andrews. "That article started it all off," he told BAe News. "It was just at that time that we were calling the first meeting of the energy conservation people at the various factories.

"I arranged for Mr. Geoff McQueen, who Is sales manager of the Infra-red division at Hatfield Dynamics, to give a presentation on the Linescan 214 system to the meeting at Preston." The presentation aroused a great deal of interest among the conservationists, and a proposal to survey most of Aircraft Group's sites went ahead; but not without difficulty.

For a start, the Twin Pioneer operated by a charter company, night One, based at Shobdon, near Leominster, was in Norway doing other work for BAe, and the Linescan demonstration equipment was at the other end of the globe In South America. At last everything was ready, the equipment Installed in the aircraft, CAA authority obtained, and air traffic control alerted In the areas concerned, when suddenly the temperature shot up in the most unseasonable way. Factory heating was turned down, large hangar doors were opened, and any survey made then would have given quite an unrepresentative thermal picture of the factories.

Eventually cold weather returned, only to be accompanied by gale force winds which would have made low-flying hazardous and reduced the resolution of the Infra-red film. On 19th March the wind abated, and a dress rehearsal flight was undertaken over the Hatfield site. "The wind returned again with renewed Intensity, leaving everyone concerned feeling a great sense of frustration," Mr. Andrews reported.

Eventually the weather cleared, and the aircraft made for the Kingston site. As well as the pilot and navigator, Mr. Andrews was on hoard as observer for Aircraft Group Resources with senior engineers Mr. Barry Woodcock and Mr. Bob Kelly from Hatfield Dynamics operating the Linescan equipment. A solar filter in the equipment, introduced to cut out heat interference from the sun, was enabling the whole survey to be carried out in daylight. This was beneficial from both financial and operational points of view.

A welcome note of light relief now crept into the proceedings as the aircraft flew over the Kingston site at 800-1,000 ft., "shooting" through an open panel in the floor with the camera used for taking reference photographs.

A number of worried residents, seeing an aircraft flying low and slow with Its wheels down, telephoned the police. Not knowing the Twin Pioneer has a fixed undercarriage, they assumed the pilot was in trouble and seeking a place to make an emergency landing!

The "heat detectives" went on to spy out Dunsfold and Hamble and, despite some more squally weather, managed to cover all the remaining factories on the list by the end of the following week. The films are now being studied and will eventually go to the individual Divisions for further study, together with reports produced by infra-red analysts. The lessons likely to he learned from the Group survey can be judged from the Bristol trial. This showed quite a lot of heat loss through the roofs, confirming the need for proper Insulation of the buildings.

Bristol Aircraft's general manager (resources) Mr. Mervyn Berry told BAe News: "One unexpected heat-loss revealed by the survey was from a large steam main buried several feet under a road that runs through the site. We have already excavated the area to insulate the pipe".

"This program of lagging and insulating roofs, along with introducing automatic boiler controls and an incinerator which puts heat back into the heating system has led, in the last year alone, to the saving of one million litres of heating oil which would have cost us In the region of £130,000." he says".

Report written by Jack Dwyer, from Bae News.

The value of Insulation In conserving heat is dramatically shown in the infra-red picture of Hatfield taken during the Aircraft Group thermal survey.

The dark corner of the main manufacturing complex on the right shows the full insulation that was carried out during refurbishment for the new machine-shop. The white traces crossing and following roads indicate underground steam pipes where heat is being lost, and further heat loss is markedly evident on one side of the flight hangar at the top of the picture.

Appendix Eleven. Summary of the Planning Sequence of events

Surrounding Milson Airstrip. It is accurate up to about 2001.

1. **Enforcement Officer's Report No 91/154**:-

This report, made as the result of a complaint from a new neighbour who had come to live close to the existing airstrip, did **NOT** recommend any action be taken due to the length of time the airstrip had already existed. The owner was however invited to make a retrospective application for planning consent which in due course was submitted. Had the initial application not been made as a sign of co-operation with the local council, the airstrip would have been entitled to retrospective planning with a "Lawful Use" certificate as it had conclusive evidence of having been in existence for more than 10 years. A movement's book of all visiting aircraft had been kept since 1971 after an aircraft had first landed at the site. The first "Fly In" event was held in 1973 to celebrate the owners 21st Birthday, and more were held during the early 1980's.

2. **Retrospective Application No 1/02005/P**:-

This application eventually resulted in planning consent being given on the 22nd April 1992, after a site meeting and two committee considerations. Amongst the conditions was a limitation on the number of flights to 8 per day plus one visitor, and a Sunday Afternoon Restriction was imposed during the summer months to appease the main local objector.

3. **Application No 1/03439/P**:-

This planning application was made after one year in order to review the existing conditions, and to ask for a number of changes in the light of experience gained the previous year. An increase to 10 flights a day plus any visitors was asked for; together with a lifting of the Sunday Afternoon Restriction. Some of these changes were **APPROVED** by the Planning Committee subject to a Section 106 being entered into. This would have prevented any further aviation related development at the site and required all aircraft to leave the visual traffic pattern after taking off; except for any emergency reasons. At the eleventh hour, the applicant was unable to accept the proposed legal agreement, as it would have, according to the council, lost him his "Permitted Development Rights" which allowed use of an alternative (Crosswind) field No 7100 should the need arise.

Accordingly, this application was withdrawn in order that an amended one could be made to allow for the use of the other field.

4. **Application No 1/04362/P**:-

The replacement application, made in February 1994, asked that the other field be included in the consent conditions to overcome the problem encountered with the previous application. Two additional "Fly-In" events were also added to the request due to the imposition of Non-Domestic Rates. Unfortunately, despite being recommended for acceptance by the planning officer, the Planning Committee **REFUSED** to approve this application despite the offer of a Section 106 agreement which was not a recommended requirement. In effect the committee was overturning their previous decision to grant permission in the withdrawn application. An appeal was therefore made against their decision, made on the 4th July 1994.

5. **Appeal No T/App/K3225/A/94/239863/P6**:-

The appointed inspector upheld the appeal and granted planning consent with the exception of the lifting of the Sunday Afternoon Restriction which had previously been approved in the withdrawn application No 1/103439/P. **However, the Inspector did not consider that the other field came within his jurisdiction, and that this field was therefore irrelevant as far as the appeal was concerned.** With that in mind, the owner did not consider that there was any planning need to withdraw the previous application after all. Since the other field has a "Permitted Development Right" on it, and it is unlikely that it would ever be used for more than 28 days in any one calendar year, the owner felt very strongly that the Sunday Afternoon Restriction should have been lifted as previously agreed, at least for a trial period. The fact that in the summer of 1993, when the airstrip users did NOT comply with the restriction, there were only 5 Take-Offs made on a Sunday afternoon shows that this restriction if removed would not be abused in any deliberate way.

6. **Attempt to Obtain an "Article Four" Direction**:-

The request for a re-consideration of the Sunday Afternoon Restriction by the airstrip owner was refused. After that, the main objector tried to have the Permitted Development Rights removed by taking out an Article Four Direction. This was also rejected. The council later tried to suggest, in a formal letter, that Permitted Development Rights never existed, which makes a complete mockery of the whole process.

7. **Rate Tribunal Hearings and negotiations to date**:-

Agricultural operations and buildings do NOT get rated but despite being classed as agricultural diversification, a formal planning application for a non agricultural activity can result in business rates being applied. The rateable value of the airstrip, which was imposed after a formal planning consent was given, was initially set at £2100, was later lowered to £2000 as a result of a Tribunal hearing, then raised briefly to £3500 but reduced to £2500 following a strong letter of complaint when the values were all revised a year or so later. Later discussions and negotiations have reduced the RV to £1650 but this is still far too high when compared to the limited level of use permitted. Attempts to get both Discretionary and Hardship Relief were rejected. Currently the rates bill is in the region of £750 annually against a potential income of around £4000. As a direct result of the rates and the planning restrictions, particularly the Sunday take off restriction, some of the resident owners left to go elsewhere. Further attempts were made to reduce it further to a rateable value of £1500 which the owner would have accepted as a final compromise.

8. **Application No 1/07734/V**:-

Owing to the loss of some resident owners and the relatively high level of rates in relation to the level of use permitted, an application to modify the conditions was made. This asked for an annual total of 1500 flights a year, excluding the two permitted "Fly-In" events, and the complete removal of the Sunday restriction. The annual total was reduced to 500 as a result of concern from local residents but despite this concession the application was rejected. The question of the high rates was deemed to be irrelevant to the application despite being one of the main reasons for making the application which was designed to make the operating conditions of the airstrip more flexible.

There was never any intention of trying to get permission for MORE flights, which was the fear of most of the local objectors: just more **flexibility** was the aim to make the airstrip more attractive to new potential residents and visitors alike. Following the rejection of this application, discussions were held with Mr. Stuart Taylor in the planning department and following his advice, another application was made immediately, which attempted to take account of the main concerns of local people.

9. **Application No 1/07848N**:-

A further planning application (No 1/07848/V) was made which included the offer of a Section 106 Agreement. This application took account of the complaints received in the previous application and the legal agreement would have specifically excluded any further aviation related development on the Milson Airstrip site. Instead of 500 flights a year, an additional clause allowing each RESIDENT aircraft owner at least one flight a day was asked for. In theory this would have allowed for more flights but in practice would only have allowed a greater degree of flexibility. In addition, the removal of the illogical Sunday afternoon take off restriction was also asked for again. As this application was also refused because of the large number of complaints received which were out of all proportion to the changes sought despite the Section 106 offer, two appeals have been made against the refusal of the Council to remove the Sunday Restriction only. It is accepted that the current 10 flights a day limitation is acceptable most of the time and that it is only likely to be exceeded on one or two occasions in any one year, if at all.

10. **Appeal No's APP/K3225/A/97/285202 & 3. Dated the 24thNovember 1997:-**

These appeals were lost due in the main to the overwhelming degree of local opposition which was out of all proportion to what was asked for. The owner tried to get a final solution by offering a re-wording of the Section 106 Agreement in return for a permanent removal of the Sunday Afternoon take off restriction. This would have concluded the matter once and for all but still allow for up to 10 flights a day including visitors which he has always accepted as being about right for the type of use the airstrip has; mainly recreational flying at weekends. Two unrestricted Fly-In weekends would also be allowed but in return all aircraft would have to fly away after taking off to reduce any disturbance to local residents (except for any air safety reason).

This is an accurate reflection of the planning issues for the Milson Airstrip up to 1998. The removal of the Sunday Restriction is the **only** outstanding item to be resolved as far as planning considerations are concerned. The rates are still far too high but that subject is a separate concern and a further letter has recently been written to a specialist Valuation Officer. His response has not been helpful but did reveal that the one home built building has been valued for over £13000 when it only cost a maximum of £2500 to construct! To conclude this summary, the bottom line is that if the airstrip is to continue the following two things MUST change:-

a) **The Rateable Value should be reduced from £1650 to £1500 (or lower)**

b) **A Removal of the Sunday Afternoon Restriction should be honoured**

In return, the Legal Section 106 Agreement/Planning Obligation as proposed would finalize the matter for good **preventing any further aviation related development** on the Little Down Farm. The daily limitation of 10 flights a day excluding the two "Fly-In" weekends is acceptable as that number of flights is rarely if ever reached.

Mr. Biggs, the council's Chief Executive was asked again to examine the evidence as the matter has not yet been concluded to the satisfaction of the airstrip owner. After an initial refusal to consider the matter, he asked the Council's Planning Advocate Mr. K Ballantyne to examine in detail the whole issue in detail. Unfortunately, he upheld the view that there were No Permitted Development Rights on the rest of the farm. A complaint was then made to the Local Government Ombudsman which was investigated.

11. **Developments since January 1998**:-

The result of my complaint to the Local Government Ombudsman was that the Official council view was that they did **not** have definitive view as to whether or not I had any permitted rights and invited me to seek a Certificate of Lawful or Proposed Use Development. (C.L.O.P.U.D.) For this the council asked for a further fee of £190 which is outrageous when all the owner wished to do, was to establish at that stage, who was correct; The Ombudsman's final report on the complaint made about the Permitted Development Rights issue concluded that there was nothing they could do to help. They did however acknowledge that there <u>was a confliction</u> in the views given by the council between 1993-5 to that given in late 1997. They also understood why the owner had been reluctant to pay yet another fee to resolve the issue formally with a C.L.O.P.U.D application. The owner initially decided not to pursue the matter for the time being, deciding to wait

xlii

until the two year period from the last appeal decision has elapsed, but changed his mind; and was fully prepared to accept a loss of my permitted rights in return for the legal agreement so long as use of field No 7100 was accepted for "emergency" landings. This was the solution suggested by one of the planning officers in 1993 (Mr. R C Mills) which, although recommended by the Chief Planning Officer, was rejected by the 1994 committee. The owner therefore tried to seek a Restoration of the 1993 consent which would have removed the Sunday Restriction in return for the legal agreement which had already cost him over £1500 in legal expenses.

To achieve this, the owner sought the permission of the council to make another application within two years of a previous appeal decision dated the 24th November 1997. He wished to get the matter of the Sunday take off restriction cleared up for good. If a further application was to be made he would also seek a slight modification to the Two unrestricted "Fly-In" Weekends which would allowed another attempt if bad weather prevented a planned event from being a success. A suggestion that if no more than 15 flights took place (5 more than the normal daily allowance) a Fly In would be considered a failure will be made. This request was however, rejected by the council.

There was never any desire to increase the number of flights and based on past experience it is doubtful that there would ever be more than 500 flights in any one year due to the various limitations and physical restrictions. For at least 2/3rds of the year, the airstrip is not useable by microlights or fixed wing aircraft because the surface is either too wet or it is too windy (or both) with a prevailing crosswind. Based on the appeal decision report in 1994 and the opinion of the Council officer's Mr. Stuart Taylor and Ken Ballantyne, the owner felt justified in seeking a removal of the Sunday restriction which serves no useful purpose as other aircraft from elsewhere can and do overfly the airstrip during the restriction period. To have **BOTH** a daily restriction and a Sunday Take Off ban is just not acceptable if at the same time the airstrip remains rated as a commercial business having to pay nearly £800 a year. A further reduction in the Rateable Value was also sought and an unsuccessful Rates Tribunal Hearing for this was granted on August 2nd 1999.

One possible option is to seek a judicial enquiry in the courts over this issue but the outcome could have serious implications for all airstrips countrywide. However a local resolution of this problem is hoped for which with a legal agreement will conclude the planning matters once and for all!

The support of all the various flying organizations was expected with a further planning application and appeal should it have become necessary. Milson Airstrip is a small Recreational Airstrip which provides a limited site for Airports in South Shropshire as allowed for in the local plan. Ironically, it is the **LACK OF REGULAR USE** which the owner believed was the problem as when there is some flying after a long period with no activity at all, it is perceived by some local people and one objector in particular to be noisy and intrusive, If there were regular flights it would eventually become an accepted activity like a nearby motorway or railway line. The next problem illustrates this well:-

12. Latest problem concerning Occasional Military Helicopter of the Airstrip:

Despite the fact that the planning consent conditions currently allows up to 10 Flights a Day including Visitors, the main objector and closest neighbour, managed to stop the occasional use of this airstrip by Military Helicopters from the nearby Defence Helicopter Flying School (DHFS) based at RAF Shawbury. This is an unacceptable development as he is trying to suggest that even a lawful activity is wrong. He made the complaint early in February 1999 shortly after there had been up to 4 helicopter movements over a three day period in late January and early February after a period of bad weather. He later stated to the press that the owner was deliberately allowing the helicopters to use the airstrip as a way of trying to get the Sunday Afternoon Take Off restriction removed. This is totally untrue and the two are totally unrelated as any military use is a weekday occurrence only.

The RAF were first invited to use the airstrip in 1995 shortly after the Government had decided on the formation of the new Tri-Service Helicopter School which was to be based at RAF Shawbury which is located some 25 nautical miles north of the Milson airstrip. They are not charged financially for their use of the site, and use of the airstrip is allowed for as a gesture of support for our armed services and the vital task the school performs in the training of helicopter pilots. In return the owner, and other landowners in the area of Shropshire who allow their land to be used, get an annual visit to RAF Shawbury which normally includes a helicopter flight. When the RAF suspended their operations an urgent and hastily arranged brief meeting was held with the local council's Chief Executive Mr. G C Biggs in which it was made clear to him the anger and concern about the latest twist in the airstrip's troubled planning history. The owner pointed out that they were carrying out a **lawful activity** and that even if there was no planning consent military helicopters are allowed to use any landing site with the consent of the landowner concerned. Mr. Biggs was able to confirm in writing that use of my airstrip by military helicopters was allowed for under the terms of the current planning consent conditions provided the daily limit was not exceeded but the council did ask the MOD and Shawbury **NOT** to use the site which was a shameful response and showed a complete lack of understanding and support for our armed services.

Notwithstanding the complaint itself, some further changes have been made to the operating conditions to try and accommodate yet again the main objector's concerns. It has also been suggested to the RAF and the DHFS that an area "Off Limits" to landing and hovering helicopters be established at the southern end and along the western side of the main airstrip field. Furthermore, it has also been suggested that use by their helicopters be limited to no more than 10 a week even though there can technically be up to 10 a day if there is no other flying activity. The fact that the DHFS is a weekday operation means that their use of the airstrip is hardly likely to interfere with the recreational use by the resident pilots which is normally confined to the weekends and during the summer evenings.

The owner has been appalled at the apparent lack of understanding shown by various local people concerning the occasional helicopter use by the RAF. He has written to all the immediate landowner neighbours and has asked them all for a degree of tolerance from them. The RAF, MOD, and the airstrip owner all recognize that they are not going to please everybody all of the time but these helicopters have to fly somewhere!

To help keep helicopters further away from the objector's property, a large 54 square metre metal helicopter landing pad was put down near to the northern end of the airstrip but that itself required yet another planning application after the objector complained about that as well. That large metal landing area cost the owner a further £1500 just a year or so before he had to sell the farm and airstrip for financial and family reasons.

As a result of being rated as a commercial business, the airstrip must be allowed to operate in the way intended within the terms of the consent conditions that have been given. The owner was no longer prepared to put up with constant harassment and would almost certainly have closed it down if the RAF had decided not to continue using the airstrip on an occasional basis. It is intolerable that he has had to put up with further complaints from the main objector who has persistently campaigned to get this airstrip closed down; despite that fact that he came to live next door to an existing airstrip which had been in existence for nearly 20 years. Admittedly, it was not a busy as it is now but it did already exist.

Note:- This appendix shows just how complex the planning issues for an airstrip can become. I hope it is an accurate summary of a 10 year planning nightmare but there may be some errors in it. Happily the RAF and DHFS continue to use the Milson airstrip on an occasional basis but not the extent they used to; mainly because they how have many more sites to choose from. The main objector continues to harass Chris Jones, the new owner, and I personally remain as angry as ever that the council took any notice of him at all and failed to give the DHFS and the military their unconditional support!

I should also like to add that the planning authority at the time was the South Shropshire District Council, which has now been amalgamated with Shropshire County Council. Any further enquiries a reader may wish to make should be addressed to them.

Hugh Thompson. August 2010.